The Improbable

Survival of a Happily

Fallible Child

Gary C. Mele, Jr.

Repercussions of Poorly Chosen Words

The Inexplicable Survival of a Happily Fallible Child: a title inadvertently designed by my siblings. Having survived the same dysfunctional childhood, I knew I needed their input. I interrupted workdays/time with spouse and/or children asking for title ideas. Over several days, each of my siblings stepped out of their normal lives to reminisce and brainstorm with me, and each other. Great suggestions were made such as *Normal Someday, The 21 Brutal Moves that Led to My Sanity, Mom's trip to the Bahamas* and the simple but poignant *Mele?* Those ideas, plus a slew of others brought laughs, praise, and poo-poos. But there wasn't one choice that all of us uniformly agreed upon as the best title for my memoir.

In addition to suggestions for what to call my book, each sibling offered frank feedback on what aspects he or she felt were important to the creation of a fantastic title. "Catchy" was mutually agreed upon because, as was pointed out, I'm not Oprah Winfrey or Madonna. No one is clamoring to read the memoir of Gary C. Mele, Jr. (Pronounced Mealy, by the way, like the bug – as some know-it-all kid pointed out the second year I attended the first grade) It's generally understood these days that everyone comes from a dysfunctional family rife with abusive spankings and neglectful missed dance recitals. To that end, a title such as *Dysfunctional Normality* would only draw

3

scoffs and jibes from hordes of potential book readers. "You want to hear about a dysfunctional childhood? *I* can tell you about a dysfunctional childhood." No. In an effort to intrigue a potential reader enough to simply open my book, I employed alliteration and near rhyme – pleasing to the ear – along with one or two unusual words to raise an inquisitive eyebrow, while still summing up the story as accurately as possible – the final, and most agreed upon, requirement.

Unlike most would-be writers, who I assume devote a significant amount of time and angst to the perfect title, once I had the formula figured out – voilà! – my title was done. The real dilemma came with writing the story. How does a forty-two-year-old man begin a story from a four-year-old boy's perspective? Use words a child would think and say, even if it limits the vocabulary of the story? Grown-up minds like to be stimulated with unusual words and interesting phrases. I suppose the set-up of the characters and plot would work better as a blend of both voices – adult and child – at least while the earliest memories are typed out and organized as best they can be. And hopefully, once the story is chugging along, the shift in voice to match the age at the time will be appreciated.

Lighting my thumb on fire is one of my earliest memories.

The grooved double metal gear of Mom's cigarette lighter reminded me of the miniature silver wheels on my train engine. I loved watching the red and silver locomotive buzz around the track, pulling flatbed log cars. It was especially fun when Dad gave a mischievous smile. "How fast you think it can go?" he'd ask, before easing the control to full speed. I'd watch, excited, while tiny white sparks popped from the wheels as the train raced along the tracks. I wondered if Mom's lighter worked the same way – if the quick flick of her thumb caused a spark, which made the flame that lit the cigarette she was about to smoke.

When I asked Mom if I could play with her lighter she gave a stern look that spoke the words before she even said them. "No, it's not a toy."

Still, I begged, "Please, please, I just want to hold it, Mom," which made her snap, "Gary, you'll burn yourself!" Then, she bent toward me and looked straight in my eyes. "Don't… Ask… Again. The answer's no."

I had given up on the idea of ever playing with one the day I found it. Mom laughed with Uncle Jim in the kitchen while I stood bored, watching Michael in his playpen, in front of the bright living room window. I reached in and set a yellow R block on the warm, sunlit square near his feet, "Michael, you stack them like this." I carefully placed a blue W block on top. He stared for a second, then grabbed the wooden blocks and began knocking them together. "He's such a dumb baby," I thought before deciding to look for change in the couch. I walked over and pushed my open hand underneath the cushions hoping to feel a cool, round coin. As I began swiping back and forth, over the lint and sand, I imagined that maybe I'd even find a quarter.

The moment my fingers touched the lighter I went completely still. I held my breath and listened to be sure Mom and Uncle Jim were still talking in the kitchen. I shot a look toward Michael, believing my quick, authoritative glance would keep him from being stupid and crying. I was relieved to see he was still drooling over his scratched-up blocks. I gripped and gently pulled the plastic BIC out as my heart began beating with excitement. I hid the lighter behind my back and slowly walked toward the basement door.

Once downstairs, I scanned the large room for a spot where I could figure out how to make the lighter work. I considered working near my train set but knew if any adult opened the door trying to find me that would be the first place they'd look. I decided the safest place would be with my back against the wall along the base of the stairs. Anyone looking for me would have to walk all the way down and turn the corner to find me. I settled against the wall, held the lighter tightly in one hand, and began pushing the gear with my thumb.

CHCK!

CHCK!

Exhilarating pride brought a smile the moment I accomplished my task. As I lifted my clenched fist to eye level, my four-year-old mind tried to make sense of the yellow flame at the tip of my thumb. Shock. Fear. Panic. I furiously began shaking my hand.

Once the flame was out, Mom's warnings, along with her stern looks, raced through my brain. I ran from the base of the stairs to the plywood toy box that Dad had built for me. My heart pounded. I knew I needed to hide the lighter. I lifted, then quickly dropped the lid as the pain seared through the tip of my thumb. I clenched my jaw, inhaled, and desperately squeezed my hand. Hiding the evidence no longer mattered. I needed to make the pain go away. I ran back to the stairs and listened.

I could hear Uncle Jim in the kitchen telling Mom, "Kathy, she's not coming back. She knows Gary doesn't want her here." I knew he was talking about Aunt Peggy leaving New Jersey for Florida because of my Dad. During one of their arguments, Dad had told Mom, "Peggy, Doreen, Jimmy – they should all be with your mother."

Mom had yelled back, "Peggy's a teenager, and Doreen's a kid," then added, "And Jimmy doesn't live with us!"

Dad disliked Uncle Jim the most. He shook his head. "He's here every afternoon gossiping with you. Why doesn't he get a job?" Then, he answered his own question. "It's because he gets drunk every day."

I knew "drunk" meant Uncle Jim drank too much beer. I hadn't figured out exactly what "gossiping" meant, but I was pretty sure it had something to do with talking bad about someone when they weren't around, which Uncle Jim did a lot. Most of the time I wanted Uncle Jim to know that I agreed with Dad about him. I'd be sure to cross my arms

7

and tighten my lips when I was around him, but that day, I kept my head low and looked at the floor as I walked by. I was glad he was gossiping. It would make it easier to sneak past Mom to the bathroom.

As I walked by Doreen's bedroom door, I felt thankful relief that she was still at school. I knew if she were home and I tried to tiptoe quietly by, she'd step out in front of me, squint her eyes and demand to know what I was doing. I was sure if I answered, "I was just trying to leave you alone," she'd become suspicious, even though she didn't want me talking to her anyway.

Doreen loved to yell at me for dumb reasons. When she was listening to the stereo – "Johnny come lately . . . the new kid in town"– I asked, "Is that about a boy moving in the night time?"

She looked at me like I was stupid. "It's not about a child."

Another time, after I realized she probably wasn't going back to Grandma's, I told her, "Doreen, you're like my older sister!" I knew she, at twelve years old, was too young to be an aunt, and I wanted her to feel like she was part of our family. She snapped, "I'm not your sister; I'm your aunt!" which made me realize that she was going to be mean no matter how nice I tried to be.

Once I made my way down the hall, I was careful to close the bathroom door gently. I imagined Mom screaming, "Gary, don't slam doors!" or worse, she'd march over to tell me to my face. "I've told you before; this isn't a barn."

Unlike Doreen, when Mom was mad, she was still pretty. From TV, it seemed that girls with light hair, blue eyes, and tanned skin were considered the prettiest. Mom had blue eyes, but her skin was pale and soft like a newborn baby. And her hair was black. Sometimes she'd pull it back under a red and white bandana. Other times she'd wear a wig, the same color as her hair, only bigger, longer, and curly. Either way, I still thought she was prettier than all the blond girls on TV.

I turned the faucet handle with the C until the water pshhhhed. The moment I stuck my thumb under the icy stream, the pain disappeared, and relief went through my body like a wonderful shiver. With the burning gone, I took my thumb out and turned the faucet off. I decided I should flush the toilet so that it would seem like I had peed. As I pressed the handle, I noticed the scorching pain creeping back to my thumb. *Why was it coming back?* I turned the water on again and dunked my hand back in. I decided to leave it under for several minutes.

As I stood on my tippy toes with my arm stretched over the sink, I noticed the top of my light brown head in the bottom of the mirror. I jumped to see how much of my face would pop up. I glimpsed my eyes and thought about the ladies at the grocery store who made happy faces and cooed, "You're so adorable!" I had blue eyes, like Mom, but one was crossed. I wore thick-framed glasses because the eye doctor had told Mom that they would straighten my lazy eye. I had a big head, bigger ears, and, to make matters worse, my hair was thick and cowlicky. Mom would brush and re-brush, determined to cover my ears. She'd face me head on, tilt her head to the left, right, then back left to be sure my ears were completely hidden by a happening, disco-era, hairstyle before we left the house.

Regardless of whether my ears stayed covered, or poked through my wavy locks, it didn't seem to affect the opinion of the women who gushed about how cute I was. Sometimes telling me wasn't enough, like when the lady at the bakery insisted I take a free brownie. "Are you sure you don't want one?" she asked in a soothing tone like she was talking to a petrified baby. I wasn't scared. I really didn't want one, at least not one with nuts on it. They were hard to chew, and the gritty bits got stuck between my teeth. Plus, they weren't sweet like frosting or chocolate chips. I didn't understand why everyone acted like they were so great.

"It's ok. Go ahead and pick one. It's ok."

I stared at the lady and stayed quiet. I knew if I explained that crushed peanuts actually made plain brownies terrible, it might prompt a worse alternative. She'd offer me something else, like a dry cookie with a rubbery red center that was supposed to be strawberries, or she'd try to scrape the nuts off, which would only roll them into the thick, dark cake. Either way, I'd end up with a treat that I didn't really want. I also knew if I didn't take something, the lady would get sad. Then, Mom would push her bottom lip out, to let me know that I was about to make the lady cry. She'd say, "Gary, that's not nice," in her saddest voice possible to be sure I understood how mean I was being.

"Are you absolutely sure you don't want one?"

I smiled and pretended to be happy. "That one!"

I have other early memories that aren't about how well I handled being the cutest little boy around or how handy I was with a lighter. I remember walking in on my grandmother sitting on the toilet, with her entire outfit around her ankles. It was a onesie with a zipper down the front, sort of like what you dress infants in, except it was black and, I think, sparkly. When it was on, it had mini sleeves, so her forearms and calves were exposed. Grandma had told Mom, that it was nineteen seventy-seven, and unlike most women her age, she still prided herself on dressing fashionable, young and cool.

Seeing Grandma hunched and naked from the sandals up wasn't fashionable or cool, it was shocking. My little mind had so many questions. Did she always have to sit when she peed? Did she pee from her butt? I could pee standing up. I'd once proclaimed, "I peed in the hoods!" which meant I'd peed behind a bush. Was she even peeing at all? Maybe she was pooping? Either way, why did her whole outfit have to come off? I was sure she must have been chilly.

Grandma didn't scold me. She said, "Close the door, Honey. Grandma's going potty," with a sweet voice so I wouldn't be afraid.

Grandma had black hair like Mom, Doreen, and Uncle Jim. She smelled like perfume, cigarette smoke, and most of the time; she had a boozy perspiration smell, too. I had wondered if the scent was stronger than when Uncle Jim smelled like alcohol because she was so skinny or because she was old.

Grandma also liked to bring me candy or toys. Sometimes she'd hold the treat behind her back and ask, "Which hand is it?" I'd giggle and pick the right one, knowing she's was going to switch and pretend I'd guessed correctly, even if I hadn't.

In a late summer memory, Grandma walked in and called, "Gary, look what I brought you." She handed me a stiff, cardboard sheet with different size boats held in place by clear plastic. Even though I wished the boats were silver passenger trains, I was still thrilled – getting to open any new toy was exciting. As I climbed down the wood steps to the backyard, I wondered why Grandma thought playing with boats in the dust would be fun. I imagined how great it would be if a stream full of darting minnows ran behind our house, then decided I'd make do. I'd just have to pretend the sand was water.

As I lined my ships up in the dirt, I heard Grandma talking loudly from the kitchen window above me. Was she upset with Mom for the way I was dressed? I'd heard that before. She'd told Mom that she'd bought me enough blue jeans and nice slacks that there was no reason for me to be running around in dirty, sport shorts.

No. It wasn't about what I was wearing. I couldn't hear exactly what Grandma was saying, but I knew she was angry with Mom about the kitchen, or maybe dinner. I tried to ignore Grandma's yelling, but my ear tensed when I heard Mom's voice, "I'm sorry Mommy. I didn't mean it that way." Hearing Mom sound like a frightened girl caused a knot in my stomach and made my chest tight.

I focused intently on my five boats. As Grandma's angry voice got louder, I imagined the biggest one looking out for the four smaller ones. I quietly whispered, "You over there, turn your boat around and follow me," and, "We need to get back before it gets dark."

I didn't understand why Mom was so scared of Grandma because when she argued with Dad, she wasn't afraid at all, and he was bigger and stronger than everyone. When Mom had to lift me, she'd groan, "Gary, you're getting too big for me to pick up." Dad would swoop me up easily and place me on his shoulders while I laughed.

Most of my memories of Dad are warm, safe, and fun. Like a clip from *The Andy Griffith Show*, we went fishing. It was sunny and cool with crunchy, orange and yellow oak leaves. I was as proud as Opie when I held up my fresh caught trout. When Mom yelled at Dad for leaving the smelly, wood fishing box in the garage, he winked at me and whispered, "I sure made your Mom mad, didn't I, Buddy?" I smiled and nodded my head, happy that we shared a secret.

Dad was largely responsible for my love of trains. He kept our locomotive and rail cars in a Dutch Masters box that had a warm, sweet, tobacco smell. Seeing the pilgrim men in their funny hats on the lid of the box would make me smile. Dad would say, "Careful," as he'd lift my favorite engine out of the box. He'd hand me a black oil car, then put his hands over my little fingers and guide them to be sure the wheels fit perfectly on the track. I knew if I rolled the train back and forth with a whisper and no clicking, I'd done it right.

Uncle Jim's being at our house and Doreen's living with us stressed Dad. He asked Mom, "Why is Doreen not with your mother?"

Mom answered, "You know my mother's not capable of taking care of her! She can barely take care of herself since my father died."

"Why is everyone in your family our responsibility?" he snapped back.

"The reason Peggy left for Florida is because she knew you didn't want her here!"

"Jimmy is here every day – and he's drunk!"

I focused on attaching the green planks to the Lincoln Log cabin that I'd built until they stopped screaming. Dad got quiet first. He shook his head, sighed, and walked toward their bedroom. He closed the door with a gentle click. I followed down the hall and knocked. He opened the door and whispered in a sweet voice, "Come on in, Buddy."

I gave an understanding look with a slight smile – the same way he did when he wanted me to feel better. "What's the matter, Dad?"

He messed up my hair and said, "They're adult problems. Don't you worry about them. Give your daddy a hug."

I knew Mom's being pregnant meant another baby would come from her belly, just like me and Michael had. The argument about that was the worst. The image type memories that flash in my mind, like a movie reel slowly stopping, show Mom and Dad at their most terrifying. Mom yelled at Dad, "I'll abort your baby!" He lunged toward her so fast that a kitchen chair bounced against the wall.

He stood in front of her and growled, "If...you...ever...!" She kept screaming as he breathed hard and started to show his teeth. I imagined him grabbing her neck and choking her, which made my heart pound. I started breathing fast and began to cry. He looked in my direction and then back at Mom. He closed his eyes, took a deep breath then turned and grabbed his keys from the kitchen table. Mom yelled, "Where are you going? Gary! Gary!" But he didn't answer. He stormed into the living room, snatched his jacket from the arm of the couch, pushed the screen door open and slammed it behind him.

My heart began racing. I couldn't breathe. Where was he going? I ran over to the door and watched him walk through the grass to his truck. He got in, started it up, and drove away without looking back at us again.

Intergalactic Station Wagon

It was probably two, maybe three, weeks after Dad had left. I was downstairs, alone, in our basement. Even with the fuzzy green paper – which was supposed to be grass – folded tight over the corners, I could still smell the plywood of our trainset. Dad always packed up the trains when we were finished playing. Still, I scanned the large oval track layout, as I always did, looking for a caboose or a boxcar that had been overlooked. Nope. Dad never forgot even one. I thought about the warm electric smell the locomotive, with the tiny, bright headlight, made when it pulled all the cars around the neighborhood that Dad and I had built together. Unlike the tracks, Dad hadn't nailed the buildings in place. He'd told me, "This way you can put them in different spots every time."

The yellow house with blue shutters and the brick train station were still lined up near the crossing gate, right where I had put them the last time with Dad. He had asked, "Why don't you want the house made out of logs there too?" I explained that a cabin was from a cowboy time, and it didn't make sense to be with the buildings that you could see in our town. He chuckled, agreed with me, and told me how smart I was.

I wondered where the pilgrim men box with our trains might be. Dad usually kept it on the top shelf of his and Mom's closet, but Mom had been moving his things around after he left. There was a box of his clothes in the basement, next to my toy chest. I dug through the jeans and tee-shirts, looking for the cigar box with the two engines and oil cars, but it wasn't in there. His brown sweater that smelled like sawdust and coffee – but mostly smelled like him – was. I thought about how much he wore it and wondered if he missed having it.

Once I gave up on finding the trains, I pulled my silver robot with red eyes from the toy box and walked over to sit at the base of the stairs. I liked being there so that I could hear the adults talking up in the kitchen. The first couple of days after Dad had left, I'd bolt up the stairs whenever someone walked in. I wanted to be the first one to greet him. Sometimes Mom would be sad. "Honey, it's not him. I don't know when he's coming home." Sometimes she'd be mad. "Gary, go back downstairs. Nobody's here." I wasn't sure if she was angry at me for wanting him to come home or angry at him for staying away. Either way, I knew running up the stairs every time the door opened bothered her. I decided, instead, I'd just listen.

The screen door squeaked as someone walked in from outside. I held my breath, listened and recognized Uncle Jim's voice. "Kath, he sent you a letter."

I ran upstairs as fast as I could.

Mom said, "Oh my God, let me see it, Jim."

"Is it from my dad?" I asked.

Mom didn't answer. She pushed her finger under the envelope flap and tore through the paper. As she unfolded the pages, I noticed there was cursive writing on the front and back of each. She began reading. Even though I knew I might get in trouble for asking, I couldn't contain my excitement. I pulled at the side of her shirt. "Is it? Is it?"

Mom snapped at me. "Gary, go downstairs and play!"

"But, is it?" I begged.

"Now! Go downstairs now."

My throat started to tighten, and I wanted to cry, but I held in the tears as I walked back downstairs. I could still hear Uncle Jim in the kitchen. "What's it say, Kath?"

Mom talked nicely to him. "He wants the boys." Then she got mad, but it wasn't at Uncle Jim, it was at Dad. "He can go fuck himself!"

I knew "fuck" meant something really angry and mean, like when someone said, "Fuck you." I didn't want Mom talking about Dad that way. Him leaving was her and Uncle Jim's fault. I hated her. I went over near the train tracks and sobbed without making any noise. I didn't want them to hear me, and I didn't care what they were saying anymore.

In the month that passed after Mom got the letter, I'd learned to stop asking about Dad. Mom got happy once when I got really mad at him for leaving. I realized, even if I pretended to be angry, she'd give me a sweet, approving look. Sometimes she'd hug me, touch her belly, which was getting bigger, and tell me, "You're my biggest and best."

I wanted the new baby to be a girl because all Michael did was sit in his playpen trying to put blocks together. I thought about Mom telling people, "He's such a good baby. The blocks entertain him for hours." She only thought he was good because he didn't cry while she packed up boxes in the kitchen.

Mom took plates out of the cabinet, one at a time, and wrapped them in crunchy newspaper before placing them in a box. I decided to look for other things around the house that needed to be packed, too. I brought drink coasters from the living room table, then magazines from the bathroom counter, and asked her if I could pack them up. She told me, "No, Honey. Don't worry about packing. We'll take care of it. Go downstairs and play." *Go downstairs! Go downstairs!* That's all I was ever told. Michael got to stay upstairs. Maybe if I were a stupid baby that only knew how to click and unclick the same two blocks, I'd be allowed to stay upstairs, too. At least I knew what was going on and wanted to help.

After Mom told me to go downstairs, she went back to packing dishes. I decided, since she wasn't really paying attention to me, I'd sneak down the hall to help Doreen. I pushed the door open to her bedroom. She was sitting Indian style with her thumb in her mouth, rocking back and forth. Her eyes were closed as she listened to the stereo with a big set of silver headphones. I knew she couldn't hear me, so I slowly sat, hoping when she did open her eyes, she wouldn't tell me to get out.

I stared at the carpet and began writing capital G's with my finger. Doreen took the headphones off. "What are you doing in here? Get out!"

I answered, "I came to help you pack," even though she clearly wasn't packing.

"I don't need your help. Get out." She paused, gave an evil grin to let me know I had one last chance to obey, and then calmly told me, "Go downstairs." We both knew that's where Mom would send me if she told on me, so I got up and went downstairs.

One of Grandpa's friends picked up our furniture in his green pickup truck. After he yanked the rope tight, to hold the mattresses and the coffee table, which was up on its end, together, he told Mom he'd bring everything over as soon as she'd found a place.

Seeing our house empty was funny. There were flat squares pressed in the carpet where the couch and the dressers had been. I screamed "Bdrrrrrrr!" like an airplane as I ran with my arms out, from the living room through the hallway and into a circle in my bedroom. Hearing my voice echo in the empty rooms reminded me of the TV show when a cowboy yelled into a cavern, "Hello down there…" Michael tried to follow behind me with his arms out, too, but he kept falling on his chin. But each time he went down, he'd pull himself right back up and keep going. I was kind of impressed that he didn't cry.

21

I knew the day was ending as the orange light from the living room windows stretched across the floor and began moving up the wall. Mom had scrubbed the bathroom counters and the kitchen floor cleaner than they had ever been. Doreen had vacuumed. I had helped by picking up torn papers and clear, plastic cigarette wrappers that had been behind the couch. Mom went into the kitchen, lit a cigarette, and picked up the telephone. I listened to the beep, beep, beep as she dialed, before holding the receiver up to her ear.

"Everything's done, Mom."

"Yes, Mom."

"I don't know when we're leaving."

"It's a long drive."

"He's at his sister, Gail's. Yeah."

"No, she's in North Carolina. His other sister, Marie, is in Georgia."

"I'll bring Doreen by later. We're going to get something to eat first."

"I will. Ok. I love you."

"Bye."

Then Mom called out, "Dor?"

"Yeah?"

"Dor, make sure Gary gets in the car."

I didn't understand why Mom wouldn't just tell me. Doreen bossed me around enough, secretly. It was only worse when she was told to.

"Gary! Come on. We're going!" Doreen shouted from outside.

"I know, I know," I said, as I walked out the front door.

Regardless of Doreen thinking she was the boss of me, I was still excited to be going for a ride so late. Plus, after we ate, we were taking her to Grandma's house. I couldn't wait until she was gone, and I knew by the way Mom had answered Grandma earlier on the phone that Mom was finally listening and taking us to see Dad. I was pretty good at figuring out what adults were talking about on the phone, even when I only heard one person.

Our Station Wagon with long wood panels on the sides was packed with big, black garbage bags full of clothes and toys. There were even two in the back seat with me. Mom was driving, and Doreen was in the front with Michael.

I loved the way the big yellow M looked like two French fries folded in half. Plus, the lights on the roof looked like giant French fries, too. Just seeing all of it made me want some! As we pulled up, Mom said, "Dor, hold Gary's hand."

Doreen opened my door, grabbed my wrist, and jerked my arm, not hard enough for Mom to notice, but hard enough for me to know she was bossing me around again. I didn't even care; I was excited to order a cheeseburger and a vanilla milkshake.

As I munched on my fries, I thought about when Mom had told Grandma that Dad wanted to kill her. It was right after he left. Grandma snapped, "He does not! You're pregnant. You should be with your husband." I was glad Grandma knew Mom was lying. I was also glad that she told Mom many times that she should be with Dad.

I took the last bite of my cheeseburger and thought about Dad being in another state. I knew it meant he was far away, and it would be hard to get there. I'd already told myself I wouldn't complain no matter how long we were in the car, and if Michael started whining, I'd let him play with one of my robots. I had two that I didn't care if he broke.

After dinner, we piled back into the car and pulled out of the McDonald's parking lot. As we drove down dark, familiar streets, I realized the air blowing in my open window started to have a salty smell. *Were we going to the beach, at night?* I loved how, on the boardwalk, you could hear the ocean as you walked along the hot, grey boards. My favorite part of the boardwalk was at the end where the rides with bright flashing bulbs were. Mom and Dad had taken me there to ride the carousel of horses with crazy faces, the flying elephant, and my favorite; the train that chugged around all the other rides.

As we turned into the quiet parking lot, I noticed that there weren't any other cars and the humming street lights made the pavement look almost white against the black night. Mom asked Doreen, "Are you sure you don't want me to take you to Mommy?"

"No, I want to stay with you."

No? Why would Doreen want to stay with us and not go with Grandma? I tried to understand her stupid thinking before deciding it didn't matter. If she wanted to go with us to North Carolina, what difference did it make to me? If I had to deal with Michael whining, I could deal with her being mean. I was not going to complain about anything until we saw Dad.

"Gary, Honey, we're going to sleep in the car tonight," Mom said like she was trying to convince me it would be fun.

I wasn't sure why she thought I needed convincing. I gave a slightly unsure, but happy, smile. "Ok!" I lay back and imagined we were in a spaceship with windows all around to look out at the dark starry night.

I woke up the next morning looking up at the window. Telephone poles and power lines were whizzing past the light blue sky and white clouds. I rubbed my eyes, sat up, and asked, "Where are we?" I was sure we had to be on our way to North Carolina – finally.

Doreen popped her elbow over the back of the seat to look at me. "It's about time you woke up. Where do you think we are?"

"I don't know. Where are we?"

"Bricktown."

What? Bricktown? I knew that was backward. That's where our old house was. I looked at the homes we were passing, which I recognized. My stomach got tight, and my throat started to close. I asked, "What about North Carolina?" As soon as I said the words, I thought I was going to cry. I didn't. I held it in.

Doreen looked puzzled and asked, "North Carolina?" like it was the first time she'd heard about us going there.

Mom said, "Gary, we're not going to North Carolina, Honey."

I tried to hold it, but my breathing got quick. *Dad. North Carolina. We weren't going??* My throat hardened as my face pulled in. Tears began running down my cheeks. I didn't want Doreen or Mom to see, so I turned and sobbed into the dirty Station Wagon upholstery. I felt Doreen's hand gently on my back. "Gar, what's the matter? It's ok. It's ok."

Mom was calm and sweet, too. "Gary, Gary, we're coming up to the train tracks. If you stop crying, we'll stop and watch the train."

I loved seeing real trains, but Mom would never wait. No matter how nicely I asked, she'd always just say, "Gary no," as she sped over the tracks.

I sobbed a few more times before wiping my nose on the back of my hand. "Ok."

"What?" Mom asked, with genuinely happy eyes looking at me from the rear-view mirror.

I sat up, said, "Ok," and, "Ok," again, sniffled and forced a smile.

DING!

DING!

DING!

DING!

My heart raced with excitement as the dirty, yellow engine barreled past with a crushing rhythm and a loud horn. Doreen and Mom both smiled from the front seat. It made me happy because I knew they were getting to experience how much fun it was to watch a real train.

The first few nights sleeping in the car were fun, but then scrunching myself against the overloaded garbage bag started to get uncomfortable. The fourth night a policeman knocked on Mom's window and told her that we couldn't sleep in the boardwalk parking lot anymore. Mom apologized to the officer then drove the car to the Cumberland Farms close to Bricktown. I thought the sign – a white tree in front of a greenish background – was boring compared to McDonald's. Plus, the girls that worked there were unhappy. When Mom had asked how much a hard roll, a small carton of milk and a pack of cigarettes were, the girl who worked in the morning huffed and answered the same way Mom answered me when I asked the same question too many times. Mom gave an apologetic smile and said, "I'm so sorry," as she counted out the pennies from the bottom of her purse.

After we had been living in the car for, I think, a week, we went to Grandma Marie's house. Mom pulled our packed station wagon along the curb in front of Grandma Marie's home.

"Dor, wait in the car with the boys. I'll be right out."

I pressed my forehead on the glass and wondered why Mom didn't park in the driveway. I also wondered why Grandma Marie didn't want all of us to come in. After what seemed like forever, Grandma Marie's front door opened, and Mom stepped out looking happy. She walked through the grass, got in the car and slammed the door. Her eyes were bright as she turned to Doreen. "She gave me five dollars and some change."

We didn't go to my other grandma's house. Mom only talked to her on the pay phone outside of Cumberland Farms. I heard her say, "Hi, Operator, I'd like to make a collect call." I knew it had something to do with the pay phone because she never said that when she called from our kitchen.

We had been living in the car for at least two weeks when Uncle Charley came. I was playing with my tiny plastic pool table – the white stick was smaller than a pencil and had a little spring to really pack power when shooting pool. Uncle Charley pulled up in a truck that looked like Dad's except Uncle Charley's was red, and the back part was empty.

Uncle Charley turned his truck off, got out, and leaned over toward Mom's window. He seemed excited to see us. "Hi, Kathy. Hi Doreen, Hey Michael, what're you doing, little guy?" He stepped back to my window, reached over the garbage bags, and messed up my hair. "How're you doing Buddy? What's that, pool you're playin?"

I burst out, "Hi, Uncle Charley!"

He chuckled. "I'm gonna talk to your mom for a minute, ok, Bud?"

Mom got out of the car, stuck her head in my window, and her eyes met mine. She gave a slight smile to let me know how much she loved and trusted me. "Be good, Honey."

They walked to the front of Uncle Charley's pickup truck and started talking. I listened, but it was hard to hear. Doreen was trying to listen, too. She even turned down the radio where a lady was singing about something turning her brown eyes blue, which I wanted to understand, but I decided I'd ask that question later. Right then, I was glad she shut it off.

I could tell Mom was getting mad when her voice got loud, and she started moving her hands up and down as she spoke. I could finally hear what she was saying. "Charley, I know it's not your fault. You're just trying to help. I am not giving you the boys."

"Kathy, no, it's not like that. It's just until you get a place. He doesn't want to take the boys from you."

29

"Yeah, well he's not. I don't care. He's not taking my kids. He'll get them over my dead body."

"No, no, Kathy. I didn't mean. I'm sorry. I didn't mean."

"Charley, it was good to see you. We need to get going."

Mom got back in the car, slammed the door, and turned the radio back on. "It's so easy to fall in love" sang from the stereo as we sped out of the parking lot.

Grandma must not have been happy that we were living in a car. A couple of days after we saw Uncle Charley, she told Mom that she had found a place for us to live in Pt. Pleasant, about three blocks from the beach – which was supposed to make it better. I didn't care about being near the ocean, but we crossed a train track on the way there. That was enough to make it good for me.

I rolled my window down and noticed the hot, wood boardwalk smell. I wondered if it was possible to smell the boardwalk from several blocks away or if the smell was coming from the dark brown power poles along the road. We turned down the street the house was supposed to be on and drove slowly. Mom said, "Look for the numbers, Dor. We're looking for 1207."

Doreen began reading off, "1197 . . . 1201, 1203."

I saw the number and yelled. "1207!"

Doreen completely ignored my outburst. "1205, 1207. There it is, Kath."

I didn't care. As we turned into the driveway, I got excited to see how big the giant peach colored house was compared to ours. I counted four windows on the first floor with six on both the second and third floors, and a wide deck, white like the shutters, wrapped around the whole house.

I opened my door, and Doreen yelled, "Gary, wait!"

Mom said, "I'll get him Dor. Here, take Michael." Mom came around to my side and took my hand. We walked up the stairs and knocked on the door.

An old lady answered with a bright, "Hello." She was shorter than Mom but stood like she was ten feet tall. She had white hair, and her yellow shirt had white dots the same color as her pants. "Kathleen?"

"Hi," Mom answered, in her nicest voice possible

"Come in, come in. I'm Mrs. Fletcher. I spoke to your mother. She took care of everything."

"This is my sister, Doreen. This is Gary, and this is Michael."

The lady looked at me and said, "You're really big. How tall are you?"

I giggled. "I don't know." I had no idea how tall I was. I was used to people telling me how cute I was or asking how old I was. Nobody had ever asked how tall I was. She was funny. I liked her.

The lady said, "Come with me. Your room is on the second floor."

She looked at me again. "Can you walk up the stairs?"

Of course, I could walk upstairs. The lady probably didn't know that we had had a basement, and I walked up and down stairs every day. After I explained that to her, she said, "Oh, really?" then opened her eyes wide. "Wow, you are a big boy!"

At the top of the stairs, Mrs. Fletcher began jiggling a key into the handle of the second door in the hallway. She pushed open the door, handed the key to Mom and told her if we needed anything to let her know.

Our room was actually two rooms. In the first room, there was a couch and a dresser with a lamp on it. The next room was bright from sunlight shining in through a big window. Mom walked over and gently swept her hand back and forth over the comforter with yellow and orange flowers – like she didn't believe it was real – then sat on the bed. I thought about how happy she must be to be able to sleep in a real bed again.

Mom got up, walked back to the first room, started taking pillows off and said, "The couch turns into a bed, Dor." I wondered if she meant Doreen could sleep on it like it was a bed, the way Uncle Jim did when he was drunk. After the pillows were on the floor, Mom began yanking at the cushions. As she pulled them off, I noticed a metal handle underneath. Before I could ask what it was for, Mom grabbed it and pulled. The bare, pillowless couch gave a loud creak, and a bed popped out. I thought about the word the lady had used downstairs.

"Wow!" I said, then asked, "Can I sleep on that one with Doreen?"

The next day Mom told me I could explore downstairs as long as I didn't touch anything. She went outside on the deck with Michael to drink orange juice at the picnic table. Doreen stayed in the room to listen to her small gray radio. I was sure she spent more time turning the dial than actually listening to music.

I loved our new home. Our old house had only one living room – the new one had three! There were all different people, mostly men, staying in the house with us. I thought it was neat that everyone had their own bedroom like everybody was brothers and sisters, but they were all adults. Mom was friendly and would talk to the men when she was sitting outside.

One day when I was setting up my green army men around a shiny, wood coffee table, a tall skinny man with a scruffy beard asked, "Whatcha doin' over there?" I quickly glanced over without turning my head. He wore an old, yellow baseball cap, and his hair curled up like wings from under the sides. Mom would have licked her fingers and smoothed the hair down if it was me. I didn't want him to keep talking to me, so I gave a short answer. "Nothing."

"You like playing with army men?"

Actually, I didn't, because they were stuck in the same position like they were glued to a base so they wouldn't fall over. Only the one lying down and holding his gun in front of him wasn't, but there wasn't much you could do with him. When you stood him up straight, it looked like he was shooting the sky. I was only playing with them because I had liked the way they'd looked in the plastic bag.

I answered, "Yeah, I do."

"I never liked them. G.I. Joes are better. Do you have any of them?"

"No." I focused on my men.

"Oh, they're more fun. You can move their arms and legs, and you can change their guns."

I was intrigued. "Really?"

We talked for a while before I learned that, in addition to being a G.I. Joe expert, my new friend used to work on a train. I was so excited; I couldn't wait to tell Mom. When he told me that he had to get going, I ran to find her. She was outside on the porch talking to another man with a beard, but his was shorter and neater.

"Mom, Mom! I met a man who worked on a train," I said with so much enthusiasm that both Mom and the man almost laughed.

"Really?" Mom asked.

"Yeah, yeah!"

"That's exciting Honey."

She pulled me close and turned me around so that I was facing the man she was talking to. She leaned into my ear and whispered, "Gary, this is Nick. Say hi."

I didn't want to talk. The man smiled nicely, squatted down, and asked, "How are you doing, Gary?" He held out his open hand toward me. I knew it was so he could shake mine. I didn't understand why grown-ups did that, but I knew it meant they were being friendly.

I put my hand out. He gently grasped mine, shook it twice, and said, "Pleased to meet you, Gary."

Burnt Tavern Manor

Doreen whispered, "Nick helped us get the new house." I wasn't sure if she told me because she knew I'd understand, or because Mom had said not to say anything. Either way, I was glad to know the secret.

When we drove into the neighborhood, I noticed the streets were wide with white lined parking spaces like a parking lot.

"Mom, why are the houses connected?"

Instead of answering me, Mom said, "Dor, can you see the number on that one?"

Doreen stretched her neck and answered, "Yeah, I think that's it."

Mom unlocked the door, and I bolted. Our new home was just like how we had left our house, empty and smelling like bleach and Ajax. There was also a funny chemical scent that reminded me of the metal cans with white drips that Dad had kept in the garage. I asked Mom, "What's that smell? Is it paint?" Doreen grabbed the post at the bottom of the railing and spun herself to jog up the stairs.

Mom looked at me. "Gary, make sure Michael doesn't touch the walls."

I grabbed Michael's hand and began walking around our new home, which was smaller than our old house and way smaller than Mrs.

Fletcher's house. The door to the laundry room looked like a closet. I leaned in and peered through the slats at the washer and dryer. They were the smallest I'd ever seen. Next, I walked to the kitchen.

"Don't touch anything, Michael." I let go of his hand and stretched my arms out to touch the yellow speckled countertops on both sides of the kitchen. I stood on my tiptoes to see if I could look through the window above the sink that opened into the living room. I loved how everything was so close together.

I took Michael's hand again and asked Mom, "Can we go upstairs to see the bedrooms?"

Doreen got her own bedroom, but I had to share a room with Michael. Once we were completely moved in, I made sure to neatly set up my robots and Spider-Man doll on my side of the light brown dresser between our beds. Michael didn't care where his yellow Tonka trucks were; that's why they were all over the floor, waiting to be stepped on by bare feet. Mom would yell when she stepped on them. Doreen would stop her step and nearly crash into a wall trying to catch herself. I already knew how dangerous his trucks were. Michael had thrown one and hit Grandma in the head once. I knew to duck when he threw them at me.

Mom thought Michael was old enough to sleep in a bed, but he wasn't. Not only would he pee the bed, which left a dried urine smell on his side of the room, he would sit on my bed in the same Hulk pajamas he'd peed in. I'd scream, "Get out of my bed. Mom!"

Mom would yell from downstairs, "Gary, I'm talking," which meant she was in the kitchen laughing with Nick.

The week before school started Grandma came to visit. She set her purse and keys on the table, hugged me and Michael, then told Mom, "I'm taking Gary to buy his school clothes." Mom tried to interject. "But Mom I've already-" Grandma gave Mom the (I mean business, and you better not try to argue with me) look, which stopped Mom cold. Mom had been telling Nick and Doreen for weeks how excited she was to take me shopping for my first school clothes. But regardless of what Mom wanted, Grandma must have figured that the first day of kindergarten was probably the most important day of my life, and she wasn't going to risk Mom messing up my look. I felt a little sad for Mom, but I was still happy to go shopping with Grandma because she always bought me a toy, like my Spider-man doll, and a candy bar. Sometimes I'd get a Milky Way or Three Musketeers, but Charleston Chew was my favorite. The first time I got one, Grandma watched as I bit down and yanked.

"If you eat that, those baby teeth will be out before you know it."

I didn't care about my baby teeth. I just loved how the bar stretched when I pulled at it. Plus, it was the biggest candy bar, and they were all the same price.

When we got home from K-mart and Sears, all I wanted to do was play with my new View-Master. I couldn't wait to look into the red binoculars, click the shutter, and watch Spider-Man beat the Green Goblin. But Grandma said, "First things first."

I tried to figure out when first things would be second, or even third. She said a lot of things that I didn't know exactly what they meant like, "What's good for the goose is good for the gander," or "It cost an arm and a leg." I wondered why she wouldn't just say, "You have to try your clothes on before you play."

Grandma took each shirt and pair of pants out of the bag and laid them on the couch. She handed me the red and yellow shirt with the white collar, which I knew was her favorite, and a pair of bell bottom blue jeans. She told me, "Go get changed to show your mother."

Mom called, "Gary, do you need me to help you?"

I yelled back, "No!" but that didn't make a difference. Mom still came into my room to pull up my pants and straighten my shirt.

I could tell that Mom didn't like the clothes by the way she tightened her bottom lip. I wondered if she didn't like them because the clothes, especially the silky purple shirt with the long, pointy collar, made me look like Uncle Jim when he went out on dates. She didn't say anything to Grandma, though. She waited until the first morning of school and asked, "What do you think, Dor? Does he look ok?"

I knew Doreen was lying because her voice was nicer than it ever was. "He looks good, Kath." Plus, Doreen wouldn't care if I got made fun of anyway. I didn't understand why Mom wouldn't just ask me, so I spoke out. "These pants are too tight, and the shirt has too many colors in it."

Mom snapped, "Gary, you look fine."

I couldn't stop thinking about getting made fun of as me and Mom walked down the school hall decorated with construction paper. I imagined kids asking me, "Why are you dressed like a grown-up? Do you think you're an adult?" Once inside the classroom though, I noticed other boys were dressed in long sleeve shirts with big collars, too. They didn't seem to care as they ran around the desks while their moms made bright, friendly faces and talked to each other. A lady, shaped like an apple or maybe a pear, (It wasn't nice to say fat) who was older than all the mothers, came up to me and Mom. She had a pudgy face, and she opened her eyes really wide when she smiled. "And who are you?"

"Gary"

"Do you know your last name, Gary?"

"Mele."

She leaned over toward me. "I'm Mrs. Davis." She put out her hand for me to hold. But I didn't want to, so I looked up at Mom.

Mom gave me a sweet look. "It's ok, Gary. Mrs. Davis is very nice, and I'll be here to pick you up in just a little while." I didn't move. Mom kneeled down, pointed up and whispered. "See the little hand on the clock? When it gets over there between the one and the two, I'll be back, I promise, Honey." She gave a smile that was meant to be reassuring, but it looked sad, like she was scared, too. Knowing she understood my feelings made my nervousness go away, so I smiled back and let go of her hand. I took the teacher's hand and walked with her. Once we were on the other side of the room, I turned back and saw Mom still watching me, with her knuckle pressed tight to her bottom lip.

Kindergarten was actually fun. I made three friends: Jennifer, Amy, and Jason. We got to drink a carton of milk and eat a chocolate chip cookie before we lay down on our mats for a nap. Some of the kids actually fell asleep, but I kept my eyes closed and pretended while I thought about what I was going to draw when we got up. As I explained all this to Mom and Doreen, I could tell Mom was happy that I liked kindergarten, but Doreen thought I was stupid for liking school. The phone rang, and Mom got up to answer it. "Hi, Tub."

I wasn't sure how Uncle Tubbo was related to us, but that's what I was supposed to call him. I wondered if he was called Tubbo because he was old with a big, round belly. Tubbo seemed like a good name for a fat person. His belly wasn't like Mom's pregnant belly, which made Mom look like she had a kickball under her shirt. Uncle Tubbo was fat everywhere, but his belly stuck out the most.

Mom asked, "She's still sick?"

"I know."

"I know, Tub."

"You know she won't listen to me."

"Yeah."

"Can you bring her by tomorrow?"

"Ok, I'll see you then."

Grandma held onto Uncle Tubbo's arm as she gingerly stepped onto the white tile in the foyer. She stopped and coughed loud and hard like it hurt. Mom went over, gently took her arm and carefully led her into the living room.

I spoke softly, "Hi, Grandma."

She tried to make a happy face like she wasn't in pain. "Hi, Honey," she said, then coughed again. I hugged her waist. I could tell she was must have been in pain because her arms only lightly touched me when she hugged me back. She moved slowly like her whole body hurt. I knew what that felt like because I had fallen down the stairs once when I was running. I'd cried. Dad picked me up, looked me over and told me, "Shake it off. You're ok." I stopped crying, but my arm, my leg, and my butt were sore for almost two days after.

As Grandma lay down on the couch, Mom turned the TV on and asked, "What do you want to watch, Mom?"

I blurted out, "Can we watch cartoons?" before Grandma could answer.

Mom whispered loudly, "Not now, Gary. Go play upstairs."

I barely had a moment to get annoyed about always being chased up or down stairs before Grandma said, "No, let them watch cartoons."

I was thrilled as I turned the channel with a chic, chic, chic until the 5 was at the top, and Woody Woodpecker was on, laughing his crazy, woodpecker laugh. I sat down on the carpet in front of the couch while Grandma began snoring softly behind me.

When Grandma went to the hospital, Nick came over to watch me and Michael. I liked Nick because the mornings after he'd spent the night in Mom's room, he'd ask, "Do you want some cereal, Gar?" He also listened when I had explained how Spider-Man's suit was red, blue *and* black – because of the webs. He'd thought about it, then said, "Yeah, I guess it is."

After Mom and Doreen left, Nick sat on the couch and asked, "Do you want to watch TV, Gar?"

I figured it was a good time for my question. "Is Grandma going to die?"

"No." Nick quickly responded, then added, "Well, I'm not sure. Why don't you find your Spider-Man?"

I realized talking about Grandma probably made him nervous, so I asked a different question. "What happens when you die?"

Nick stood and began scratching the back of his neck. I thought about how he seemed shorter than Mom, but he always stood straight up. He also had his light brown hair combed straight back, not to the side, the way Mom brushed mine. I started to feel bad for making him uncomfortable, and I was going to say, "Never mind," but he answered. "I don't know for sure."

I continued. "Do you go to Heaven?" Mom had told me that's where Grandpa was. She said it was wonderful, that Jesus and the angels were there and that we should be happy Grandpa was there, too. But I didn't believe Mom was really happy Grandpa was in heaven because she looked like she wanted to cry when she had told me that.

Nick said, "Let's watch TV. Maybe *The Incredible Hulk* is on. You like *The Incredible Hulk*, right?" I could tell he didn't want to talk about Grandma, or dying, or Heaven, either.

I answered, "Michael likes *The Incredible Hulk*." Turning green and dumb just to become all muscly seemed pretty stupid to me. I liked Spider-Man because he was smart and beat his enemies in ways they weren't expecting. Still, I climbed on the couch and smiled because I knew Nick was trying to be nice.

Mom didn't make any sound when she cried. The smudgy, mascara colored tears just streamed down her cheeks. Doreen cried so loudly it almost sounded like screams. I was sure she would have

45

crumpled to the floor if Mom hadn't been holding her up. Seeing her shoulders shake as she sobbed put a hard knot in my throat and made me want to cry, too. Michael did start crying. He didn't understand that Grandma had died. He was just crying because the adults were crying. Even though he had no reason to be sad, I still grabbed his big, blond head and squeezed him tight.

A few days after Grandma died, the doorbell rang. When Uncle Jack came in, I thought about how Mom told everyone he and Uncle Jim were twins. I wondered why, if they were twins, he didn't get drunk as much as Uncle Jim and sleep on our couch. He also got married. When Aunt Aida walked in, she grinned really big, like she was happy to see me, but I could tell she wasn't. She was wearing a dark blue dress that was much prettier than the black dresses Mom and Doreen were wearing. Even though it was flowy and loose, I could still see her pregnant stomach. I wondered why she wanted to hide it. Mom rubbed her pregnant belly like she had a round, silver trophy under her shirt.

Aunt Aida hugged Mom and asked, "How're you holding up?" then gave the same fake smile she had given me. Usually, after Uncle Jack and Aunt Aida left, Mom and Uncle Jim would talk about how "phony" she was. I still hadn't figured out what that meant, but I thought it had something to do with her pretending to like someone when she really didn't, or maybe it was about her yellow hair. I doubted they would talk about it that day anyway because everyone was so sad.

As the adults cried and told stories, I thought about the time when Michael had thrown his truck at Grandma. I remembered how I'd laughed when he did it, which put a lump in my throat. I wanted to tell her I was sorry and explain that the reason I laughed was because Michael did something that he'd get spanked for. Even though telling her would have meant I was in trouble, too, I wanted Grandma to know I wasn't laughing at her getting hit in the head. I also thought about when she lay down on the couch, and I had asked to watch cartoons. My stomach felt empty, like a card house ready to collapse, as I remembered that I hadn't cared what she wanted to watch. I wished I had turned on *General Hospital* for her. I should have sat right near her and got up to change the channel as many times as she wanted, but all I cared about was stupid Woody Woodpecker.

I looked at the reflection of the patio in the dark curved glass of the TV and thought about how I was sent to bed as soon as *Charlie's Angels* or *Three's Company* came on. Sometimes I would lie awake until the sounds turned from TV shows to the news. I knew by then that Mom would be asleep on the couch snoring. I would slowly slide out of bed, careful not to wake Michael across the room, and quietly open my door to see the blue lights flickering through the wood railing at the top of the stairs. Once, I even snuck out to the hall, looked down and saw Mom sleeping with her mouth open and her hand on her belly. I felt safe with her downstairs, Doreen in the next room, and the chatter from the TV filling the house.

After the adults left for Grandma's wake, I imagined what it would be like if Mom died. Just thinking about it made my chest hard, and I knew I would cry louder than Doreen if it ever really happened. I wondered who would take care of me and Michael, and now, Doreen, too.

I was glad Nick was watching us. "Nick, why do people go to a wake?"

"Well, it's so they can see someone who's died one last time before the funeral."

"Why do they want to see them? Are they in a coffin?"

"Yeah, they're in a coffin, and they look very peaceful."

"Do they look like they're asleep?"

"Yeah, that's exactly what they look like."

When I asked Nick questions, he usually gave good answers. Other adults – and Doreen – would say "Because," or "Just because," or ignore me.

We were watching TV when the phone rang. Nick got up to answer it.

"Hello?"

"Really."

"Her water broke?"

"Uh huh, uh huh."

"Sure, I'll be here."

I asked, "What happened?" wanting to know what "water broke" meant.

Nick was very calm. He turned toward me with cheerful eyes and said, "Everything's ok. Your mom's going to have another baby."

I folded my hands together and jumped up and down with crazy excitement! "Please! Please! Please! Please! Please!" I squealed. I was going to have another brother or sister. I wanted it to be a girl so bad.

I was sure she smiled at me because she knew I was her brother. Mom asked if I wanted to hold her. "Yes!"

Mom said, "Ok, sit next to me. Put your arms like this, and don't move them. You have to hold up her head. And you can't touch her head because it's still soft."

Her head was soft? We better keep Michael away. He might throw one of his trucks at her or worse; he might pick up a coffee cup from the table and try to hit her in the head. At least Grandma had a hard head. I was not going to let him hurt my new sister. I yelled, "Michael, get away from us!" The excitement drained from his face, and his dumb bottom lip started quivering.

Mom scolded me. "Gary, that's not nice," then called, "Michael, come here, Honey. He can see her, too." She pulled Michael to her other side, safely away from Christina.

Patriarchal Uncertainty

Dad?

Really?

That would feel weird. Nick had moved in with us shortly after Christina was born. He and Mom weren't married, but Mom asked if I wanted to call him Dad. "Why, Mom?" I asked.

"Well, you can if you want to, Honey."

I didn't want to. I liked Nick. He was one of the nicest adults around, but I knew he wasn't my father. I could tell from Mom's tone like when she'd ask me to rub her feet, she really wanted me to do it – call him Dad. I just didn't understand why it should be my idea.

Michael had already started calling him Dad. He didn't understand that Nick wasn't our father. He just did it because it made Mom happy, like the first time he pooped on the pot. Mom had squealed with a big, approving smile. "Good boy! Did you go poopy on the potty?" Michael laughed and clapped.

Regardless of why, Michael calling Nick, Dad, it made the situation even more uncomfortable for me. I didn't want Nick to think I wanted him to be my father. I could just imagine how stupid I'd feel if I called him, "Dad" and he told me, "I'm not your Dad." He'd be right, and I'd look like a fool. I didn't understand why Mom was doing this to me, but I still told her, "Well, I guess so."

I decided I'd say it at breakfast. Nick asked, "Do you want Alpha Bits or Lucky Charms, Gar?"

I stared intently at the stupid light blue flowers of my cereal bowl as I gave my answer. "Lucky Charms… Dad." My heart began pounding.

Nick smiled. "I like Alpha Bits, but Lucky Charms are my favorite, too."

It sure made Mom happy when I got comfortable calling Nick, Dad. It seemed really important to her that Nick liked me, and I liked him. Mom would say, "Gar, why don't you show Dad the train you drew at school?" Then she'd whisper, "He told me he drew it for you, Nick," which wasn't true. I didn't like her making me look like a needy baby, but at least Nick… *Dad* always said nice things like, "Look at that! What a good job!"

Talking about my father, Gary, at school was uncomfortable. Once, my teacher asked me if I was a junior because I was named after my dad. I told her that I was, but he was gone. She made a sad face like she wanted to hug me. After I started calling Nick, Dad, I didn't know how to explain it, especially since he wasn't married to Mom. So, whenever Dad dropped me off at school, I'd jump out of the car, yell "Bye," and run.

There were other things that Mom didn't want me talking about at school. After I'd learned that Uncle Jim always being drunk meant he was an alcoholic, she didn't want me talking about that. She also didn't want me saying that Uncle Dan was in jail. I questioned, "What should I say if someone asks?"

She looked at me all serious. "No one's going to ask if you don't talk about it."

On our last day of kindergarten, we had to line up to give Mrs. Davis a hug. She squeezed me really tight, then told me, "You're a really smart boy, Gary. Do a good job in first grade." When I looked back as I was walking out of the classroom, she smiled and waved. I waved, too, and felt a little sad that I wouldn't be in her class again, but also happy that I wouldn't have to think about what I couldn't and shouldn't talk about anymore.

While Uncle Dan was in jail, Mom had helped me write letters to him. In his last letter back to me before he got out, he had told me that he was going to buy me a monkey when he came home. I was thrilled when Dad left to pick Uncle Dan up to bring to our house. I couldn't wait to ask him if he had to wear striped clothes and dig with a chain on his ankle. When the door handle turned, I jumped up. "Is he here? Is he here?" Uncle Dan walked in holding a dark green duffle bag over his shoulder.

Uncle Dan was younger than Mom, Dad, Uncle Jim, and Uncle Jack. I thought it was funny that he only had hair around the sides of his head, just like Uncle Tubbo, except Uncle Dan's hair was still black. Doreen, the only one younger than him, gave a big hug. "Hi, Dan."

Mom was next with a hug. She put her hand on his bald head and asked, "What's up with this, Dan?" She laughed, and he laughed, too. I could tell he was really happy; I could also tell that he had no front teeth!

Even before saying hello, I asked, "Why are you missing your front teeth?"

"Woah!!!!" I screamed. Uncle Dan grabbed me and picked me up above his head so fast I couldn't help but giggle. It was like being on a ride.

"You've gotten so big!" he said, as he pulled me to his chest. "You were a baby the last time I saw you." He pushed his tongue through the part of his mouth where his front teeth should be and put me down. "You talkin' bout this, Champ?" He bent down like a boxer and pretended to fight me.

I laughed. "Did somebody punch your teeth out?"

"They sure did, Champ, but you should see what they look like!" He pretended to punch me again, which made me giggle some more.

Wow! It was just then that I noticed that Uncle Dan had a tattoo of a skull and crossbones on his arm just like a pirate. It wasn't even in the normal spot. It was on the lower part of his arm.

Uncle Dan was my favorite! I was so happy he was staying with us that I didn't even care about not getting a monkey. I burst out, "Do you want to sleep in my room?"

He gave a loud chuckle, then asked, "Where will Michael sleep, Bud? No, I'll crash on the couch."

I wanted to say, "Let Michael sleep on the couch," but I knew Mom wouldn't risk his peeing the bed in the living room, even though she didn't sleep there anymore anyway. I asked, "Mom, is it ok if I sleep in the living room with Uncle Dan? Please!"

She answered, "You can watch TV with Uncle Dan, Gar."

I stayed up until almost midnight watching movies with him before falling asleep on the floor.

I woke in the morning with the pillow from my bed under me and the blue, purple and white blanket made out of yarn over me. Someone had made it for Mom, but I didn't remember who. I didn't like it because it had little holes which let the cold air in when I slept. As I pulled the blanket tight under me, I could hear Uncle Dan in the kitchen talking with Mom and Dad. "Hey, Kath, can you spare a fin?"

Mom said, "Let me get my purse, Dan." She pulled out her money and counted out three dollars. "That's all I have, Dan."

"I see you have a sawbuck in there. Why don't you give me that? I'll bring you change."

Mom laughed. "Yeah, right."

I ran into the kitchen and asked, "What is a fin and a sawbuck? Is it money?"

Uncle Dan answered, "It sure is, Champ," then grabbed my neck to pull my head toward him. He whispered above my ear, loud enough for Mom to hear. "Tell your Mom to give me the sawbuck."

"Mom, give Uncle Dan the sawbuck!"

Dad sucked on his cigarette, turning the tip bright orange, before running it under the faucet. He threw the wet butt in the garbage, took one last sip of his coffee, filled the cup with water and left it in the sink. I wondered why adults always rinsed their cups and plates but didn't finish washing them. Dad said, "Alright, we need to get going." He kissed Mom on the lips and grabbed his tool belt with the hammer and razor in it. Uncle Dan pretended to box me one last time before walking out the door with Dad.

Mom didn't want to hear that I didn't like peanut butter and jelly sandwiches. Once, she made me one with a red spread that had tiny black seeds and chunky strawberry pieces that made me gag when I chewed it. Even though she got mad when I told her I didn't like it, she still bought grape jelly the next time she went shopping. I wondered why the grape jelly had lumps. *Were they supposed to be grapes?* I knew they weren't. I also knew Mom was watching me as I bit into it. I could see her next to the refrigerator as she smoked her cigarette. She told me, "There's no grapes in it. I don't want to hear it." I thought that maybe I should explain that I just wanted a smooth jelly that tasted like fruit without stringy bits or rubbery lumps, sort of like what they put in a jelly donut, but I knew she meant it when she said she didn't want to hear it. So, I tightened a delighted grin on my face, chewed, and forced myself to swallow the peanut butter jelly mush.

Normally, I didn't like when Uncle Jim came over, but that day, I knew his being at our house would distract Mom from focusing on my sandwich halves with only one bite taken out of each one.

The front door opened. "Kath?" Uncle Jim always just walked in like our home was *his* house.

"I'm in here, Jim."

He shut the door behind him. "What's going on?"

"Nothing. What're you doing?"

"Eh, nothing. I just came from Jacky's."

"Really?"

"Phew!" he said, as he rolled his eyes. "Boy, that Aida is something else."

"What happened?" Mom asked.

I knew they were going to talk about how Aunt Aida is a "real bitch" and thinks she's better than everyone. I asked Mom if I could go watch TV. She said, "There's nothing on, Gar. Why don't you go play outside?"

Uncle Jim butted in. "I would never be inside on a day like this when I was your age." I didn't really care what he did when he was my age. I wondered why he was the only man I knew who could spend the afternoon gossiping with Mom, while other men were working. I went into the living room to turn the TV on.

After I'd clicked through every channel twice, I realized Mom was right. There was nothing on but boring soap operas like *Ryan's Hope*. I grabbed my Spider-Man and went back to the kitchen table where I could hear Mom and Uncle Jim talking. Sometimes, when they knew I was listening, they'd tell me to go upstairs or outside. Other times, like that day, when I focused intently on my Spider-Man, they didn't realize I was paying attention.

I heard Uncle Jim say, "No, I'm not sure. I just know what John told me."

"But he's working, Jim."

"Maybe. Listen, maybe it's nothing."

I could see Mom over the kitchen counter. She looked like she had lost something important and was trying really hard to remember where she had put it. I didn't understand why Uncle Jim liked to make Mom worry. He always did it then left before Dad came home.

Uncle Dan and Dad usually came home when it was still light out. That night, Michael and I had watched all the afternoon cartoons and played with his Hot Wheels track during the news and then with my Lincoln Logs while Doreen watched *Different Strokes*. Mom made hot dogs after it got dark outside. Doreen took hers to the living room, but Michael and I had to eat at the kitchen table. Mom didn't eat. She stayed in the kitchen near the telephone smoking cigarettes. She only came out when Christina cried to give her a bottle or change her. Uncle Dan and Dad still weren't home when Mom said, "Come on guys; it's time for bed."

I didn't want to go to bed before Uncle Dan came home, but I could tell something was making Mom upset, so I decided not to argue with her. I said, "Come on, Michael."

I could hear the front door open downstairs. Michael was still awake. "Gary, is Dad-"

"Shhh!" I cut him off. "Be quiet, Michael!" I listened.

Mom asked, in an upset voice, "Where were you?"

"We went out. We've been working all week."

"Is Danny still out?"

"Yeah, I don't know."

"Where'd you go?"

"Out, I said." I could hear Dad click the top on a beer can.

I couldn't hear anything again for a few minutes except the news, which meant it was really late. Mom said, "Doreen, go upstairs."

When Mom was serious, she would say Doreen's full name. For me, she would say "Gary Charles." She didn't have to say that to me a lot.

Doreen answered, "I'm not tired."

Mom yelled, "Doreen, go upstairs now!"

Then, I heard Dad's voice. "Don't yell at her."

I heard a loud walk, like stomping. Doreen hollered, "Ow! Get off of me!" My heart raced. I hoped Michael would stay quiet as I pressed my head down in the pillow. It sounded like a stack of boxes falling over when Doreen screamed, "I hate you!" Doreen ran up the stairs, and I clenched my eyes shut. She slammed the door next to us and started crying.

Mom yelled at Dad. "Did you go to the go-go bar again? Did you see that fucking pig?" I wondered what a go-go bar was. Uncle Jim went to the bar a lot, but I'd never heard "go-go" before. It sounded like something for a kid, like a pogo stick. Dad stayed quiet. I could hear the next time Mom spoke that she had started crying. "That's really nice, you fucking bastard! I'm at home with three babies, and you're at a fucking go-go bar!"

Dad said, "I only went to drop Danny off." He put his keys and wallet on the counter, then walked upstairs. Mom yelled from the kitchen, "Yeah, that's why you're home at midnight!" then sobbed.

I heard Uncle Dan come in even later. He knocked a chair as he made his way to the kitchen to open the refrigerator. Then, he stumbled into the living room to turn the TV on. I knew he was drunk because he turned the TV up louder than it should have been that late. He didn't care if he was too loud, and he didn't care if he was the reason that Dad had made Mom cry.

The next morning, I was the first one up. Uncle Dan was lying on the couch in his white boxer shorts with one leg on the floor. He slept with his mouth open like Mom. His jeans and tee-shirt were thrown over a kitchen chair. He opened his eyes and looked right at me like he knew I was watching him.

"Hey, Champ, go get me a blanket."

I wanted to tell him to get it himself or give him the cold, blue, yarn blanket. Instead, I went up to my room and brought down my blanket for him. He took it and turned toward the back of the couch.

Mom pretended the fights never happened, but Doreen didn't. She would answer Mom's questions with only a "Yes," "No," or "I don't know" without even looking at her. Mom didn't seem to care unless Doreen started slamming doors. Then Mom would yell, "Doreen!"

Dad kept going to work every day. Uncle Dan would only go with him some days. Other days he'd sleep till it was almost lunchtime. Sometimes he'd take his blanket from the couch and go sleep in my bed after I'd gotten up. He'd say, "Go play downstairs," between snores if I went in my room to get my Spider-Man or my Star Wars X Wing fighter pilot.

The day we were getting ready to move, I watched TV in the living room with Michael. Dad and Uncle Dan were upstairs taking beds apart. Doreen, who had been upstairs, too, came down to get a can of Pringles, then jogged straight back up to her room to listen to music. Uncle Jim came over and went into the kitchen where Mom was placing dishes in a box. After he chuckled a few times with Mom about stupid things that I knew he didn't care about – like the traffic on the parkway and the crowds down the shore – he asked Mom about the new apartment. I wondered if he was "phony" like Aunt Aida. He didn't say anything bad about Dad or Uncle Dan when they were around.

Uncle Dan yelled from upstairs. "Kath, we need a Phillips head screwdriver."

Mom walked over to the bottom of the stairs and asked, "Where would I find it, Dan?"

He walked into the hall. "Look in the drawer next to the fridge."

Uncle Jim hopped over, rustled through the drawer as if he were working, too, and yelled, "I found it!" He then called to me. "Gar, take this to Uncle Dan."

I kept watching Tom and Jerry, wondering why Tom didn't die when Jerry dropped a heavy weight on his head. He only grew a banana-shaped bump that birds would chirp around. "Gary, take this to Uncle Dan," Uncle Jim said again. He could take it himself, I thought, before saying, "I'm watching TV."

"What did you say?!" Uncle Dan's voice.

He grabbed my arm and jerked me up.

WHAP! WHAP! WHAP!

My body froze in terror…

WHAP! WHAP!

Michael looking at me…

WHAP! WHAP!

Mom… Please… Mom…

WHAP!

"Don't you ever talk to your uncle like that again!" Uncle Dan yelled. He yanked me toward Uncle Jim, as the sting and shock to my body closed my throat. My face collapsed into a hard cry that I wanted Mom to hear. *Where was she?* In the kitchen? *Why wasn't she coming?*

"You want something to cry about?!?" Uncle Dan growled.

WHAP! WHAP! WHAP! He dragged me over to Uncle Jim, as I screamed and sobbed.

"Say you're sorry!"

"I… I… I…"

"Say it!"

"I... I'm... I'm so... sorry."

"Now, go up to your room!"

Motherly Ilk

It looked slimy like the two lines of boogers that would drool out of Michael's nose, down his upper lip. It wasn't yellow, though. It was dark green, and when she moved slightly, it squished through both the cushions on the couch. I leaned in to smell, and my throat closed shut. *It was throw up!* Uncle Dan had brought Veronica over to our new apartment a couple of weeks after we had moved in. Veronica had long brown hair that Mom had said was "A beautiful shade of red." It only looked reddish sometimes when it shined under the fluorescent light in the kitchen. Veronica had given a proud smile and answered, "Oh, thank you! I color all my girlfriends' hair. I could do yours."

Veronica tried to talk like she was an adult, but she was only a little older than Doreen, like maybe 16 or 17. Regardless of how old she was, I was pretty sure Mom wasn't going to let Veronica touch her curly black wig.

"My hair's naturally black, Hon," Mom had said, which I thought was really smart. Mom didn't like people knowing she wore a wig. She didn't lie. Her hair was naturally black… underneath. Mom had touched the sides near Veronica's face and told her that her hair was beautifully feathered, too. I thought maybe that meant she put white feathers in it sometimes. I'd seen pictures in a book where girls sitting in a field had white and yellow flowers in their hair. Maybe some girls put feathers in their hair instead.

Veronica didn't have feathers in her hair when she was lying on our couch. She had gooey, green puke with chunky strands dripping from her shoulder and neck. Her pretty brown hair looked like black oil stuck to her head. *Maybe she's sick?* The last time I had gotten sick and threw up, it hurt so bad I wanted to cry. I wondered if I should get her a towel.

I also wondered why Uncle Dan had left her alone on the couch. He had woken me and Michael when he came into our room laughing with her the night before. The bright light from the hallway had made it hard to see their faces, but I could tell Veronica was wearing her puffy rabbit fur coat that Uncle Dan had bought for her from the outline of the furry collar around her neck in the hallway light.

Uncle Dan had said, "Come on. Get up. Go sleep downstairs." Normally, he'd just make me sleep with Michael, and he'd sleep in my bed if it were just him. When he came over with Veronica, he wanted both beds, so he made us both leave. He also shut the door because he wanted to kiss her. Maybe he made her sleep downstairs because she got sick, I thought. I was trying to figure it out when I heard my bedroom door open upstairs.

I froze. I was sure I would be in trouble for looking at her instead of getting ready for school. I wondered what time it was then realized I might have already missed my bus. After Uncle Dan had marched us out of our bedroom the night before, Mom took us to

Doreen's room. Mom opened her door and whispered, "Dor, the boys are gonna sleep in here tonight."

Doreen replied, "I don't want them–" but Mom cut her off with a hard whisper. "Doreen!"

I closed my eyes and lay quietly on the floor, so Doreen wouldn't yell, but I didn't fall asleep for at least an hour.

Doreen's bus came a long time after mine, so she slept later than me. Dad could go to work whenever he wanted, so he didn't have to get up early. I was the only one who had to catch a bus at 7:30 in the morning. Even though I was still the first one up, I knew I had slept later than I was supposed to.

I ran to make a bowl of Alpha Bits so that it looked like I was trying to get ready. Uncle Dan walked into the kitchen. His face was puffy, and his eyes were almost closed like he was still sleeping. He asked, "Who's getting you ready for school?"

My hearted pounded. "Um, I am."

"Did you miss your bus?"

"I don't know. I don't think so."

"Kath!" He hollered up the stairs. "Kath, Gary missed his bus!"

Mom yelled, "I'm coming down."

Mom came into the kitchen in her light blue robe. She lit her cigarette and asked Uncle Dan if he was making coffee. He was. I could see that. If I had asked him that, he would have told me, "Don't ask stupid questions," or "Don't worry about it."

I was never sure if I was going to school when I missed my bus. Mom would talk about it like she was going to take me, but some days it would get too late, and she'd say, "I'll give you a note tomorrow saying that you were sick, Gar." She'd give a sweet look and touch my face to let me know she wasn't mad.

Whenever Mom took me to school late, she would dress me in my best clothes. That morning, she told me to put on my red corduroy pants and my red, white, and brown striped shirt. As she brushed my hair and looked me in the face with her cigarette dangling from the side of her bottom lip, I thought about how ugly it made her look. I asked, "Mom, why do you smoke?" She didn't answer. Instead, she said to Dad, "Nick, we need to take him back to the doctor about his eye."

"We will," he answered. "We need to get going. It's almost lunchtime."
Mom asked if I wanted to get lunch at K-mart, which I happily answered, "Yeah!" I hoped that we would shop for so long that I wouldn't have to go to school.

I got into the back seat of our station wagon and slammed the door shut. I liked going for rides, plus I wanted to see our new neighborhood. As we drove past a Dunkin' Donuts, I thought about how neat it was that they made the pink words look like a donut dipping into a cup. When we drove by Pathmark, I decided it should be my favorite food store because its sign looked kind of like a passenger train engine.

We pulled into the K-mart parking lot. Mom got out and took my hand as we walked up. I thought about the toy aisle and started to feel excited. When we walked in, Dad told Mom that he was going to get Woolite and Lysol. Mom said, "Ok," and told Dad that she was going to take me to get something to eat. We walked right to the cafeteria – no toy aisle that day.

Mom asked, "Do you want macaroni and cheese and a hot dog, Gar?" The yellow, sticky mush in the silver pan didn't look like the macaroni and cheese Mom made. Her macaroni and cheese was liquidy, and the macaroni never stuck together, like a delicious cheesy soup. "Can I just get a hot dog?"

Mom got frustrated. "Gary, you can't just eat a hot dog." She smiled at the lady and ordered both. The macaroni and cheese tasted even grosser than I thought it would.

When we got to school, the lady at the front counter told Mom, "His class is outside at recess. You may take him back if you like."

As we walked down the hallway, I started getting a nervous feeling in my stomach. My first-grade teacher, Mrs. Grossberger, wasn't nice like Mrs. Davis. When I was late or missed school, Mrs. Grossberger would speak to me with a mean voice through clenched teeth. She'd tell me to sit down then speak nicely to one of the girls who smiled all the time because they never missed any school. Dad pushed the metal bar on the door. It clicked, banged, then opened to the playground behind the school where kids were running, laughing, and screaming in the sunlight. We walked over to Mrs. Grossberger. Mom smiled. "Hi, I'm sorry he missed the bus."

Mrs. Grossberger gave a smile that I knew was phony and said, "Its ok. I'll take him."

She took my hand and waived to Mom and Dad as they walked back into the school. As soon as the door clicked behind them, she squeezed my hand hard and jerked me. "Don't you ever be late again! Go wait over near the wall until recess is over."

I didn't miss the bus the next day. Dad woke me when the sky was just starting to turn from black to dark blue. He gently shook my shoulder and whispered, "Gar, come on. Time to get up." I walked downstairs. The couch had wet towels covering the cushions, and the living room still smelled like Lysol. Uncle Dan wasn't there. Neither was his girlfriend. I wished it could always be like that.

Dad poured milk into my Alpha Bits and handed me a spoon. I finished eating, went upstairs to get dressed and put my coat on. I grabbed my book bag and walked outside to the bus stop. It always felt funny with the other kids after I'd missed a day – or several days – of school. Most times they'd talk to each other and act like I wasn't there, but that morning, Stephen said, "My Mom said I shouldn't play with you anymore."

I wondered if his mom knew that Uncle Dan's girlfriend threw up on our couch. Or maybe she thought I missed the bus too much. I answered, "I don't care," even though I really did.

Stephen leaned toward his friend and pointed to me. "Your eyes are crossed!" *What? My eyes?* They weren't actually both crossed. It was just one. I had been born with it crossed.

"Nuh-uh. They are not," I answered back, then looked away so he couldn't see them anymore.

Doreen got home from school after me. She usually took a bag of chocolate chip cookies or potato chips into her bedroom to listen to music. I was tired of sitting on the floor in the living room. No matter how many times Mom told me the couch was clean, I wasn't going to sit where Veronica slept in her throw up. I decided to go to Doreen's room.

I could hear music from outside her door. "We don't need no education," the music boomed. Dun da da. "We don't need no thought control."

I opened the door. "Hey, teacher! Leave them kids alone!"

I was sure she was going to scream, "Get out!" but she didn't. She was sitting Indian style on the floor near her stereo, rocking back and forth with her thumb in her mouth, like always. I walked over, sat next to her and listened to the whole song. I told her, "I love you, Dor."

She said, "I love you, too, and Mommy shouldn't let Danny hit you."

A few days later Mom took me to the eye doctor. "It's called a lazy eye," the doctor said.

"Does that mean there's something wrong with it?" Mom asked.

"No, it's fully developed. Think of it like this. It's like a perfectly good engine. It's just not on."

"How do we turn it on?"

"Well, we can put a patch over his good eye. That might work."

So, the next day I had to go to school wearing a patch that looked like a big, round band-aid over my left eye. I couldn't see anything but blurry colors from my uncovered lazy eye. I was afraid I'd fall down in the hall or trip over a desk in the classroom which, I was sure, would prompt Mrs. Grossberger to yank me up and yell in my face. I had to hold my breath when she screamed at me because her breath smelled almost as bad as Veronica's throw up. I held my hands out in front of me as I took one small step after another.

Mrs. Grossberger hollered, "Move!" as she pushed me forward. I stumbled, and there wasn't even a desk in front of me. Then she said,

"You have to concentrate." I really tried, but no matter how hard I thought about it, I couldn't make my eye see.

After a couple of days, I realized if I peeled out the inner part of the band-aid patch that was stuck to the top of my nose, the small opening was enough for my good eye to see out. I had to walk around with my head turned all the way to the left for it to work, but it was enough to keep me from crashing into anything.

I fooled Mrs. Grossberger, but I didn't fool Mom. She noticed the slight opening under the patch. "Gar, come here, Honey." She gently pressed the patch back down with her finger which sealed me back up in darkness. Maybe it was my hands opening right out in front of me; she knew I couldn't see. She said, "Come here." She pulled the patch off, and the whole world opened up again. I had forgotten how much I liked seeing everything. She asked, "Is it getting better, even a little?"

I shook my head. "No."

"Do you want to stop wearing the patch?"

"Yes."

"Ok, come here."

Mom picked me up. "Oh, you're really getting big," she said, as she sat me on the kitchen counter. She held her finger up in front of my right crossed eye. "Close your good eye. Can you see my finger?"

I couldn't see her finger exactly, but I could see a big peach-colored blur. I answered, "Yeah."

She slowly moved her finger to the right. "Can you still see it?"

"Yeah," I said again.

"Try to follow it."

It was easier to focus and concentrate on one color and make my eye move to follow it from the safety of sitting on my own kitchen counter. Trying to see a whole classroom of running kids, desks and book bags thrown on the floor along every wall was too much work for my poor lazy eye.

Mom did this exercise with me every day for several weeks. My eye never turned on like the engine the doctor talked about, but it did get strong enough to move in the same direction like it was looking at the same things as my good eye. Nobody ever told me my eyes were crossed again.

Tidings of Melancholy

The end of nineteen seventy-nine was the first New Year's I was allowed to stay up for. Dad told me it was the start of a new decade, which made it more important than a regular New Year's. He said we were going to have a lot of people over for a party. I already knew Uncle Jim would be there. He had been sleeping on our couch since Thanksgiving. I asked Dad, "Is Uncle Jack coming?"

"Yeah, he's coming with Aunt Aida."

"Is Uncle Dan coming?"

Dad answered, "Yeah." He didn't say he was coming with a girlfriend, though. Uncle Dan's girlfriend, Veronica, was around when I turned six in July and when Michael turned three in September, but she was gone when Christina had her first birthday in October.

After Veronica, Uncle Dan had a different girlfriend every time he came over. He didn't like when I would ask, "What's your name again?" or if I told the new girl about his other girlfriends. One of his girlfriends, when she had met me, bent down and asked the name of my Star Wars figure. I'd answered, "C-3PO." She smiled. "I bet you like him better than R2-D2."

I did. I told her, "You're the first girlfriend Uncle Dan's had who has blond hair."

"Really? How many girlfriends has Uncle Dan had?"

I started counting out on my fingers when Uncle Dan hustled over. "Run along before I bust your ass!"

I didn't have to worry about saying something wrong (that I didn't even know was wrong) on New Year's Eve. Uncle Dan did bring another new girlfriend, but he didn't introduce me. She had on bright red lipstick and wore a big, furry coat like Veronica's, but hers was made of black, brown, and white rabbits. She also looked old, like probably 30. I knew if I told her that she was older than all of Uncle Dan's other girlfriends I'd get in trouble for sure.

When she came in, Mom said, "I'm so glad to finally meet you," which Mom said to every one of Uncle Dan's new girlfriends.

Uncle Dan's girlfriend asked, "Where'd you get that dress? I love it!" I had realized that women liked to tell each other how good their dresses, pants, and shoes looked, but men never said anything about each other's clothes. I imagined a guy telling Uncle Dan that his brown slacks made his butt look good and made myself chuckle.

Mom told Uncle Dan and his girlfriend, "Come on in. Get yourselves a drink." She brought them to the kitchen table where bottles of clear and brown alcohol were mixed in with cans of Ginger Ale, Coke, and plastic cups. Uncle Jim had been at the table all night, talking louder and louder every time he had another drink. Uncle Jack, Aunt Aida, plus other adults I didn't know, were standing around drinking and talking to each other, too.

Over the music Mom practically hollered. "Gar, I want you to go upstairs with Michael and play with him near Christina's crib, ok?" Of course, I wanted to stay downstairs with the adults, but Mom seemed so happy with the party she'd put together that I didn't want to give her a hard time. I smiled and nodded. Once upstairs, Mom asked me to listen for Christina's crying because the talking and stereo would make it hard for her to hear. Then, Mom added, "Be a good boy, Gar. I'll come get you before it turns midnight."

Michael asked, "What about me?"

"You'll be sleeping," I answered for Mom.

Mom smiled. "I'll get you, too, Michael."

I knew she was just saying that to keep him from crying. He'd be sleeping.

After Michael fell asleep, I lay on my back and looked up at the ceiling at the little white pebbles stuck in the paint. I noticed that some looked like faces with different expressions – one was laughing, and another looked like it was winking. I realized if I looked away and then back, it was difficult to find the same face again.

I turned to my side and wondered why New Year's Eve was supposed to be fun. It wasn't like Halloween where I got to dress up as Spider-Man and Michael as the Hulk. Before we went trick or treating, I ran around our front yard pretending to shoot webs. Mom had said, "Good job, Gar," and Dad had added, "Ooh, you're gonna get me." I was quiet like Spider-man. I only shook my head yes or no when someone asked me a question. The only way it would have been better is if I had had a mask that pulled over my head like a sock instead of a plastic face held on with a skinny rubber band. Michael didn't care that the tiny mouth on his Hulk mask kept most of his breath inside the plastic face and made his cheeks wet. He still ran around yelling, "Grrrr!"

When we were done trick-or-treating Mom and Doreen dug through our pillow cases and took almost all the small Snickers and Milky Ways, but there was still plenty of good candy to last for over a week. By the time I had to start eating the powdery candy necklaces and the hard red candies that you couldn't bite into, I really didn't want candy anymore, anyway.

Christmas was my favorite holiday. Even though I knew Santa wasn't real, I still pretended to believe in him because it made Mom happy. Mom was thrilled to show me the half glass of milk and chocolate chip cookie with a bite out of it which we'd left for Santa on Christmas Eve.

"Gar, look! Santa was here!"

I knew it was probably Uncle Jim who had taken the bite out of the cookie, but I still smiled. "Wow! He was here!" Then, I ran over to figure out where my pile of presents was. I picked up every package under the tree to read the name. I wanted to be sure none of my presents got mixed up in somebody else's pile. I also made sure there was a line where you could see the carpet between mine and Michael's gifts. I knew he'd get so excited he'd start opening any present around him.

I had asked for Donnie and Marie dolls, but I only got Donnie. I was pretty sure the football and the remote-control car – which I didn't ask for – were given in place of the Marie Osmond doll. I also got Chewbacca and C-3PO, which I really wanted. After all the presents were opened, I neatly restacked all of mine back in a pile to remind myself how happy I had been when I first saw them under the tree.

I loved looking at the colorful lights blinking around the tinsel and garland while the radio played. Some of the songs were especially for kids, like "Rudolph the Red Nose Reindeer" and "Frosty the Snowman." I knew the words to Rudolph because Mom had sung it to me with a bright, happy face after the TV show. "Rudolph the Red Nose Reindeer had a very shiny nose."

"Gar, Gar. Honey, wake up." Mom whispered as she shook my shoulder. "It's almost New Year's. Do you want to come downstairs?"

I did want to. I sat up, yawned, and looked to be sure Michael was sleeping. He was. I would have been really mad if I had slept through New Year's and he was up to see it. When we walked downstairs, everyone got even louder.

"Hey, Buddy," said Uncle Jack.

Dad smiled. "Oh, I thought you were going to sleep right through it."

Finally, Uncle Dan, who was as drunk as Uncle Jim normally got, said, "Hey Champ, come here!" He picked me up, turned me around, and placed me on his shoulders. I was so afraid I was going to fall that I grabbed his chin.

"Here it comes!" Mom said with a big smile. On the TV there was a city with a lot of people screaming and laughing, and there was a ball on top of a building with lights all over it.

"Where are they?" I asked.

"Times Square," Mom said. "The countdown's going to begin."

Everybody started together, "10... 9... 8..." I couldn't help but smile. "7...6... 5..." I started counting, too. "4... 3... 2... 1... Happy New Year!" 1980 started flashing on the screen as everyone screamed and clapped. I wobbled as Uncle Dan leaned over to kiss his girlfriend. Mom kissed Dad. Uncle Jack kissed Aunt Aida. Even the strange people I didn't know were kissing each other. Mom took me off of Uncle Dan's shoulders and gave me a big hug and a kiss, too.

"You have to kiss someone when it turns New Year's," she said.

Doreen's best present came a few weeks after all the holidays were over. I could see Uncle Tubbo's car in front of our apartment from my bedroom window. I heard barking and saw a tan colored dog jumping from the front seat to the back. I ran downstairs as Mom opened the front door. Two dogs came racing in – the tan one, and a black one. They were almost as tall as Michael but thin with feet that looked a little too big. The tan one was kind of white on the bottom, with a darker back that went to the top of its head and came to a point above its eyes, kind of like Dracula. The other one was completely black. The tan dog ran right up to Christina and started licking her face. She wobbled and then fell on her butt, which put a mad look on her face. The black dog looked toward me on the stairs, then looked at Michael, then came over to me and started licking my face, too. I giggled and ducked my head toward my shoulder

After Mom picked up Christina, the tan dog ran over to Michael and started licking his ear. Michael put both of his hands on the dog's head like he was going to jump on and ride her. I wanted to see that. I knew she'd run away, and he'd tumble backwards right onto the floor. Michael asked, "What's his name?"

"That's Sheba," Uncle Tubbo answered. Then he pointed to the black one near me. "That's Soya. They're both girls."
I decided I liked Soya better because she came to me first and she didn't have the funny looking point above her face.

Doreen bent down, put her hands out, and called in a high, sweet voice, "Come 'ere! Come 'ere, girl!"

Sheba and Soya both stopped, turned, and took off toward her. Doreen rubbed each one's back as they licked her cheeks. Doreen closed her eyes and laughed like she was the happiest she'd been in her entire life. From that point on, she would take them out to play fetch with a tennis ball every morning and afternoon. Her enthusiasm stayed the same, day after day, as the winter snow melted to small icy patches in the corners of the yard.

We'd learned in school that there are four seasons. Summer was my favorite, mostly because there wasn't any school, but also because that's when my birthday was. Summer was also the last time we had moved. I was pretty sure it was every time we had moved. But, it was spring when I heard Mom and Dad talk about moving again. I was setting up Chewbacca and Han Solo at the top of the stairs when Mom said, "We haven't paid the electric since November."

Dad asked, "Did you call them?"

"Yes, I called them. They said if we don't pay December and January's bill at least, they're shutting it off. We haven't paid it in five months."

"What're we going to do?"

To keep them from realizing I was paying attention, I looked down the stairs without moving my head. Mom opened a newspaper and laid it out on the table. "There's a house for rent right off of 71 in Manasquan. Nick, hand me the phone."

Beep, beep, beep . . .. Beep, beep . . .. Beep, beep.

"Hello?"

"I'm calling about the house for rent."

"Yeah."

"Three bedrooms is great. Yeah, we'd like to see it."

A few days later, Mom was in the kitchen packing with Uncle Jim. I was in the living room thinking about how spring had no good holidays. Even though we got candy on Easter, we also had to search for dumb hard-boiled eggs which were hidden under the couch and inside closet doors. Then we had to pretend to be happy as we peeled them to eat – well, at least I did. Michael bit in his like he was expecting white chocolate, then stuck out his tongue. "Ewww."

As *Scooby Doo* ended, I wondered why Fred, Daphne, and Velma weren't in the episodes with Scrappy Doo. Plus, I thought it was stupid when he'd yell, "Puppy power!"

Mom reached up and opened the cabinets between the stove and the refrigerator. She asked, "Jim, will you hand me that box?"

Bzeeeooo!

The house went silent except for the sound of Mom holding plates. The TV was dark. The light upstairs was off. The refrigerator had even stopped humming. Doreen opened her door. "What happened?"

Mom walked over to the front door and looked out. "Shit!"

I knew better than to ask Mom a question right after she said "Shit," so I walked over to the kitchen and asked, "What happened Uncle Jim?"

He didn't look at me but still answered, "They cut the power."

I asked, "Why?"

Mom came back into the kitchen. "Don't worry about it, Gary. Take Michael and go play in your room."

"But I don't want to."

"Gary! Now! Go up to your room!"

I turned to grab Michael's hand. "No!" he screamed and pulled his hand away.

I yelled, "Mom!"

She called, "Doreen, take Michael up to his room."

Doreen jogged down the stairs with a ba dum ba dum ba dum. She picked Michael up as he started screaming. "Stop it!" she yelled, then brought him to our bedroom. I walked in just as she set him down. She stepped out and shut the door.

I always used to wonder, if you watched the sky without looking away if it would really turn to night. As I lay in my bed looking out the window, the sky turned from light blue to dark blue, and then I saw a tiny star. *Were they always there, even during the day?* Once the sky was dark and the shadows had completely covered the entire room except the part of my bed where I was lying on my pillow, I listened. It was so quiet that I could hear the electric box, which the neighborhood kids would sit on, buzzing outside. I heard a car, sat up and saw Dad's truck. The headlights were bright as the truck pulled up to our dark apartment. Dad and Uncle Dan both got out and slammed their doors. I looked at the apartments across from us and both ways down the street. Every apartment had lights on. You could even see flickering TVs in some windows.

I turned around and sat back against the wall. My eyes moved around our dark room. The area at the bottom of the door where I could usually see light from the hall was black. I sat still and listened. I heard a creak from our closet, and my ear tensed. Then, I thought I heard a knock in Doreen's room, but she was downstairs with Sheba and Soya. Questions raced through my mind. *When were the lights going to turn back on? What if everyone left Michael and me alone in our dark home?* My heart started beating faster. I got up and opened our bedroom door to look out. It was so dark in the hallway that I could barely see across to Mom and Dad's room. I called out, "Mom?"

"What?"

"Where are you?"

It was hard to see, but I could hear her coming up the stairs.

"Gary, I need you boys to stay in here."

"Why can't we go downstairs?"

"Because we're working."

"What about Doreen?"

"She's helping me."

"Can I help?"

"No, I need you to stay up here with Michael."

"Why can't Doreen stay with Michael?"

"Gary."

"But what about Christina?" I added, asking any question to get her to stay with us longer.
"Christina's downstairs. Lay down and try to go to sleep like Michael. I will come up and get you in a little while. I promise."

I wanted to cry as she shut the door. I ran back to my bed, climbed in and pushed my back up against my pillow near the window where I could see the street lights. I held my knees and kept wishing –

please, please – for the lights to come back on as I told myself over and over there's no such thing as monsters.

I wasn't sure how long I'd been sleeping when Mom opened the door, but I felt relief as I realized the sky was turning blue again. Mom whispered, "Gar, come on Honey." She picked Michael up out of the bed. I wondered if I was going to school, but I wasn't going to say anything. I didn't want to remind Mom if she'd forgotten. I walked out of our bedroom and looked down the stairs. The apartment was still dark but almost empty. The couch was gone, the TV was gone, and the kitchen table and chairs were gone. There were newspapers and blankets on the floor in the living room. There was still a box open on the kitchen counter, and the front door was open. I wondered where Sheba and Soya were. Uncle Dan walked in wiping his forehead with the front of his tee-shirt. Uncle Jim followed.

Mom said, "The boys are ready to go, Dan. You guys can do their room."
Uncle Dan asked, "Are you putting them in the car?"

"Yeah."

Mom handed Michael to Uncle Jim, so she could put my jacket on. Next, she put Michael's coat on him. He moaned because he didn't want to wake up. When we walked outside, I noticed frost on the grass, and there was a big yellow truck with the back open right in front of our door. Inside was our couch, kitchen table and chairs, piled up next to stacks of boxes. We walked around to our car where Doreen was holding Christina in the front seat. Sheba and Soya were both in the back seat with their tails wagging. Mom opened the backseat door and told them, "Get in the back. Come on. Get in the back." Only Soya hopped in the way back. I climbed in next to Sheba. Mom walked around the car and lay Michael down on the other seat. Dad came out of the house. "We're almost done."

Mom said, "Ok, I'm going to take them to the house. I'll see you there," then got in the car. I looked at the two dark windows and open door of our apartment and realized that the front of our empty home looked kind of like a sad face. I remembered Halloween, then Christmas and especially New Year's and felt a little sad, too. Doreen turned the radio on. "Do that to me one more time," played as we backed away.

Determining Sibling Allowances

Mom liked the house in Manasquan because there was a pool, and it was near the ocean. She said, in a proud voice, when she spoke to Aunt Aida on the phone, "Ade, we are right near the water. You can walk to the beach." I didn't think Mom would ever walk to the beach. She didn't even walk to the mailbox. She always sent Doreen, Dad, or me to get the letters. Even if we never walked there, I knew we must be near the ocean because the air had a sandy, salty smell, and white seagulls with black wing tips glided over our new home.

I knew what seagulls were because I'd asked Dad one time when we were at the beach with Uncle Dan and one of his girlfriends. The birds had started walking around us when Mom opened the cooler to take sandwiches out. I took a piece of crust off my bologna and cheese sandwich to throw to them. Two of the birds almost got in a fight over the bread – they cacked at each other with their wings in the air. Uncle Dan got up and waved his hands at them. "Get atta here!" he yelled before saying to me, "Don't feed them. They're nasty." I didn't understand why they were nasty. I thought they were really pretty. Plus, they were smart. They knew we had food in the cooler, even before we took it out.

It was the most fun when we were first moving in. You could see the lines in the carpet from where it had been shampooed, and it had a spongy feel when you walked on it with bare feet. I loved the smell of the new paint in my bedroom. I also couldn't wait until summer when Dad would take the cover off the pool, so we could go swimming. Mom liked that the house was nicer than the apartments we'd lived in and she wanted to be sure it was decorated beautifully with modern furniture. She told Dad and Uncle Jim to put a dresser, Christina's crib, and an end table that looked like it was made out of mirrors in the garage with the boxes she didn't want to unpack yet.

Uncle Jim was only supposed to spend the first night in the house because he'd helped us move. He'd told Mom that he had a room to rent down the shore. I wondered if that meant the beach like the Jersey Shore. He also wasn't supposed to drink in our new house. The second night, after all the furniture had been moved to where Mom wanted it, Uncle Jim said, "We should get a pizza."

Mom turned to grab the telephone. "I'll order it. Nick, where's the phone book?"

Before Dad could start looking for it, Uncle Jim said, "Nah, let me go get it, Kath. Where are your keys?" Mom answered, "Jim, you know I don't want you drinking in the house."

"I'm not gonna get drunk, Kath!"

Mom looked at Dad. "Nick, why don't you go with him?"

I could smell the delicious, cheesy pizza the moment Dad and Uncle Jim walked in the front door. Dad was holding two white pizza boxes stacked on top of each other, and Uncle Jim was carrying brown paper bags. "I got Coke," he said as he placed one of the bags on the dining room table. I loved Coke, but I wasn't allowed to have soda unless it was a birthday or a holiday. Moving into a new house was kind of like a holiday, I thought. Mom always tried to make it feel that way.

Even when I was allowed to have soda, I wasn't given the whole can like Doreen was. As Uncle Jim walked into the kitchen with the other bag clutched under his arm he hollered back, "We got extra cheese and a sausage. The Cokes are on the table." I already knew that because the cans had started to make the bag on the table wet. Then he said, "Damn, that move was rough, wasn't it, Nick?"

I got a knot in my stomach. Dad had told me that's what you call the feeling in your belly when you know something bad is going to happen. I had it whenever I went to school after I'd missed two or three days in a row. I also got it whenever Uncle Dan would ask, "What did you say?" That night, the knot in my stomach was because I knew Uncle Jim talking so much meant he was going to start drinking.

Mom walked into the kitchen and came back out shaking her head. She set two red plastic cups down on the table and whispered to Dad, "Did you take him to the liquor store?" Even though she was being quiet, I could tell she was upset like she wished Dad hadn't done that. It seemed like Dad got in trouble for a lot of things Uncle Jim and Uncle Dan asked him to do.

He whispered back, "What was I supposed to do?" Mom popped the Coke can and filled my cup. She turned and looked out the

91

window for a couple of seconds while my fizz popped down. Michael asked, "Can I have some, please?" Mom didn't even answer him. She just started pouring his soda. Uncle Jim walked out of the kitchen holding a white and blue can. I knew it was beer.

I thought that maybe if I helped Mom put out the pizza, she'd be able to sit down, eat, and not think about Uncle Jim being drunk in our new house. I stood up and took the paper plates out of the soda bag and started pulling them apart. I gave one to Michael, one to me and then asked, "What about Christina? Should I put one for Doreen?"

Doreen was in her room. Actually, it wasn't just her room anymore. Now that Christina could sleep in a bed, she had to share a room with her, which kind of made me happy.

Mom told me, "No. Go ahead and sit down." As she grabbed two crusts to pull apart my slice, I watched to be sure she didn't pull any of my cheese off. Sometimes a big glop of cheese would pull off one of the slices. Mom would grab it with her fingers and smush it back on, usually the slice she was going to eat. Mom handed me my piece of pizza, licked her finger and thumb then started pulling Michael's slice off. I didn't care if she took his cheese.

Doreen came out of her room, looked at Uncle Jim and asked, "Where'd you get the beer, Jim?"

"Nick took me to the store," he answered, then added, "Actually, don't you worry about it."

Mom cut in. "Jimmy, you told me you weren't going to drink here."

Uncle Jim's voice started getting loud. "I've been busting my tail for three days moving you, and I can't have a goddamned beer?!" Then he went into the kitchen and started slamming cabinets and talking to himself.

Mom looked at Dad. "Are you going to do something?"

"What do you want me to do?"

Mom looked at me. "Hurry up and finish your pizza."

I started, "But what about Michael–" before I realized he wasn't in his chair. He must have snuck away when Uncle Jim started yelling. I usually had to take Michael to our room when a fight started. I could usually take my time by pretending he didn't want to go so I could listen longer. Not that time. Mom handed me my paper plate and marched me down the hall, right into the room. Michael was already in there on the floor. He didn't even look up from his matchbox cars when we walked in.

I hated Uncle Jim. Every time he got drunk, it caused a fight. Even though Mom said my real dad was a bastard for leaving her with two babies and pregnant, I knew he wouldn't have left if Uncle Jim hadn't been around so much. Now, Nick Dad was getting yelled at because of Uncle Jim. I thought, he'll probably leave, too.

The worst part about Uncle Jim drinking was how much he talked. Sometimes he'd try to cause a fight by asking people questions while he drank his beer. He did it so they couldn't pretend they didn't see him drinking. Sometimes he would spend a lot of time explaining the same thing over and over, like when he'd told Aunt Aida she didn't understand equal rights. She had said that men should still be gentlemen by opening her door, lighting her cigarettes, or taking out her trash. He told her if she wanted to vote and work the same jobs as men she shouldn't expect men to do those things for her. When she told him she disagreed, he said, "You can't have your cake and eat it, too." The more drunk he got, the more times he would say, "You can't have your cake and eat it, too."

I had wanted to ask him why men couldn't take out the trash, but women were supposed to do the dishes. I had thought of at least three times when he had gotten drunk and used every pan and bowl in the kitchen to make scrambled eggs. His pile of dishes would sit in the sink, sometimes for three days, until Mom or Doreen would finally do them. I had also wanted to tell him that what he told Aunt Aida was the dumbest thing he'd ever said, and if he stopped drinking, maybe he wouldn't sound so stupid. But I knew I'd get in trouble. Mom expected me to respect my elders no matter how dumb or drunk they were. I lay in bed and listened to the adults yell until I fell asleep.

The next morning, when I woke, I stared at my bedroom window and wondered why the sunlight shined in brightly, but in our apartment, it didn't shine in until the afternoon. I pulled myself up and listened. The house was quiet. I walked out of my bedroom to the living room where the TV was on, but the sound was almost completely off. Uncle Jim was snoring on the couch with one foot on the carpet, and one arm spread out straight toward the floor, like someone had dropped his lifeless body from the ceiling. I knew he wasn't dead as he struggled to pull in a sticky breath. I looked at the cigarette burned down to the light brown filter, still in his hand, and remembered Mom screaming, "Jimmy, do not fall asleep with a lit cigarette – you'll burn the house down!" I wondered why Mom expected him to think about causing a fire when he didn't even think about getting changed. He slept in his tee-shirt, blue jeans, and dirty socks. Uncle Dan slept in his boxers. I slept in pajamas and Mom slept in her light blue nightgown, which flowed like a thin curtain over a kitchen window as she walked around dumping coffee grinds before filling the coffee pot.

I loved being the first one up, so I could explore the house before an adult would tell me to go play in my room or outside. Uncle Jim's beer cans were on the kitchen table, the counters, and there were even two on the floor near the couch. Some were crushed like he was trying to be tough when he finished them. Sometimes when he got drunk, he would say, "You have a problem? You have a problem?" like he wanted to fight, but everyone knew he didn't really want to. The last time he did that, Dad had told him, "Calm down, Jim. No one wants to fight you."

There were also Coke cans on the kitchen table. I thought about how adults hated when soda got warm. I didn't mind. I looked around then slowly picked up one of the cans. It was almost full! I knew if I swallowed a bunch of times really quick, I'd be able to finish it before anyone else got up. I listened for Mom, Dad or Doreen then stared at Uncle Jim to be sure he was still dead asleep. I gripped with both hands then lifted the Coke can to my mouth.

Gulp, gulp, echh, blech, krechhh.

I took the can away from my lips and coughed into my shoulder. *Cigarette ashes and butts!?* Gross! I shook the can and heard the cigarette butts swishing around. I stuck my tongue out and wiped it on my hand. I needed water, but I didn't want anyone to know why. If I told them what had happened, they'd say, "That's what you get for sneaking Coke." I put the can back on the table and ran to the kitchen to turn the water on. I quickly decided, if someone walked in, I'd tell them I was really thirsty. I poured a glass of water, took a big swig and spit it out. I took another swig and gargled like mouthwash before spitting it out.

Could I die from drinking cigarette ashes? Should I say something to Dad? He'd probably be the least mad, but he'd still tell Mom. I put my hand on my heart and breathed in and out several times. I decided I'd say something only if my chest started hurting.

I went back to the living room and looked over where Uncle Jim was sleeping. I didn't have to worry about him catching me snooping. If Uncle Dan caught me, he'd grab the top of my shirt, yank me close, and say, "What do you think you're doing?" Uncle Jim got so drunk that nobody sneaking around would wake him up. I was pretty sure I could bang a wooden spoon on one of his beer cans right near his ear, and he still wouldn't wake up. There was a glass bottle on the floor. I knew he snuck beer in, but I didn't know what that was. I reached down and picked up the empty bottle to smell. It stopped my breath. The label spelled vodka, which I wondered how to say. I'd never seen a word with a "d" and a "k" next to each other.

I hadn't been to school since we left our apartment, but still, I knew it was the weekend as lawnmowers hummed and buzzed outside. Michael came out of the bedroom rubbing his eyes. "I'm hungry."

I told him, "Go sit at the table. I'll make you cereal." I looked around our new kitchen. *Where would Mom put the cereal?* I opened all the cabinets below, but there were only pots in them. I pulled a chair over to climb up and look in the higher cabinets. I found a box of Honeycomb. I put it on the table with two bowls. Then, I thought that I should make Christina a bowl of cereal, too. I went back and got another bowl. Doreen usually slept late on the weekends, so I could probably sneak into her room and wake Christina up.

I opened Doreen's door. It creaked, so I stopped. I pushed it just a little slower, so it wouldn't be as loud. Doreen was still asleep. Christina was already sitting up looking at me. *How long had she been awake?* "Christina," I whispered, "come on. Do you want cereal?" She looked at me like she didn't understand. I made my face really happy like you're supposed to do with babies. "Come on," I said in a bright whisper, but she still just stared. Stupid Christina, I thought. Doreen's going to wake up. I knew Christina probably just wanted to be carried, so I decided to creep in and pick her up. I took five tiptoe steps toward her bed, then turned toward Doreen. I imagined how much safer I'd feel if her long, black hair that was spread out all over her pillow were covering her face – like Cousin It from *The Addams Family*. Still, I could see that her lips were slightly open, and she was snoring. She didn't snore as loud as Mom and Uncle Dan. It was more like heavy breathing. As I pulled Christina up, her blue eyes met mine, and she smiled. She knew I'd never picked her up before. Ewww, I thought as my nose scrunched – she smelled like poop. I had forgotten about her diaper. And she was heavy, too. I put her and her squishy diaper down, took her hand and led her out of the room.

I barely got to eat because I had to keep running around the table wiping milk that Christina splashed all over. She was so excited I was letting her eat with me and Michael that she kept smashing her spoon in her cereal. Even her soft, light brown hair was wet to her cheeks with milk and cereal bits. When I finally calmed her down enough, so I could sit and eat my own cereal, Michael asked, "Can I have more?"

I wanted to yell at him, but I thought it would be better if I acted like a grown up. I answered calmly, "No. You've had enough." He crossed his arms and frowned which made me mad. I told him, "Don't make me give you something to cry about."

Michael popped out of his chair and yelled, "You can't hit me!" then ran to the bedroom and slammed the door.

I was so angry I wanted to run right in there and spank him for talking to me like that, but his stupid slammed door woke everyone up. First, I heard Uncle Jim snort a few times like he couldn't breathe, then Mom and Dad's door opened, then Doreen's.

It was sometime after lunch when I was playing on the back porch with my Star Wars figures. I'd wanted to play in the grass, so it would look like a jungle, but I wasn't allowed to go near the covered pool. Sheba kept coming over and sniffing Chewbacca and C-3PO. Every time she did I told her, "Get away."

There were plenty of big monsters in Star Wars but nothing that looked like a giant mutt. Dad had told me that Sheba and Soya were mutts when I asked him why they looked different from each other. When I tried to explain that to Doreen, she yelled at me. "They're German Shepherds!"

"Gar!" I heard Mom calling me.

"Yeah?" I yelled.

"Is Michael with you?"

"No!"

She came out onto the porch, turned her head both ways and looked around the yard. Then she walked over to the side of the house that you couldn't see from the back porch.

"Do you know where Michael is?" she asked.

"No, I don't."

"Have you seen him?"

"No."

Mom looked upset as she walked back into the house. I got up and followed her.

Mom said, "Nick, he's not in the backyard."

Dad asked, "Are you sure?"

Mom put her fingers near her lip. "Yeah, it's just Gary." She yelled down the hall. "Dor, are you sure he's not in his room?"

"He's not in here," Doreen yelled back.

"Oh my God!" Mom said as she held her chest. She walked over, opened the front door and hollered, "Michael... Michael!" Uncle Jim, who had been sitting on the couch for most of the day, looking sick, said, "I'll go look down near the tracks, Kath." He walked out the front door calling, "Mi-chael! Mi-chael!"

Mom picked up Christina and grabbed my hand. "Oh my God, oh my God," she said over and over.

Dad walked to the back door. "Michael!" I knew he wasn't back there. I'd been playing there by myself for at least an hour after lunch.

Mom led me over to the couch and sat Christina next to me. "Aaaah," Christina whined as she slid off the sofa. Mom picked her up and sat her back next to me.

I tried to calm her. "Christina, just stay here." But she kept squirming.

Mom asked, "Dor, please watch her. I'm going to go check with the neighbors," then stopped, put her hand on her chest, and shut her eyes. "Oh, my God," she said again, then started crying.

Just then, Dad came in and hugged her. "We'll find him. We will find him."

Mom sobbed, "I have to go ask the neighbors," as she walked out the front door.

Dad turned to Doreen. "I'm going to go look near the beach. Stay here with Gary and Christina, ok?"

I wondered why everyone was so upset if Michael was just lost. Someone had to find him. I wished I could look for him. I knew Mom would smile big and laugh with relief if I was the one who yelled, "I found him!" Then, I thought about how scared everyone was and wondered, what if no one ever found him? *What if he was really gone forever?* My throat got tight. I had wished he wasn't my brother every time I caught him playing with my C-3PO and whenever Mom gave him the same amount of macaroni and cheese as me. I thought about his happy face when he got seconds. I remembered breakfast when he wanted more cereal. *Why did I tell him no?* Please, I thought, please, please. I was sorry for wishing he wasn't my brother. Everyone loved him except me. I knew it would be my fault if we didn't find him.

When the police came, Mom could barely talk. She held her fist to her mouth crying. The officer asked, "Is it ok if we search the house, Ma'am?" She nodded.

A tall officer with a gray mustache walked down the hall toward the bedrooms. A younger officer looked at me. "Are you sure you didn't see your brother when you were playing?"

I remembered one day when I was at a basketball court with Uncle Dan. He had kneeled down next to me and pointed at a police officer across the street. He'd whispered in my ear and told me to call him a pig. Because I was a stupid five-year-old, I yelled out, "Pig!" Uncle Dan and his friends laughed so hard they sounded like little girls. Thank goodness that police officer didn't hear me. I knew these police officers were there to help us find Michael. I answered, "I didn't, Sir."

The older police officer opened the glass door to our backyard. "We need to take the cover off the pool, Ma'am. You should probably wait in the living room." Mom called me over to the couch and told me to sit next to her. I hugged her waist as I wished over and over that they wouldn't find Michael in the swimming pool.

When the police officer walked in from the backyard, I held my breath. He smiled at Mom. "He's not in there. We're going to look through the garage." Both officers stepped down into the cool, concrete room. I heard them moving boxes and pushing furniture before the younger officer's voice got bright. Mom ran to the door as the police officer walked in – holding Michael. "He was sleeping in the bottom drawer of the dresser."

Mom laughed "Oh my God!" She took Michael in her arms, brushed his dark, blond bangs from his eyes, hugged him tight and kissed the side of his head. She held him in front of her. "What were you doing in there?"

Michael giggled. "I was hiding!"

Doreen asked, "Where was he?" as she came down the hall.

"He was in the dresser," Mom said, then "Oh, my God," again. She held him in front of her. "Michael, you almost scared me to death." She hugged him again. He didn't stop smiling. He just turned his head toward her chest. Mom asked, "Where's Nick and Jimmy?"

Doreen answered, "They're outside looking for him. I'll go get them."

Dad came in first. "He was in the dresser?"

Mom nodded. "Yeah, the bottom drawer. I don't know how he got in there."

Uncle Jim came in with Doreen. "Oh, my God Kath, I'm so sorry. I'm so sorry." He sat down shaking his head.

"It wasn't your fault, Jim," Mom said.

"No, No I know. I just–" He stopped for a moment then, "I'm just glad he's ok."

I thought to myself how it *was* Uncle Jim's fault. Michael hated the fighting. He was hiding because he didn't want any more fighting. I was sure of that.

I was glad Uncle Jim left to go live down the shore. I was also glad Uncle Dan went back to jail for beating somebody up. I was the gladdest that I didn't have to go back to school before the summer came. It was right after my seventh birthday when Mom and Dad called me into the kitchen. Mom smiled, "Gar, we want to tell you something."

"Ok."

"You know your dad and I got married, right?"

What? Who? "Do you mean my real dad?" I asked.

Mom bent down with a sad look. "I thought you wanted Nick to be your dad."

I didn't want to hear about how my real dad left, so I just said, "I do."

Mom said, "We got married, and I'm having another baby."

I smiled. "Really?"

"Yeah, really."

"Do you think it'll be a girl or a boy?"

"We don't know, but it doesn't matter."

Before we lost Michael, I would have been disappointed at the idea of another brother, but now I agreed. I would love the new baby the same no matter if it were a girl or a boy.

Educating Ambivalence

"I don't want to be left back." I almost started crying. I was supposed to be going into the second grade.

"Gary, Honey, you're not being left back. You didn't go to school enough to finish first grade."

I begged, "Please, Mom, please. I don't want to be in a class with kindergartner's just starting first grade." I was sure the kids would laugh at me, and the teacher would treat me like a dummy. My throat got tight. I could feel water filling my eyes. I tried to breathe in and out and look up, but the tears still ran down my cheeks.

Mom stood up and said to Dad. "We can't do this. I'm taking him to the school." I thought, oh my God, please, I don't want to be left back, please.

As we walked up the stairs toward the brick building, I saw kids walking by themselves. I pulled my hand away from Mom's hand.

"Gary, give me your hand."

"Mom, I'm not a baby."

She stopped. "Give me your hand."

Mom opened the door, and I looked around. The building was different, but there were bright papers on the wall, just like at my other schools. There was also a big Indian head on the brick wall in front of us. Mom walked up to a lady in a white shirt holding a clipboard and asked where the office was. She pointed down the hall. Off we marched. It was quiet as we walked in. Two kids were sitting in blue plastic chairs, and a mom was talking to the woman at the desk. Mom held my hand as we waited.

Bdddrrrrrrnng!

I looked through the window into the hallway, knowing it would be empty after the bell rang. I wondered if I was going to start late that day or the next morning. I was just about to ask Mom when an old lady with short blond hair came from the back.

"Mrs. Mele?" she asked. "Hi, we spoke on the phone. Come back to my office." She smiled and offered me and Mom a seat before sitting down. She listened to Mom explain how Grandma had died, how Dad had been out of work, and how we had to move. Grandma died when I was in kindergarten, I thought. I wondered why Mom said that. I didn't remember Dad not working, either.

The lady started, "Listen, I completely understand, but Gary's other school has him marked incomplete for everything."

Mom said, "But it isn't his fault."

The lady added, "I'll tell you what I'll do. I will call the other school to find out if they can give us grades for what he did complete. We really should get Gary in class until I hear back from them."

I looked at Mom, hoping she'd say something else, but she gave me a defeated smile. The knot in my stomach felt like it went right into my chest as I walked down the hall with the principal to the first-grade classroom. As soon as she opened the door, I could tell all the kids were way younger than me.

Embarrassed and ashamed weren't vocabulary words I learned in the first grade. I learned that "c" sometimes sounds like "s," which meant city was a place with tall buildings and a lot of people. It wasn't a baby cat. I also learned about blends like "sh" and "ch." Both of my first-grade teachers thought "ph" was the neatest blend because it was part of one of the most important words of all – telephone. The first time I was in first grade, I had asked why "telephone" wasn't just spelled with an "f." The teacher mouthed "fa," then "fa" with her lips a little different each time. I questioned, "But it's still the same sound." She kept explaining until I finally agreed that they *were* different sounds. The second time I was in first grade, I didn't ask any questions about it. Blends and letters that had two different sounds created great first-grade vocabulary words like lunch, recess, and schoolwork, but the words that described my life weren't in the vocabulary books.

When we lived in a car, it was because we were homeless.

When Uncle Dan hit me, it was because he was abusive.

When we had to move in the middle of the night, it was because we were evicted.

When Uncle Dan went back to jail, it was because he had committed assault and battery.

Mom and Dad were having a baby out of wedlock.

Uncle Jim, one time when he was arguing with Mom, told her that everyone knew that she and Dad weren't married. He said she could try to act like her life was perfect, but she was no better than anyone else. When I had asked Mom why he had said that, she said it was because he was an alcoholic.

I thought about the kids whose parents drove them to school every day. Even most of the students who rode the bus talked about how their parents got them ready for school in the morning. Sometimes they'd complain about the clothes their moms had picked out for them or the snack that was put in their lunchbox. I got myself ready almost every morning, and I thought I did a pretty good job until Bobby asked me why I wore the same brown pants all the time. When I told him that they weren't the same, he pointed to a dark ketchup stain on my knee and said, "That stain is there every day. Billy and Patty have seen it, too." When they all laughed, I was so embarrassed I wanted to die.

I was surprised to see Uncle Jim at our house when I got home from school on Christina's second birthday. Mom said, "Jim you look really good."

He smiled. "I feel really good. I'm taking it one day at a time."

"I'm really happy for you. How long have you been sober?"

"It's been two months and three days. Every day I focus on my sobriety."

I guessed that sobriety must mean he's not drinking anymore. I was happy for Uncle Jim, but mostly, I was glad for Mom. I knew it upset her the most when he got drunk.

That was the first time I remembered Uncle Jim not drinking at all. The adults laughed while they ate chocolate cake off of tiny blue plates. "I'm working my way back to you, Babe," played on the stereo while everyone talked at Christina's party. Even Sheba ran around barking. Soya, who was pregnant, was always calmer than Sheba, anyway. That day she just lay in the corner and watched everyone dance.

I wanted to watch when Soya had her puppies, but I wasn't allowed. Doreen cleared out half of her closet and put an old white and red comforter on the floor for Soya. Her belly was stretched with eight, tight lumps and her tiny nipples had grown fat and pink. I wondered if the puppies would come out of her nipples. I imagined that they would grow long, and a puppy would pop out of each one. The night that Soya went into labor, only Mom and Dad were allowed in the room.

The next morning Doreen let me and Michael in to see the puppies. They made little yelping sounds as they crawled around the blanket with their eyes closed. As soon as they found a nipple, they went still and quiet. I asked Doreen if I could hold one.

"Not yet," she said. "If you touch them, they won't smell right, and Soya won't take care of them." I wasn't sure if that was true. I thought Doreen just didn't want anyone else holding her puppies. I hated when she was selfish.

After two weeks, the puppies' eyes opened. Doreen said we could hold them, but only one puppy at a time. She made me and Michael sit on Christina's bed next to each other. I noticed Christina's bed smelled like pee, sort of like Michael's, and I wondered why they both peed the bed. Mom had told me that I never peed the bed once I was potty-trained.

I stretched my neck to see in the closet. Some of the puppies were white – or maybe tan. The others were black. I thought it was funny that some looked like Sheba. It must have been because Sheba and Soya were sisters. Doreen picked up a tan one and placed it in my lap. It was the cutest thing I had ever seen in my life, and it had a warm, sweet scent. I told Doreen, "I like the way she smells."

"That's puppy's breath, and it's a boy."

"Are we keeping any?"

"No, we can't," Doreen answered like she wasn't sad, but I could tell that she was.

After we gave all the puppies away, Soya didn't want to come out of the closet. Doreen sat on the floor petting her for hours. "It's ok, girl. It's ok." After a week, she and Dad took Soya to the hospital for dogs – "the vet," Dad said. When they came home, Doreen's eyes were puffy and red. I knew she'd been crying.

I asked, "Where's Soya? Is she ok?"

Dad answered, "She's fine. She went to live on a farm."

On a farm? Why would they send her to live on a farm without us? I was sure Soya was sad about all of her puppies being taken away. Plus, she was sick. I asked Dad where the farm was and if Soya had a new family. Dad answered, "It's in the country, and she has a lot of other dogs just like her to play with. She's very happy."

Michael had gone to the hospital several times because of his asthma. He was allergic to so many things; dogs, dust, even chocolate. Mom called it wheezing when his breathing made a constant noise, sort of like buzzing. I could tell it was hard for him to breathe because he would sit with his mouth open and his chest and back expanding out, then back in. I imagined it felt the same as when I popped up to take several huge breaths after I'd held my breath underwater to count to thirty.

Whenever Michael went to the hospital with Mom and Dad, I had to stay home with Doreen and Christina. Doreen would tell me to play with Christina, so she could watch *Too Close for Comfort* or *Bosom Buddies* while she ate Chips Ahoy right out of the bag. One time, while Doreen stuffed her face, I decided to teach Christina to play with her doll.

I cooed, "Christina," as I walked the doll toward her. She grabbed it, banged the plastic baby's head on the floor, and threw it toward the kitchen. Then, she reached for Michael's Matchbox cars. I told her, "No!" She wasn't allowed to play with them because the small black wheels could come off and choke her. She screamed louder than I ever remembered Michael being when I put them on the table where she couldn't reach them.

Doreen yelled, "Keep her quiet!" with a mouth full of chocolate chip cookies.

I was so mad I yelled back, "You keep her quiet!" then ran to my room. I knew there was no way Doreen would give up her TV show and bag of cookies to chase me.

When Christina was born, I had to wait for Mom to come home to see her. Mom and Dad said I was old enough to go to the hospital to meet my new brother, Vincent. The day after Mom gave birth, Dad took us all there. I was so excited because I'd never been in a hospital before. When we stepped through the doors that slid apart, I thought it was probably the cleanest place I'd ever seen. The walls and the floors were white and smelled like bleach, and I loved how bright the long fluorescent lights were. We walked into Mom's room. She was wearing a pink gown that tied in the back, and she was holding Vincent. After Doreen held him, Mom asked if I wanted to. When I said yes, Mom told me, "You have to be careful. He can't hold his head up yet."

"I know."

"Ok, come here. Hold your arms like this."

I could feel his warm little body through the blanket. He wasn't like a puppy. His eyes were already open, and he was looking right up toward the ceiling and around the room. I thought Vincent was a funny name, so I asked Mom, "Why did you name him Vincent?"

"We named him after my baby brother who died."

"You had a brother Vincent?"

"Yeah."

"He died?"

"Yeah, when he was a baby."

I looked down at Vincent and wondered why so many babies were named after other people. I was named after my first dad, and now my new brother was named after Mom's dead brother.

When Mom and Dad started talking about moving again, I wondered if the electricity was going to go off or if a policeman was going to tell us that we had to leave. I walked in while she was changing Vincent and asked, "Mom, why do we have to move so much?"

"Grab me a Pamper out of that bag," Mom said, as she held Vincent's tiny legs in the air. "We're moving to Arizona because of Michael's asthma."

"But we've already moved. I don't want to move again."

"This is going to be the last time."

"When are we leaving?"

"In just a few weeks when you and Doreen finish school."

Mom handed me the dirty diaper and told me to throw it away.

Till next time, New Jersey

When I saw the "Welcome to Pennsylvania" sign, I knew we had left New Jersey. It was the first time I'd ever been to another state. I looked at the leafy green fields along the edge of the highway. I could see that the plants had green tomatoes under them, which I knew were hard. I'd picked one up at the grocery store one time and asked Mom if we could get it. She said, "No, they're not ripe. You can't eat them."

I had asked, "Why do they sell them, then?"

She didn't answer because Uncle Jim was telling her Aunt Aida's parents had a lot of money, and they were going to make sure Uncle Jack got none of it. I wondered when the tomatoes would turn soft and red.

I broke my gaze and came back to the car. Doreen was in the front seat with Mom, turning the radio knob. Bu Dee I Roo Ah. I listened to the chopping sounds – Eee Ah Zu Me Doo – and wondered if she'd ever find a song that made her happy. Finally, – "Everybody's got a hungry heart." Michael, Christina, and I were packed around Vincent's car seat while Sheba shared the back seat with the suitcases and diaper bag. Dad and Uncle Jim were in the U-Haul behind us. "Everybody's got a hu hu hungery heart."

Doreen loved Bruce Springsteen. I remembered her carefully placing the needle on the record to listen to "Candie's Room" over and over. I thought he looked like Uncle Jim on his album cover – just not as drunk. I had asked her if that was why she liked him.

"Don't be stupid," she'd said. "He doesn't look like Uncle Jim. I like him because he's from New Jersey."

Wasn't everyone from New Jersey? That was the first time I had realized people lived in different states. I knew Aunt Peggy moved to Florida with her boyfriend, Bruce, who became her husband. They moved to Iowa because that's where Uncle Bruce's family was from. We were going to stop and see them on our way to Arizona.

I asked, "Mom, when do tomatoes turn red?"

"At the end of the summer," Doreen butted in.

"I was asking Mom."

"Why do tomatoes turn red?" Michael asked, followed by Christina popping up with "What's tomato?" She thought asking a question meant she should stand up.

"Gary, make her sit down," Mom said.

Even though Michael got a whole seat for himself, and I had to sit on the same side as Christina, I didn't mind. Michael wasn't capable of watching her. Plus, she never listened to him anyway, and I could tell she trusted me more than anyone else.

As we pulled off the highway, into crunchy stones along the side of the road, I looked to be sure the U-Haul was still behind us.

Mom stepped out. "Dor, I'm going to call Peggy. Make sure the kids stay in the car."

As Mom walked toward the pay phone, I remembered when it was just me, her, Michael, and Doreen in the car after my real dad had left. Now we had Christina and Vincent, and Sheba, too. It was going to be a much longer drive this time, but at least we had a place to go.

I heard Mom outside. She had to hold her finger over one ear and talk loudly because cars and big trucks were zooming by.

"Peg?"

"Yeah, we're on the road."

"We should be there the day after tomorrow."

"No, Jimmy's with us. He can't wait to see you."

"No."

"I can't wait to see you, too."

"Ok, ok. Love you. I'll call you tomorrow night."

After Mom hung up the phone, she walked to the U-Haul, where Uncle Jim opened his door. I could see Mom's pink flip-flops under the orange door, as she talked to Uncle Jim and Dad, for what seemed like several minutes. She walked back to our car and got in. "We're gonna stop as soon as we make it to Ohio."

Did that mean we were there? When I had asked Dad how long the drive would take, he'd told me, "Two, maybe three days." He had said we couldn't drive straight through with a baby.

I asked Mom, "Are we going to be there tonight?"

"No, Honey."

"But you said we'll be there tonight."

"Gary, sit down and make sure Christina's not eating fries off the floor."

Doreen looked back over the seat and asked, "Where do you think we're going?"

"Aunt Peggy's."

"No, what state?"

I knew she was trying to make me look stupid. I was sure there was an "o" and an "i" in the name. I said, "The state we're stopping at tonight."

"Ohio?" She laughed. "We're going to Iowa. They're two different states."

"I know that!"

"Really? Then why do you think we'll be there tonight?"

"Doreen, stop," Mom said.

A couple of weeks before we had left, Uncle Jim was talking to Mom about Doreen when she was at school. "Kath, she's getting big."

Mom gave a concerned look. "I know, Jim. I've been telling her to eat carrots and celery sticks instead of cookies."

Sure, Doreen's legs and butt were bigger than everybody else's, but I didn't think that made her fat. Plus, I was pretty sure she didn't care if she was fat, anyway. There was no way Doreen would give up her bag of Oreos while she watched TV on the couch. *Had I ever even seen her exercise?* I imagined her wearing a red sweatsuit, white headband – with her long black hair in a ponytail down her back – and doing jumping jacks in the middle of the living room. I chuckled.

Doreen snapped, "What're you laughing at?"

"Nothing," I said, as I smiled at Christina, who gave me a big smile back like she knew the joke.

Aunt Peggy was supposed to be thinner than Mom and Doreen. Mom liked telling people that Aunt Peggy had been a teenage model. "Beautiful, with long black hair," she'd say. Then Mom would get serious and talk about herself. She'd say the only thing fat on her was her belly because she had had four kids. She also told people that I had caused all of her stretch marks, and her body never went back to the way it was before she had me. I didn't think she looked fat at all. Her legs and arms looked normal. Plus, her boobs stuck out farther than her stomach, anyway. You couldn't really see her belly, but Mom didn't care. She still wanted to be sure everyone knew her fat belly and stretch marks weren't because she ate too many Oreos.

Uncle Jim had to ride in the car with us the next day. Mom said it was so he could help her with the kids. I thought it was because he liked gossiping, and Mom would ask questions to keep him going. Dad probably just said, "Really?" or "Oh, yeah?" which, I was sure, bored Uncle Jim. Uncle Jim riding with us meant everyone got shifted around. Doreen was in the back seat. Michael and Christina were on the same side next to each other, and I was in the way back where Sheba had been. She got to ride with Dad.

I wished that I could ride in the U-Haul, but Mom had told me, "No," when I had asked and, "Stop asking," when I asked again. She'd rather tie one of her kids to the roof of the car than let us ride in a vehicle she wasn't driving.

With Doreen not in the front seat, Mom was in charge of the radio. She wasn't as picky with songs. She quickly found one she liked. "Oh, I love Sheena Easton!" she exclaimed, then started singing, "My baby takes the morning train. He works from 9 to 5, and then." I could see her blue eyes and black eyebrows looking at me in the mirror as she pretended to be a singer. She made her voice airier than Sheena Easton, which I wasn't sure if she thought sounded better or because she wasn't that good at singing.

Sometimes in music class, we'd sing songs like "A Hunting We Will Go" or "Itsy Bitsy Spider." The kids who sang the best would sing loudly, so everyone heard them. The kids who sang the worst also sang loudly because they thought they were singing the best – like Bobby McDonald. I hated standing next to him because he would scream in my ear and then smile really wide like he was the best singer in the world. I usually sang just loud enough so my music teacher wouldn't say, "Gary, I can't hear you," but soft enough so I blended in with the good singers.

Michael bopped up and down and swayed his head. He loved Mom singing. Christina was too serious about removing the arm on one of my old X-Wing fighter figures to care about Mom pretending she was Sheena Easton. Doreen stared out the window, and Vincent slept. I smiled so that Mom saw me in the rear-view mirror. I wanted her to think she did a great job, even though it was just ok.

I turned around to look at the U-Haul behind us. Sheba was sitting up on her seat, looking forward, like she was a person. Dad was staring forward with one hand on the steering wheel and the other out the window smoking a cigarette. I wished we had our windows open. Since he stopped drinking, Uncle Jim was always smoking. Sometimes he would even light his new cigarette with the one he was about to put out. I asked Mom, "Can we roll down some windows?"

Bvvt.

She barely rolled it down an inch. "I don't want to let the cold air out."

"It stinks like smoke in here. I can't breathe."

"It does not, Gary. Stop complaining."

Then Mom asked, "Jim, will you crack your window a little?"

Bvvt

Once we made it to Iowa, it seemed like there was nothing but cornfields. I was amazed at how tall the corn stalks were and that they grew in perfectly straight rows. I thought, Iowa must be the corn capital of the entire world and wondered how many people it would take to eat that much corn on the cob.

When we pulled into Aunt Peggy's apartment parking lot, Mom said, "Jim, she told me it's third from the end. Do you see it?"

"Yeah, I do. Is that her? Look how short her hair is."

"Oh, my God. She cut her hair."

I looked out and saw Aunt Peggy. She was still skinny, and she did have really short hair that was kind of curly on top. Everyone started getting out. Mom gave her a hug first. "Oh Peg, why did you cut your hair?"

"It's the style, like Olivia Newton-John. It'll grow back, Kath."

Aunt Peggy hugged Uncle Jim and Doreen. Then, she bent down to me and looked in my eyes. "Gary, you've gotten so big. Can I have a hug?" I wondered if it was the black eyelashes and hair that made her blue eyes look almost gray. Still, even with the short hair, that

Mom thought was ugly, Aunt Peggy really was beautiful. I smiled and squeezed her tight.

It was different living with Aunt Peggy. Her son, Josh, was a little younger than Christina. If he asked Aunt Peggy a question when she was talking to an adult, she'd turn right toward him and say, "What do you need, Honey?" Then she'd get up to get him a glass of water or help him look for one of his toys – whatever he wanted. It didn't matter if she was talking to Uncle Jim, Mom, or even her husband, Uncle Bruce. If Josh needed something, it was more important than whatever the adult was talking about.

Mom never interrupted Uncle Jim bad mouthing Aunt Aida to get us a glass of water. She'd say, "Wait a minute!" or, "Go play," or worse; she'd call Doreen. Doreen would take a cup out of the sink (because that's where they all usually were) fill it up one time, dump it, fill it again and hand it over. I knew better than to question Doreen on whether the cup was really clean. Christina would gulp it down, then say, "The water tastes funny."

Michael would just say, "Never mind. I'm not thirsty anymore," and run away. He'd rather climb up on the bathroom sink to drink from the faucet than have Doreen get him a glass of dirty water.

Aunt Peggy also kept Josh on a schedule, which we quickly became part of. I couldn't believe she would get up every single morning to make us all cereal. Lunch was always around the same time, and so was dinner. She'd yell out the front door, "Come on guys. It's time for dinner."

We had never eaten dinner at the same time before Aunt Peggy's. Sometimes it would be dark with the street lights on when we decided to go home. Mom would say, "Nick, make them cereal." Michael would look like he was falling asleep while we ate, and Christina would lie on the floor.

Aunt Peggy made all the other kids go to bed at 8:30. She told me, "Because you're eight, you can stay up later than the other kids, but you have to go to bed right after The Dukes of Hazzard. Ok?"

I told her, "Aunt Peggy, I wish I could live with you forever."

She smiled. "Aww, I wish you could, too."

Aunt Peggy was friends with the lady across the hall who had a son. Joey was younger than me but older than Michael. We would all play tag with him in front of the apartment while Sheba ran around us, barking. I had to tell Joey to let Christina and Josh get him sometimes. "They're only three. It doesn't count if they tag you." But it didn't matter what I said. Joey would still run really fast away from them, and when he was "it," he'd go right after either one, sometimes knocking them down when he tagged them. Josh would get right back up and laugh, but Christina would yell. "No pushing!"

Joey also liked to tease Sheba. He thought it was funny to try and grab her tail when she ran over because he had pushed Christina down. I told him, "You shouldn't do that. She'll bite you." Sheba was very protective of us, probably because anytime somebody walked by our house, Doreen, Uncle Jim, and sometimes Mom would say, "Sic 'em! Sic 'em, girl!" Sheba would growl, show her front teeth, then bark like crazy. They'd pet her afterward and say, "Good girl." I knew Sheba didn't like Joey because she'd run faster when he tried to touch her.

I didn't usually agree with Uncle Jim, but when he said, "That kids a fucking brat!" I thought he was right.

Aunt Peggy said, "Jim, don't swear." I didn't understand why Aunt Peggy and Uncle Bruce called cursing, swearing. They also called soda, pop.

The first time Uncle Bruce asked me, "Do you want some pop with your pizza?" I thought he was talking about a cheese bubble.

I had answered, "No thanks, that's ok."

"Do you want water?"

Why would I want water when everyone else was drinking soda? When I asked, "Can I have soda?" he replied, "You mean pop?"

I thought it was a good idea to explain to Joey that soda was the right word, not pop. We were in the front yard debating while Michael was playing with Sheba. "That's fucking stupid," Joey said, which prompted me to let him know something else.

"You're not supposed to be cursing. And yes, it's cursing, not swearing!"

"Cursing?" he asked like he wasn't sure if what I'd said was stupid or funny. He laughed. "Oooo, I'm gonna place a curse on you," then started laughing even harder. "Are you a witch? Are you?"

I was so frustrated by how dumb and bratty Joey was that I turned to walk back inside. I heard a growlish bark from behind me. When I turned around, Joey wasn't laughing anymore. He looked scared and was holding his butt. Michael pointed. "Sheba bit him." I ran inside to get Mom.

Sheba had to go away for quarantine for two weeks to be sure she didn't foam at the mouth and go crazy. If she did, that would mean she had rabies, and then Joey would have to get a bunch of painful shots in his belly. Doreen was the most upset. "Somebody should beat his ass!" she yelled about Joey. I kind of thought she was right. Even though I didn't see it, I was sure Joey had done something to make Sheba bite him. We didn't stay with Aunt Peggy long after that. By the time Sheba was out of quarantine, we'd found our own house to rent.

Procurement of the Ghost House

When Mom and Dad went Christmas shopping, Mom would tell me, "We're going to see Santa." I already knew I couldn't go with them, so I wasn't going to ask. I just wanted to talk to Mom before she left us with Doreen and Uncle Jim. When I walked into her bathroom, she was leaning toward the mirror to put mascara on while her cigarette burned in the ashtray. It stank like perfume and smoke. I waved my hand in front of my face, so she knew how much I hated her smoking. "Mom?"

"What, Honey?"

"How long are you guys going to be gone?"

"I don't know. Just a couple of hours."

"I hate staying with Doreen."

"Uncle Jim's here, too."

At least when Doreen bossed me around, it only lasted for as long as she could yell. She would scream, "Go play in your room!" or "Go play outside!" and then smile in a way that made her look even meaner than she was.

One time, Doreen had said to Mom, "It must be nice to have a built-in babysitter."

Mom yelled, "I'll wipe that smirk right off your face!" before chasing her down the hall. The next day I asked Dad what a smirk was.

"It's kind of like an evil smile," he said. Doreen hardly ever smirked at Mom after that, but she sure smirked at me, a lot.

Uncle Jim was worse than Doreen. He'd say things in a really nice voice like, "Gar, change it to channel 7," or "Gar, hand me that ashtray." If I didn't jump up, like he was the most important man in the universe, he would try to get me in trouble later. He would say, "Boy, that Gary's getting too big for his britches," to whomever he thought I'd get in the most trouble from. Before Uncle Dan went back to jail, it was always him.

Mom didn't understand when I tried to explain all this to her. She just said, "Well, you should listen to Uncle Jim – and respect him, too." At least she understood when I told her Doreen was mean.

Mom asked me, "Do you like my outfit?"

It was flowy and red, and I did like it. I said, "You look really pretty." Mom tilted her head to put on a silver earring.

Dad stepped into the doorway with Christina right behind him. Her soft brown hair was long, almost to her butt, but it was scraggly and always in her eyes. I wondered if Mom would ever cut it. Doreen was only allowed to trim her hair, so it had an even, straight edge, but hers was down to her butt, too. She was really good at putting it in a ponytail, though. She'd brush it fast, lean over, scoop it back and forth, and then flip a hair tie around twice before standing back up with her black hair pulled tight to the back of her head.

"You ready to go, Kath?"

"Almost. Give me one more minute, Nick."

Dad and I both knew that "one more minute" probably meant twenty more minutes. He looked at me. "So, we're gonna tell Santa you want a train set, right?"

I got excited. "Yeah, I want a freight train with trestles. And make sure there's an oil car."

"Ok, we'll make sure Santa knows."

I watched out the window as steam came off the hood of the car. Dad put his arm behind Mom's seat to look back before pulling out over black, icy snow at the edge of the driveway. They drove away.

Mom and Dad were gone way longer than a couple of hours. After I got bored playing with my toys, Christina, and then Michael, I went to Vincent's crib. He was going to be a year in one month. He knew how to stand up, but he couldn't walk yet. I asked Doreen, "Can I take Vincent out of his crib?"

"No."

"Why? I want to play with him."

"Play with him in his crib."

Normally, I wouldn't do what Doreen told me to do, but there was nothing else left to do, anyway. Even though Vincent couldn't speak yet, he still tried to talk. He was always making sounds and chattering from his crib. I couldn't remember what Michael had done as a baby, but Christina would either be really quiet, or she would scream. I noticed Vincent didn't have anything in his crib except a yellow blanket. Maybe he wants something to play with, I thought. I looked around the room. I knew I couldn't give him one of Michael's toys because they were too hard, and he might choke on the little pieces.

I tried to figure out what would be a good toy for Vincent. I needed something soft – that he couldn't hurt himself with. I had it! I remembered Doreen's short, white socks that she called booties. They had a puffy yarn ball at the back, near the heel. I knew that sometimes the balls would get loose, so I snuck into her room and found one of her booties on the floor. The green yarn ball with the little red dot in the middle wasn't as loose as I thought it would be, even after I pulled on it a couple of times. I decided to sneak into the bathroom to cut it off. I looked in every drawer, but I couldn't find scissors. I thought that if nail clippers cut fingernails, surely, they'd cut yarn. I grabbed a pair and stretched the ball away from the booty and clipped and clipped until it popped off. I didn't want Doreen to find her yarn-ball-less booty, so I stuffed it behind the toilet before I snuck back to Vincent's crib.

I handed the puffy, yarn ball to Vincent. He looked at it and dropped it. I handed it to him again. He held it, dropped it, then plopped down on his butt. What a waste of time, I thought. I'd destroyed one of Doreen's stupid looking booties for nothing. As I was thinking about what other things would make good toys, I realized that Vincent was quiet. I turned around. He'd stuffed the whole booty ball into his mouth. I could see the green with the red dot right in the center. *He's choking!* I ran out to the living room. "Vincent's choking! Vincent's choking!"

"What?" Doreen shot up and ran to the room.

She stuck her fingers in his mouth as he squirmed. She pinched the booty ball and pulled it out with a long string of drool. Vincent started crying. "How'd he get this?" Doreen yelled. "I don't know. He had it when I came in here."

Doreen looked at me like she knew I was lying. "Well, he better not get anything else!"

It was almost dinner time when I heard the car pull up. I ran over to the window. Doreen ran over, too. Uncle Jim opened the front door. "Kath, what's going on?" Mom was getting out of the car, but I didn't see Dad. Mom came into the house with black mascara smudged all around her eyes.

"Oh my God. He was arrested, Jim."

"What happened?" Uncle Jim asked.

"The police started following us. I told him not to run. I said, 'Nick, don't run.'" Then Mom started crying.

"Holy shit! What happened, Kath?"

"They made me go to the police station with him. They said he has warrants for his arrest in New Jersey."

What's a warrant? I wondered. *Dad in jail? Was Mom going to jail?* My throat got tight, but I wouldn't let myself cry. I didn't want Mom to think I couldn't handle it.

I walked over. "Is Dad in jail?"

Doreen said, "Take Michael, and go to your room."

No wonder she loves dogs so much, I thought. She barks just like them when she tells people what to do.

"No," Mom said, "Its ok. Yes, Dad is in jail." Then she started crying again.
"What did he do?"

"Nothing, Honey. It's a mistake. We're trying to get him out."

Mom took out the phone book. "I need to find a bail bondsman. God, I wish we were in New Jersey. I'd call Danny's."

I wanted to know what a bail bondsman was, but I didn't say anything. I knew Doreen wanted me to go to my room and asking questions would give her a reason to send me. Mom picked up the phone and started dialing.

Whatever a bail bondsman was, it didn't seem like they could help us. They all asked questions that Mom answered the same way.

134

"No, we don't own a house," and, "It's a 1976, but it's in great condition." I thought they must be asking about our car. I knew 1976 meant when it was made, and I'd heard Mom tell Aunt Peggy and Uncle Bruce our car was in great condition because it made it all the way from New Jersey to Iowa.

Mom called Aunt Peggy and cried while talking to her.

"Peg, I don't know what to do."

"No, we're not coming back to you. You and Bruce are fighting enough already."

"He's trying, Peg. He was going to work with Nick."

"I know. I love you, too. I'll call you tomorrow."

I got my train set for Christmas. The track was shaped like an eight, and it came with trestles, just like I wanted. The oil car didn't come with the set, but I still got one. It was wrapped separately.

When the phone rang in the afternoon, Mom picked it up. "Yes, operator. I'll accept the charges."
We took turns talking.

Christina started with, "Hi, Dad. Where are you?"

When it was Michael's turn to talk, he told Dad, "I got a Teddy Bear and named him Duke. When are you coming home, Dad?"

135

As Michael was finishing, and I knew it was going to be my turn to talk, I got choked up. I knew what choked up was because I'd asked Dad when I heard Mom say it once. I knew what choked up was, I knew what smirked was, I knew what so many things were because Dad always answered my questions.

When I talked to Dad, I told him, "Thank you for making sure my train set has trestles and for getting me an oil car." I didn't care if Mom knew I didn't believe in Santa. I thought about the first time I told him I loved him. I did it because Mom wanted me to. I said it every time I told Mom I loved her after that. As we were about to hang up, I said it, and for the first time, I meant it. "I love you, Dad."

"I love you, too, Son."

When we ate dinner, Uncle Jim kept getting up to go outside. He didn't even put his coat on. He just said, "I need some fresh air." When he came back in, he would rub his hands together and blow in them. "Damn, it's cold out there!" I got a knot in my stomach. I could tell by the look on Mom's face that she knew, also. I took Michael to our room to play with his Legos. As I sorted out the pieces for him to build a fire station, I heard Mom and Uncle Jim in the kitchen. I snuck to the edge of our door to listen.

"I can't believe you're drinking, Jimmy."

"It was a couple beers, for Christ's sake!"

"I want you out. I can't do this anymore. I want you out, Jimmy!"

"Fuck you. I'm not going anywhere!" A plate crash into the wall.

Doreen yelled, "I'm calling the cops! He's a drunk."

Uncle Jim's voice got angry. "What did you say to me?"

Doreen yelled again. "Go ahead! Hit me!"

I got up.

My heart was racing.

I started walking out the door.

Christina was standing in her room, holding her hands to her mouth, crying. Michael began crying behind me.

I grabbed Christina and hugged her. "It's ok." I brought her into our room. I tensed my hands to keep them from shaking. I had to be as much of an adult as I could be. I put my hands on Michael's shoulders. "Michael, stay with Christina and Vincent, ok?"

He begged, "Don't go out there, please."

"It's ok." I hugged him. "Just stay here. I'll be right back."

It was the most scared I'd ever been in my life, but I had to go. *What if he hurt Mom? Or Doreen?* Step after step, I walked toward the yelling, toward the kitchen. Then Uncle Jim came into the living room.

137

My heart froze. He looked at me and then turned toward the closet. He pulled out a jacket, opened the front door, went out, and slammed the door behind him. The whole house shook.

Doreen stormed into the room. "He's lucky he didn't put a hand on me!"

Mom came into the room right after and saw me. "Gary, what are you doing? Go to your room."

The next morning, Uncle Jim was passed out on the living room couch. *Why did they let him back in?* I hated him. I'd *always* hated him. I stared at him and wished he would never wake up from his drunken sleep.

When Uncle Jim would get really drunk and act the craziest, he would stay sober for several weeks after. Mom would try to believe that he wasn't ever going to drink again. Doreen would never talk about it, but I knew she didn't believe it – just like I didn't believe it.

In February Mom started talking about moving, I knew, because we hadn't paid our rent since Dad went to jail. Mom was able to get food stamps because she had four kids, but we weren't going to have a place to live if we got evicted. Just like the other times we'd moved, she opened the newspaper on the kitchen table. She circled every house with three bedrooms and called them. I listened from the hallway as I put together my train set.

"They want references," Mom told Doreen.

"Why don't you give Peggy?" Doreen asked.

"I can't, Dor. She just moved herself, and she lives in an apartment. Besides, that's not the big issue. Who's going to rent to a single mom with four kids and pregnant?"

Pregnant? Really? I remembered when Mom had told my first-grade principal that I'd missed so much school because Grandma had just died. That wasn't true. She said it because she wanted the principal to feel sorry for me. Was she trying to make people feel sorry for her by saying she was pregnant?

"Mom?"

"Yeah?"

"Are you really pregnant?"

"Gary, why are you listening to our conversation?"

"I wasn't trying."

"Yes, I'm pregnant. Now stop listening to adult conversations."

I wondered whether Mom was going to have a boy or a girl then thought about Christina. If Mom had another boy, Christina would have two older, and two younger brothers which I didn't think would bother her at all. I wondered why Christina didn't care about being pretty. When Mom brushed tangles out of her hair, Christina would say, "Ow, ow, ow." Mom would tighten her lips and say, "Stop moving!" Aunt Peggy had given Christina a Barbie for Christmas. She showed her how to brush the blond hair with a tiny, pink comb, but the poor doll's hair was more matted and tangled than even Christina's hair. The only thing Christina cared about was playing kickball or T-ball with the boys on our street. I decided that I wanted Mom to have a girl.

I could tell Mom was worn out from calling, being really nice and everyone telling her that they wouldn't rent their house to us. As the last phone call ended, she said, "Ok, thank you. I understand. No, it's ok. I understand." She leaned her forehead on her hands and shut her eyes. She sat at the table for several minutes before standing up and closing the newspaper. "Doreen, get ready. We're going to get one of these houses." Mom put on her wrapped blue dress, which came down in a V, so that her collar bones and the very top of the crease where her boobs squished together could be seen, high heels, mascara, and lipstick. She made Doreen change her clothes two times. "No, put on your tan sweater." Mom walked over to Uncle Jim. "We'll be back, Jim. Watch the kids." Mom then kissed me, Michael, Christina, and Vincent. She opened the door, turned to me and gave a slight nod, to let me know it would be ok before walking out.

After Mom and Doreen had been gone a few minutes, Uncle Jim said, "Gar, I need you to do me a favor."

"Yeah?"

"I need you to go ask the neighbor if I can borrow some beer."

What? Beer?

140

"Really?" I asked, even though I already knew he meant it.

"Yes, really. Just tell them we're out and ask if we can borrow a six pack."

Oh my God. Why did Mom leave me with him? I wanted to die.

I put my hands in my pockets and walked toward our neighbor's house. Please, please, don't let any kids answer the door, I thought. Maybe I could just *say* I did it. I turned and saw Uncle Jim watching me from the window. *Was it possible to have a heart attack at eight years old?* My heart was beating so hard I could feel it, even though my hand wasn't even on my chest.

DING DONG

Please don't come to the door. Please don't come to the door.

Click

"Hello."

"Uh, Hi. Um… My uncle wants to know if he can borrow some beer."

"Who's your uncle?"

"Um… We live over there."

"I'm sorry. I don't think we have any." The man leaned out the door and looked both ways down the street.

I was so relieved to walk back to our house.

141

"Did you get any?"

"They didn't have any."

"Well, try the other neighbor."

At the next house, there was no answer. The house after that –
three girls answered the door with their mother. They laughed when I
asked. The mother said, "We don't drink beer. You should go home."
At the house after that, an old man asked me if the beer was for me.
Finally, at the fifth house, they gave me two Budweiser beers to take
back to Uncle Jim.

When they pulled into the driveway, I could see Mom laughing
with Doreen. I knew she had done it. She had gotten our new house.

Overarching Despondency

The only times I remembered going to church before Dad went to prison was on Easter Sunday and when Vincent and Christina were baptized. When we went, Mom would dress me and Michael in white, short-sleeved, dress shirts. I thought we looked like the religious boys who rode up to our house on their bicycles, except that we weren't wearing ties and name tags. When they rang the doorbell, Mom went, "Shhh... Shhh!" and scurried us all into the bedroom. Sheba must have thought we were afraid of them because she barked like a lunatic every time they rang the bell. I think it was three times total. Fortunately for those boys, Mom didn't intend on answering the door no matter how many times they rang the doorbell. I was sure Sheba would've ripped a chunk out of their butts just like she did to that brat, Joey.

Mom started calling churches after she found our new house because we needed help moving. "We can't afford a U-Haul, and we don't know anyone with a truck," she said, as she flipped the phone book open to the yellow pages. "I think it'll be under 'c.'" One of the churches she called must have said we should be going to church if we expected help. I think that was the first time she ever made sure all four of us were wearing neat, clean clothes. She used a wet rag to scrub dirt stains out of Michael's good pants, and she put Christina's hair in pigtails before loading us up in the car on Sunday morning.

Everyone smiled and acted like they were really happy to be there even though the organ, which I thought was a big piano, made haunting, scary music, and there were statues of Jesus being whipped and beaten. It was the most depressing place I'd ever been. After church, a blond lady a little older than Mom came over to us. "Oh, Kathleen, I'm so glad you came."

Mom introduced us. "This is Gary, Michael, Christina, and Vincent. This is Mrs. Winter."
"Don't be silly." The lady smiled. "Mrs. Winter is my mother-in-law. I'm Carol." She kneeled down to Christina. "How does it feel to have so many brothers?"

Christina hid behind Mom. "I don't care."

Carol smiled at each one of us. "Well, you are all adorable."

In the weeks before we moved, Carol brought us cans of soup, cheese, and bread. The food was great. I never knew cheese came in a box before. Then she brought over big, paper grocery bags full of clothes for us to go through. At first, I was excited, but then I imagined how horrified I'd be if some boy pointed at me and said, "Hey! That's my Pac-Man shirt. My mom gave it to the church for poor people." I picked out only plain colored shirts for myself and let Michael take all the shirts with characters on them, even if they were my size.

Carol also expected us to pray to Jesus, Mary, and the saints. To help us pray better, she gave us each a small plastic bag with a necklace made out of blue beads with a cross in the middle. When Michael put it on, she got serious. "Michael, you don't wear that around your neck. It's a rosary."

He gave me a funny look and said, "It looks like a necklace." He was right. It clearly was a necklace no matter what she called it. I wasn't going to tell him that, though. I just wrapped it around my hand and pretended to pray like Carol and Mom did.

When we moved, Carol's husband helped Uncle Jim move the furniture while Carol unpacked boxes with Mom and Doreen in the new kitchen. I wondered what she might be telling Mom. When we were packing at our old house, I had heard her tell Mom, "Kathleen, I know it's a habit, but you really should try to quit smoking while you're pregnant." Mom stopped smoking the next day. I thought to myself that maybe Carol was telling Mom that Uncle Jim needed to leave. I'd pray every single day with the rosary to make that happen.

Everywhere we'd lived before had a front and a back door. Instead of a back door, our new home had a side door which went right into the kitchen. From the kitchen, you could see the front door, and if you walked straight toward it and then looked to the right, our living room was right there. There was another door in the kitchen that looked like a closet, but when you opened it, there were stairs. I got excited as I looked down. "Michael!" I called.

"What?" He came running through the living room and into the kitchen.

"Look!"

We both ran down the stairs. The really big room was carpeted, so it looked like the rest of the house, but the laundry room and the back storage rooms had concrete floors, so they looked like a regular basement. The windows were all the way at the top of the walls, and you could see grass growing at the bottom of each one. It felt like a hidden army fort. I pointed and said to Michael, "Look, you can see people's feet if they walk by."

He ran right up to the wall and started jumping. "I can't see! I can't see!" I thought how even for five years old, he's stupid.

I yelled at him. "No! You can't run right up to the wall. You have to stand back like this, so you can see."

Mom liked the basement because there was only one door in and out, so she knew exactly where we all were. She put the TV down there, too, so we could watch it when we were finished playing. She didn't want there to be any reason for us to be in the living room where we could listen to her and Uncle Jim talk while they drank coffee. She didn't realize I could still hear their conversations when I crouched at the top of the stairs and listened under the door.

As Michael and Vincent watched TV at the bottom of the stairs, I waited. It wasn't long before Uncle Jim started talking about Doreen. "Kath, I'm sure I smelled pot on her jacket." I wondered if it was the same smell that came from the bathroom when Doreen watched us. I thought she was sneaking cigarettes, but the smell was funny. When she sprayed Lysol like she'd just taken the biggest poop in history, I knew she was trying to cover up the smell.

Mom said, "I don't think I've ever seen her high. Have you?"

146

Uncle Jim started, "Are you kidding–" when Christina walked in.

"Mom, where's Gary?"

Stupid Christina! I crawled back down the stairs as quickly and quietly as I could. I was almost at the bottom.

Click.

I sat on the bottom step and acted like I was playing. "Gar?" Christina called from the top of the stairs.

"What?"

"What're you doing?"

"Come down if you want."

"You come up here."

"No. You come down here."

She shut the door.

A few minutes later, the door opened again, and Mom walked down with Christina behind her. "Gary, play with Christina down here, ok?"

"Ok."

Vincent had learned to run almost as quickly as he'd learned to walk. He would chase after Michael with his laughter echoing through the hard, cold walls of the basement storage rooms. When he fell on the concrete, he would get right back up and keep running. I wished Christina would leave me alone and play with Michael and Vincent, but she sat near me asking annoying questions.

"Do you want to watch TV?"

"Nope."

"Do you want to help me build a fort?"

"Nope."

After a little while, she wanted to go back upstairs. I ran over to her as she started climbing the stairs. "You're not allowed up there, Mom said."

"You're not the boss of town," she yelled back.

"Mom!"

Click.

"What?" Mom yelled. I knew she was mad that she even had to answer, and Christina was going to be in trouble.

"Christina's not listening!"

Thump, thump, thump, thump, thump.

Even pregnant, Mom still got up and down the stairs with no problem. It seemed like a lot of pregnant women held their backs and sighed a lot. Mom didn't, probably because she'd been pregnant so many times.

"Christina, get away from the stairs. Go play over there."

"I wanna go upstairs," Christina whined, then dropped to her butt and started kicking her feet.

Mom walked over to her. "Stop it!"

She didn't.

"Stop it! Goddamn it!"

She grabbed Christina's wrist and yanked her up so hard her feet came off the floor.

WHAP! WHAP!

Michael and Vincent stopped running.

WHAP! WHAP! WHAP!

Stop, I thought, please stop! It was just like Uncle Dan. She was so angry. The hate in her face was scary.

WHAP! WHAP! WHAP!

The terror on Christina's face melted into a cry as Mom dropped her to the ground. *Why had I tried to get her in trouble?* I'd gotten Michael in trouble probably a hundred times, and Mom had never done that to him. Christina wasn't even four years old yet. She was still a baby. I wanted to run over and grab her, but I was frozen as I looked at Mom. Her chest heaved. "When I tell you to stop, you stop," she said before turning to go upstairs. Who was she? I thought. Who was she? Then I thought... she's just like Uncle Dan.

Doreen had to watch us when Mom went into labor. We were all downstairs watching TV, and Doreen was at the top of the stairs talking to Sheba with a baby voice. "Come down with us. Come on, girl." Sheba didn't like the basement. She liked sitting upstairs where she could see the living room and the kitchen door. "Come on," Doreen said one more time, then, "Alright, stay up there if you want."

I was lying on the floor focused on *That's Incredible* trying to figure out if a man could really catch a bullet with his teeth when Doreen asked, "Did you hear that?" I looked over. She was getting up from the couch and walking toward the stairs.

I sat up. "Hear what?" She kept looking toward the top of the stairs as she turned the TV down.

"Shhh," she whispered, then called, "Jim?" in her normal voice. She walked halfway up the stairs. "Peg?" When she got to the top of the stairs, I listened. The only thing I heard was her footsteps and the floor creaking as she walked around the living room above us.

Carol brought Mom home from the hospital. She had a cheery look on her face as she opened the kitchen door for Mom. "Say hello to your new sister!" I was so happy Mom had had a girl, and I was thrilled she named her Michelle. I thought it was the prettiest name ever. It was also the first time I'd seen a baby with really dark hair. Vincent and Christina were both born bald, and from the pictures I'd seen, so were me and Michael.

"Can I hold her?" I asked.

Mom, with a genuinely happy look in her eyes, answered in a sweet tone. "Of course. You're the oldest, and she's the youngest."

I was nine. I calculated that I'd be ten when she turned one.

I already knew to hold up Michelle's head with my arm and to squirt the bottle on the back of my hand before feeding her, but I got the most excited when Mom told me that she was going to teach me how to change her. Mom pulled the white tapes open from the front of the diaper. Then she held her two tiny feet together with one hand, lifted, and pulled the diaper out. She explained that girls are different than boys and I needed to wipe from front to back – not from back to front like I wiped my own butt. Mom said, "Once she's clean, pull the clean Pamper under her. Make sure the tapes are at the back."

I remembered every step and asked to change her every time I smelled poop. Sometimes her poop was yellow, and sometimes it was green. I asked Mom if that was normal.

"Yes, it's normal. Babies poop all different colors."

A couple of weeks after Michelle was born, I heard Mom talking with Doreen in the kitchen. "Dor, are you sure you heard footsteps?" Doreen was serious. "Somebody was in the house. I heard it. They were walking back and forth through the living room."

"Doreen, that's crazy. Sheba was in the house."

"I'm not crazy. I know what I heard."

"What do you think it is?"

"I don't know."

The next time we were all downstairs watching TV, Sheba started whimpering at the top of the steps. I'd never heard her cry before, and I didn't think she was afraid of anything. Maybe there's a ghost in our house, I thought. In all the stories I'd seen about ghosts haunting places, the houses were old, but our house was new – at least it looked new. Uncle Jim, not realizing that I was paying attention to their conversation, said to Mom, "She does not like this house."

Mom whispered back. "It's crazy. Sheba doesn't want to be upstairs alone, and she won't come down here."

Going to school wasn't as bad as it normally was because Carol knew some of the moms. Even though it felt weird having kids be super nice for no reason, it was better than being made fun of. Michael even told me that three different kids asked if he was Michael Mele and if he wanted to play tag. He knew nobody wanted to know his name before.

One day when we were walking home from the bus stop, I noticed Mom sitting outside on our steps with Christina, Vincent, and Michelle.

"Hi, Guys. Did you have a good day at school?"

Michael was puzzled. "Why are you outside Mom?"

"I was waiting for you guys to come home."

I asked, "Can we go inside?" I knew something had scared Mom inside the house.

Later that afternoon, after Uncle Jim came home from wherever he had been (not working), Mom told us to go play downstairs. After a few minutes, I crept up the stairs to the door to listen to the adults. Mom wouldn't tell us, but I knew she'd tell Uncle Jim. Mom began, "I swear to God, Jim. The picture was moving."

"What do you mean?"

"I was in the kitchen talking to Peggy on the phone when I saw it tilting in the reflection. I walked into the living room, and it was straight. I went back in the kitchen, and it started moving again. Oh my God, Jim. I walked up to the corner, and I heard it scraping on the wall."

"Holy Christ! There is something in this house. Have you told Nick?"

"Jim, I tried. He doesn't believe in that stuff."

"Doesn't he get out in two months? He'll believe when he's here. There is something in this house."

Did our house really have a ghost, I wondered? Doreen had heard footsteps, and Mom had seen a picture move. I listened. "Creak." *I heard a creak!* "Thump." *I heard a thump!* I realized if I was really quiet, I could hear all sorts of noises in the house. Was it all the ghost? Later on that day, I decided to tell Doreen when she was getting ready to take Sheba for a run with Uncle Jim. Surely, she'd believe me. She had asked me if I had heard the footsteps upstairs. I should have told her yes, I thought.

"Dor."

"What?"

"I heard noises downstairs earlier."

"Really? What kind of noises?"

"Like a creak and a thump."

"What do you think it is?"

"I don't know. It was weird. I've never heard noises like that before."

"Do you think it was a ghost?"

"Yeah!"

"Maybe it was, or maybe it's just normal noises a house makes."

I should have known she wouldn't believe me. She would only believe it if she had heard the noises herself. "I don't think it was the house," I said.

Doreen ignored me and started talking to Uncle Jim. "You coming with me, Jim?"

"Yeah, I need some fresh air. Let's take her up to the overpass they're working on. She can run around."

A couple of hours later, the car pulled up. I ran to the window and saw Doreen sobbing as she got out of the car. When they came in, Mom asked, "What happened?"

"It's my fault. It's my fault," Uncle Jim said, as he held his head. "I didn't think she would jump after it."

"Oh my God, what happened?" Mom asked again.

"We were playing with her on the overpass, throwing the stick. When we were done, I threw it over the side. She jumped for it. Oh my God, she jumped for it. I never thought she'd jump. I never thought she'd jump."

Mom started crying and hugged Doreen.

"We... took... her to the vet... She broke her back... She broke her back," Doreen said between sobs. My throat closed the moment I realized. Within a moment, me, Michael and Christina, even Vincent we were all crying. Sheba was gone.

Popsicle Stick Christmas Tree

That was the first year we couldn't afford to buy our own Christmas tree. Mom said in an excited voice, "Carol has spoken with the local Boy Scout troop. They're going to bring us a Christmas tree!"

I sighed. "Oh, man."

"What do you mean, 'Oh, man'"?

I'd heard it on *Happy Days*. I liked saying it because it made me feel like Richie Cunningham. Most of the kids I knew liked The Fonz, but I thought saying "Aye!" with your thumbs up looked stupid. Plus, The Fonz didn't have a lot of reasons to say, "Oh, man." Richie was bothered by bullies or in trouble with his folks all the time. He had plenty of reasons to say, "Oh, man."

I knew Mom didn't want to hear me complain about a pack of Boy Scouts bringing us a Christmas tree. She'd say, "Gary, that's so ungrateful. Carol has done a lot for us," like when I asked if we could eat at home instead of going to the church for Thanksgiving. Actually, I knew Carol had done a lot for Mom. The church had given us food, clothes, and I was pretty sure they'd given Mom money, too. I knew Mom couldn't work because she had five kids, but she could tell Uncle Jim to get a job. All he did was lie around watching TV or read paperback books when he wasn't gossiping about Aunt Peggy's husband, Uncle Bruce, or Doreen's new boyfriend, Gene.

The community college that Doreen had started going to wasn't like regular school. Sometimes she'd have classes at night, and some days she had school in the afternoon. I wasn't sure if Doreen had met her boyfriend, Gene, at college, but Uncle Jim didn't like him. He whispered to Mom as he stirred sugar into his coffee. "I think he's hiding something, Kath."

Mom didn't care if he was hiding something. She just didn't like how old he was. She asked, "What would a guy in his forties want with an eighteen-year-old girl?"

I didn't care if Doreen wanted to date an eighty-year-old man with gray hair. The only thing I cared about was how embarrassed I'd be if the Boy Scouts delivered our Christmas tree, and I knew any of them. I imagined them pointing at me in school, saying, "We brought a Christmas tree to his family because they're poor." I decided I'd wait downstairs until they were gone.

"Gar!" Michael yelled from the top of the stairs. "Come up. They're here!"

"I don't want to!"

Michael ran back to the living room and left the door wide open. He was always doing stupid things. Thoughts raced through my brain. Should I hide in the laundry room? I could shut the light off and hide next to the washer. No, you could see right into the laundry room from the couch. The back storage rooms were too creepy. Maybe I should sneak up and try to close the door? I was panicked, trying to figure it out when I heard Mom. "Gar? Are you down there? Come on up, Honey," followed by Michael's "He's down there. I heard him."

I sighed and began walking up the stairs. I crossed my arms and sat on the living room couch and thought about how I could get back at Michael. He, along with Christina and Vincent, were running around laughing with excitement to have a free Christmas tree brought to our house by Boy Scouts. Christina and Vincent were too young, but Michael was just too stupid to realize we were getting the tree because we were poor. We all should have been hiding in the basement.

KNOCK, KNOCK, KNOCK

Click

"Merry Christmas!!" Carol, about ten boys and four men, probably some of the dads, started maneuvering a Christmas tree through our front door. I could see the boys' Scout uniforms under their coats. I put my hand on my head like Mom did when she had a headache. I could see a few of the boys through my fingers. *Thank God!* They looked older at least, like eleven or twelve. Carol asked, "Hi Jim, are you here for Christmas?"

He answered, "Oh yeah, just a couple of days."

"Where do you live again?"

"Just off of 16th."

What a liar, I thought. I wanted to tell her that, actually, he lives on our couch. Then I thought I could be really funny and ask, "Is our couch located on 16th street?" Regardless of the chuckle I'd get out of embarrassing Uncle Jim, the last thing I wanted was everyone in the room looking my direction.

"Gar," Mom called, "help those boys with the stand." I peeked my head up to see four older boys staring at me with goofy grins on their dumb Boy Scout faces. I quickly dropped to my knees and grabbed the one leg of the stand that didn't already have a Scout holding it. They pushed the tree up into it. One of the dads, clearly making sure none of the "poor" children had to work for the wonderful Christmas miracle, said, "Let me get that for you, Bud." I happily got out of the way.

Instead of garland, the tree had paper chains made out of yellow and red construction paper. The Popsicle stick stars that were supposed to be ornaments looked like they were glued together by kindergartners. There was a crazy thing at the top made out of paper plates and macaroni that I think was supposed to be an angel. *Where did these come from?* Did they recruit elementary school art classes to make decorations for poor families? Did these Boy Scouts do them the days they weren't camping or hiking?

I was sure there was no way the night could get any worse when Carol said, "Everybody hold hands. We're going to pray and sing a Christmas hymn." I quickly looked around for Mom, Doreen,

Michael, I would have even held Uncle Jim's hand at that point. On both sides were goofy Boy Scouts smiling at me. As I took each of their hands, I could see Michael across the room looking at me. He was happy enough to get a Christmas tree made with homemade decorations, but even he realized singing was ridiculous. We made it through Carol's prayer, but it was too much when the Boy Scouts started singing, "Si…ilent night…Ho… oly night..."

I clenched my jaw and held my breath to keep from laughing, but Michael wasn't able to hold it. "Hee hee . . .. Hee hee hee."

Mom growled, under her breath, from across the room. "Michael! Stop it!"

That was the second Christmas Dad had missed. It seemed like so much had happened since he went to prison. We had moved to a new house that Mom and Uncle Jim were sure was haunted. Michelle was born, and Sheba died. Doreen finished high school and started college.

When the car pulled into the driveway, I could see him in the passenger seat. Mom came in the door looking as happy as ever, followed by Dad, who also had a big smile. He looked mostly the same – beard neatly trimmed, glasses resting on the curve of his nose. Only his light brown hair still brushed straight back, looked a bit higher on the sides of his forehead. Christina said, "Hi, Dad." He reached down and gave her a hug.

Then he grabbed Vincent. "My God, you've gotten so big!"

Vincent held up his fingers. "I'm two!" Dad gave Michael a hug, then said to me, "Did you take care of everyone while I was gone, Gar?"

"I did."

I wasn't sure if Mom let us stay upstairs because she really wanted us to spend time with Dad or if it was because she didn't want him to know she kept us in the basement when we weren't at school or sleeping. I was just happy to be in the living room where I could hear their conversation without listening through the basement door. I knew it wouldn't be long before Mom and Uncle Jim would start talking to Dad about the ghost. I couldn't wait to hear what he'd say. Mom put an Entenmann's coffee cake on the kitchen table. Dad put three spoonsful of sugar in his coffee, sat down and lit a cigarette.

Mom called, "Vince, come here Honey." Vincent ran right into the kitchen. Mom said, "Tell Daddy about the lady downstairs." Vincent just grinned and held his hands up like he didn't know.

Mom got serious as she explained. "Nick, he came upstairs going hup two three four. I said, 'where'd you learn that?' He said, 'the lady in the basement.'"

Dad gave a disbelieving look. "Kath, it was the TV. You're being silly."

"No, I'm serious. The TV wasn't on. We've heard footsteps – and Sheba, my God, Sheba."

Uncle Jim butted in. "Nick, I swear to Christ. Sheba was afraid of whatever is in this house."

"Sheba?" Dad asked. "No way."

I didn't know if Sheba had liked the house or not, and I must have been at school the day Vincent shared his army march story with Mom and Uncle Jim. I agreed with Dad; it wasn't that crazy for a two-year-old. I thought that maybe he'd seen *Private Benjamin*. It was a little weird, though, when he talked about the lady like only he could see her. One time, when we all went down to the basement to watch *Flash Gordon*, Vincent had yelled as Mom was about to sit. "Don't sit there!"

"Why?" Mom asked.

"The lady's there."

Dad didn't think it was silly after he'd been home a couple of months. One day, after watching TV downstairs, we all had to come up to get ready for bed. I heard him talking to Mom. "It was one hanger in Doreen's closet, swinging back and forth. I went to grab it, and it stood on end." He added, "Christina keeps taking her angel pictures down because she says they're moving."

Mom got serious. "Nick, I told you. Maybe we should go to the church and ask to speak to the priest."

163

Mmmmm, I loved the smell of cake. Mom and Dad waited for a day when Doreen didn't have school to go see the priest about our haunted house. The only thing Doreen liked better than Chips Ahoy or Twinkies was baking her own cake. The kitchen had a sweet, toasty smell. I wondered what made cold, lumpy cake batter smell so good as it cooked. We all knew we'd get a piece as long as we followed Doreen's instructions like she was the emperor of yellow cake.

After she'd flipped the second round pan over a plate, Doreen barked, "Don't touch them. They need to cool." She went into her room to listen to Bruce Springsteen. The four of us stood on each side of the table staring, as the round cakes cooled.

Michael whispered, "Christina, touch it." She shook her head no as Vincent stood on his tippy toes and looked up over the table. He was happy to take on Michael's challenge. He didn't realize being a big kid meant risking the wrath of Doreen.

As he reached over, I stopped him. "Vincent, no. Don't." A secret touch behind Doreen's back was one thing, but Vincent might give it a two-year-old smash. Plus, he probably had buggers all over his hands.

"Ok, I'll do it," Michael said.

It was right then that I realized it was a risky game that we probably shouldn't be playing. I started, "Michael, don't–" just as his finger pushed down the middle of one of the cakes like a round pillow with a button. It wasn't even a second before it popped up into three triangle sections. *He had broken it!* Christina gasped. Vincent jumped up and down to see. Michael had a look of horror on his face. I had to act. "Quick, quick! Go downstairs!"

Bum bum bum bum bum bum bum boom boom boom

After the four of us were downstairs, I turned the TV on, and we all jumped into a sit to pretend like we'd been watching TV the whole time. My heart raced. I knew it was coming when I heard Doreen's footsteps through the living room. Her voice boomed from the kitchen. "What happened!" The door flung open, and she yelled from the top of the stairs. "Who touched the cake?!" She started coming down.

Vincent said, "I dunno," followed by Christina, "We've been watching TV the whole time."

Doreen scanned each of us. "I know one of you little bastards touched it! Who was it?"

Doreen took a giant step like she was about to chase us. Everyone screamed, "Aaaaah!" and scattered. Vincent and Christina ran right into the storage room. Michael ran to the laundry room. Doreen started toward Michael. As soon as she was off the stairs, I knew that was my escape, so I darted.

She turned around as I raced up the stairs. "Where do you think you're going?" She turned and began chasing me.

"Aaaaah!" I screamed, as she pounced up the stairs behind me. I zipped through the living room to my room and slammed the door. She swung open the door and panted. I couldn't help it. I started laughing. She tried to hold it, but she laughed too.

"You better hope I can frost that mess you guys made."

I'd heard Uncle Jim talk about *The Amityville Horror* a bunch of times with Mom. I think he secretly liked that our house was haunted and wanted more bad things to happen, so it would be like the movie. Before the priest came, the worst thing that had happened was when something grabbed Christina's foot from under her bed. I remember it because I was playing with Michael in the living room. Christina was in her room playing next to her bed. She'd made a half tent from her blanket. As we were playing, she screamed, then came into the living room, crying.

Mom walked out of the kitchen. "What happened?"

Christina pointed. "Michael grabbed my leg."

Michael looked puzzled. "It wasn't me." He liked teasing Christina as much as I liked teasing him. He knew that was something he would have done but not that time. He added, "I've been here the whole time." Christina didn't like it when she thought someone was lying. She stomped her foot and pointed again. "He did it! He did it!"

"I bless this house in the name of the Father, the Son, and the Holy Spirit," the priest said, as he sprinkled water in each of the rooms. The house didn't moan or shake like Uncle Jim wished it would. Nothing happened.

After the priest was done, Mom said, "Thank you so much, Father. Would you like a cup of coffee?" He told her he had to get back and said everything should be fine.

I liked the weekends because I could watch TV downstairs late after all the other kids had to go to bed. Because I was by myself, I could watch whatever I wanted without having to listen to Michael's mouth. He'd arch his head back and moan like he was being tortured. "We've seen this movie a hundred times already!" *Clash of the Titans*, which I'd probably seen only three times, was one of my favorite movies, and I never got tired of watching it. The gold robot owl, Bubo, was so cool. I loved the way he clicked and burred, and Perseus knew exactly what he was saying. I imagined if I had a robot owl, I'd know exactly what he said, too, like telepathy. As I lay on the couch watching TV, I felt my eyes get more and more tired, but I didn't want to miss the show. I thought that if I shut my eyes for just a couple of seconds, the tired would go away.

BANG!

I shuddered awake, every muscle tight with fear.

BANG!

What was happening? Where was that sound coming from?

BANG!

The dryer door slamming.

Nobody there!

I jetted up the stairs as my heart clenched furiously in my chest. Mom asked, "What are you doing down there!?" I put my hand on my chest to feel the crazy pounding of my heart, as I tried to steady my breathing enough to speak.

"Nothing… It was the dryer… I didn't do it."

It wasn't long after that when Vincent got hurt. I heard Mom tell Dad and Uncle Jim about it. "Somebody pinched his hands. He was playing at the bottom of the stairs by himself like he always does, when I heard him scream. I ran down to get him, and his hands were purple like somebody just dug their nails in."
Dad said, "That's it. We're moving."

Good by Myself

"Kath, can I take Gary with me?" Uncle Jim asked as he loaded the vacuum, broom and dustpan into the car.

"Sure, Jim," Mom answered.

"I want to set up my new room, and I don't want Vincent touching my toys." I begged Mom, "I don't want to go."

"Gary, just go and help Uncle Jim, and stop whining."

I wondered why he had volunteered to go sweep and vacuum, but mostly why he wanted to take me with him. *Was he afraid to be alone in the ghost house?* Oh jeez, I thought, he probably wants me to ask the neighbors for beer. I blurted out, "You know, Michael loves talking to people and asking for things. Maybe *he* should go!" Neither was true, but I figured it was worth a try.

Uncle Jim ignored my outburst. "Come on, Gar. Let's go."

The house looked so normal when we rolled into the driveway, like all the other houses on the street. But when Uncle Jim opened the kitchen door, the smell of cardboard boxes and dust reminded that our former home was vacant. I looked around the corner to the empty living room as Uncle Jim brought in the vacuum. He opened the door to the basement.

"Gar, grab that broom. We're gonna start down here."

169

What? The basement? I asked if I could start in the living room even though I didn't want to be anywhere in the house.

"No, come on. There's nothing."

Nothing? Uncle Jim didn't think there was nothing when he had told Mom he'd seen a shadow figure standing outside the basement window. He also didn't think there was nothing when he'd said the German Shepherd next-door barked at Doreen's window when there was no one in the room. At least I wouldn't be alone, I thought, as I followed him down.

He handed me the vacuum. "Start here in the family room. Once you're done, you can sweep the laundry room and the storage room. I'll be up in the kitchen working."

Oh my God. My mind raced. He wasn't really going to leave me in the basement alone, was he? My heart started pounding. Should I beg him? Cry? I could. I was that scared.

No, not with him. I'd rather be killed by a ghost than beg Uncle Jim for anything. I took a deep breath and stood frozen in the empty basement. A shiver ran up the back of my neck, and I felt the little hairs on my arm stand. I imagined turning around and seeing a white, misty lady with hollow eyes staring at me when I heard the kitchen door open. *He's leaving??*

I ran to the laundry room.

Through the laundry room window, I saw Uncle Jim walk down the steps toward the backyard. I bolted out of the laundry room and into the storage room, so I could see what he was doing. I recognized the red and white vodka label on the bottle he pulled out of the dirt. He stood up and walked to the other side of the house.

I ran again, but I was unable to see him from that window. I went up to the wall and listened. I heard him dig up something else; then it got quiet. I started backing up from the wall when I noticed a shadow in the window above me. Uncle Jim's face – with his hand up to the glass so he could see in! I flung myself back and pressed against the wall, hoping he couldn't see me below.

I listened and waited until I heard him stand. He brushed the dirt off his knees before he started walking back around the house. I darted to the vacuum, clicked it on and began pushing and pulling in wild, uneven thrusts that made a crazy, deformed starburst pattern in the middle of the basement carpet.

When we got back to our new house, Uncle Jim told Mom, "It's all clean, Kath. The whole house has been vacuumed and swept." He didn't tell her that I was the one who did the vacuuming and sweeping while he ran around digging up bottles of booze.

"Oh thanks, Jim. That was a big help," Mom said.

The last time I saw the ghost house was a few weeks later. We had to go back to get our mail every couple of days after we'd moved. Vera lived next door, but we hadn't talked with her much when we'd

lived there. That day, Vera was working in her rose bushes. I knew Dad
was nervous because he stood at the mailbox for several minutes
staring at the letters like he wanted to ask her something but didn't
know how. I thought he probably felt silly asking Vera about the house
since he had told Mom, "There's no such thing as ghosts," when he first
came home. It wasn't until he saw a Coke bottle drop off of Doreen's
dresser and slowly roll across the floor to under Christina's bed that he
started believing. Dad finally said, "Hi Vera," then asked, "Do you
mind if I ask you something… did anyone ever die in the house, Vera?"

Vera tightened her lips and looked at the ground as she thought
about Dad's question. She answered, "Well, I'm not sure." Vera had old
lady white hair that I knew she curled with rollers. Sometimes at night,
I could see her in the kitchen doing dishes. She also wore glasses, and it
seemed like every shirt she owned had little dogs or flowers all over
them. That day, she had thick, yellow gloves on, too.

"You know what?" she began, as she walked toward us. "A
few years ago, there was a young couple that bought the house. The
wife couldn't have been older than thirty. She got cancer. I'm not sure if
she died at home or in the hospital."

Dad questioned, "Really? You don't remember at all if she died
in the house?"

Vera put her fingers on her lips and stared toward the ground.
"Mmmm, no, I'm not sure, but the husband sold it right after she died.
The family that bought it only lived there about six months before

172

renting it. You know, I don't think anyone that lived there has stayed longer than six months. Your family was the first. How long were you there, a year?"

Dad nodded. "Yeah, a year."

Vera probably wondered why a nice, normal family would live in a haunted house for a whole year. She probably thought Doreen was my older sister. Uncle Jim didn't have his own car, so she would have never wondered why he never went home. She also didn't know that Dad was actually in prison half the time we had lived there. A couple of days before he came home, I had heard Mom tell Vera, "Vera, remember I told you my husband was working out of state? Well, he'll be home in two days."

Vera gave Mom a big smile as she clipped her bushes. She answered, "Oh, yeah!" but I could tell that was the first time she'd heard that, and she was pretending to remember just to be polite.

The normal neighbors, like Vera, never really spent time getting to know our family. They'd say, "Good morning" or "Hi" as they walked to their cars in the morning or carried their groceries inside in the afternoon. It was people like our new neighbor, Judy, who quickly became friends with Mom and wanted to know all about our family. She was super friendly when we moved in.

"Hi! You guys from New Jersey?" Judy asked when she saw the license plates on our car. "My ex-sister-in-law is from New Jersey. Or do you say Jersey?"

Mom laughed. "We say Jersey or New Jersey, Hon."

I knew when Judy laughed back that it wouldn't be long before she was over at our house.

Judy was about the same height as Mom, but heavier with a pudgy face. Her hair looked like tiny black springs coiled all over her head, and she wore black tights and really baggy, long shirts. Judy explained to Mom that her husband only hit her one time. "I beat the shit out of him and told him to get out."

Mom asked, "Really?"

"Oh yeah! I said if he ever came near me again, I'd shoot him."

They also talked about Doreen dating an older guy. Mom said, "Judy, I don't know what to do. You know, at that age, she's going to do what she wants."

Judy said, "I know. I know," as she shook her head. "I think she's got a low self-esteem."

Her son, Jason, was my age. Judy tried to get us to play together by saying, "Jason, show Gary your Atari."

Mom didn't like the idea of us being alone at Jason's house, so she told me, "I want you back in ten minutes."

"Kathleen, they'll be fine," Judy said like Mom was being silly.

She *was* being silly, I thought. "Mom, I'm ten, and they're right next door."

Mom gave me a serious look. "I don't care. I want you right back."

Jason's basement had toys scattered everywhere. He had the *Dukes of Hazzard* car, He-Man figures, and a bunch of Tyco black race track pieces all over his carpet. I wondered if he had a train set somewhere. As I looked around his playroom, he called, "Come here!" He was under his stairs. He said, "Look at this," and pulled out a blue lighter. He pulled out and opened a Monopoly box lid to show me a small plate with black marks and ash all over it. He took a pink five-dollar bill, held it up, and lit the corner.

I asked, "What are you doing?"

"Watch, Watch."

"We shouldn't be doing this."

"Are you gonna tell on me?"

"No, but we shouldn't…"

He dropped the bill on the plate once it was halfway on fire. I looked around, wondering if there was another way out in case the stairs caught on fire. I was just about to run when the flame flickered down to nothing. "See?" he said. "Nothing happened." I didn't care if nothing had happened. I decided that was the last time I was going over to his house or playing with him at all.

Michael wasn't allowed to play outside due to his asthma, especially in summer. He didn't mind, though. He'd rather shoot his rubber dart gun at the windows or the glass door on the stereo in the living room. Christina and Vincent both loved playing in the backyard, which was perfect because our yard had a chain-link fence, and Mom could see them no matter where they were.

I liked sitting in the kitchen listening to Mom talk to Judy. I realized if I pretended to understand everything they talked about and didn't ask questions, Mom wouldn't send me to play. I came up with a great idea to be sure they really considered me one of the adults. I made sure I announced every time I was taking care of the kids. I would get up and say, "Do you smell that? I need to change Michelle's diaper. I'll be right back." As soon as Mom said Vincent and Christina needed to come in; I'd jump up. "I'll get them." I'd bring them into the bathroom to wash the dirt off their hands and face with a wet washcloth.

Christina never struggled, but Vincent would scrunch his face and try to pull away when I held his chin. I wondered if Mom would ever cut his hair. When it started getting thick and curly, she had told Dad, "Nick, it makes him look so cute. I can't cut it."

Dad replied, "It makes him look like Shirley Temple. Do you want him getting made fun of?"

Christina and Vincent, I could handle, but Michael would disrespect me. When I told him to stop shooting darts at the stereo, he yelled, "You're not a grown up, so stop acting like it."

176

I wanted to grab his arm and slap his butt like Mom would have, but I knew he would fight back, making both of us look like stupid kids. Instead, I just breathed. "Michael, you heard me." Even though Michael tried to embarrass me, my plan still worked.

As I walked back in the kitchen, I heard Judy telling Mom, "God, I wish Jason would help me like that."

One day Mom and Judy started talking about Uncle Jim. Judy said, "You know, I'd date Jimmy if he could get the drinking under control." I knew, even if he were sober, he'd never date her. He always said she looked like a fat hamster with frizzy hair.

I almost laughed when Mom said, "Oh, Judy, you'd be perfect for him." Then, I decided to follow Mom's lead.

I added, "Uncle Jim always says you're really pretty."

"Really?" Judy asked.

I thought it was funny that she seemed surprised because she had just said she'd date him like it was her choice, and he'd been waiting to date her the whole time. I thought that maybe I wasn't believable enough, so I beefed up my lie. "Oh yeah, he said you're the most beautiful girl he's ever seen." She got a big smile on her chubby face as she turned to pour more coffee. I was grinning, too, thinking about the look on Uncle Jim's face the next time he saw Judy. As I imagined her saying, "Hi, Jimmy, I think you're handsome, too," I felt Mom's hands on my shoulders. She turned me around and marched me right into the living room. "You've spent enough time with the adults. Play in here with Michael."

A few days later Judy came over wearing light green eyeshadow and red lipstick that almost looked orange. I wanted to ask her if she was trying to look pretty for Uncle Jim, but I didn't want to risk getting chased into the living room, so I kept my mouth shut. When Uncle Jim came home, Judy smiled and laughed at almost everything he said. That didn't surprise me. I'd seen almost every one of Uncle Dan's girlfriend's do the same thing – except Veronica. She had acted the most normal around him. I thought that was why he had liked her the best.

I was shocked when Judy told Uncle Jim that the right woman would make him want to stop drinking. She's crazy, I thought. Miss America in a red bikini with a crown of sparklers couldn't stop him from drinking. I waited to hear what Uncle Jim would say to that, but he just stared for a few seconds. Then he said, "Yeah, well I'm gonna go for a walk," and left. Go for a walk meant go to the garage and dig out one of his bottles of booze. When he walked back in a while later, I knew it was going to be trouble.

Uncle Jim started. "Judy, why'd your husband leave again?"

"He left because I made him leave."

"Heh." Uncle Jim gave an airy chuckle, then said in a low voice, "Best thing that ever happened to him."

Judy's face turned red. "What did you say?" which turned into an argument. She called him a loser and a drunk. He called her a fat busybody.

Mom kept yelling, "Jimmy!" "Judy!" "Jimmy!" "Stop!" but it didn't matter.

They kept going until Judy screamed, "I don't have to listen to this!" grabbed her keys and slammed the door behind her. The next day, Judy knocked on our door to tell Mom that Jason wasn't allowed over our house anymore. They talked for a few minutes before Mom shut the door and said, "Fuck her, fucking bitch!"

Even though Mom and Judy stopped being friends, Jason would still play with Vincent through the fence. I didn't understand why Jason wanted to play with a two-year-old, but Vincent loved it. He'd run and grab the Nerf football Jason had thrown over and throw it back like a little gladiator throwing a boulder. I was in the kitchen listening to Doreen tell Mom how she was going to be a veterinarian when Vincent screamed.

Mom stood up so fast her chair fell over. "Oh my God!" she screamed as she yanked open the glass door. Vincent was running with fire on his back. Mom grabbed him and threw him down. The fire was out.

Doreen yelled, "What happened?"

"What is this?" Mom picked up a melted, black and plastic wad from the ground. "A milk container?" Jason was at the fence crying.

Judy stormed out screaming. "What did your son do?"

Mom yelled back. "*Your* son stuck a lit milk container on Vincent's back!"

Judy growled, "Don't blame my son. Your son is a brat!"

Mom ran to the fence, grabbed the bar, and vaulted over better than any boy I'd ever seen. Doreen screamed, "Kath!" and ran after her. Mom pushed Judy down, grabbed her hair, and started hitting her as Doreen – who wobbled her way over the fence – finally made it to her. She grabbed Mom's arm. "Kath, stop! Stop! We have to get Vincent to the hospital. He's burned!"

As Doreen pulled Mom away, Mom growled, "If you or your son *ever* come near my kids again, I'll kill you!"

Once the doctor cleaned up the burn, the worst part was about the size of a quarter with bright pink skin around it. He told Mom the middle was third degree and would leave a scar, but the areas around would heal.

After the fight with Judy, Mom wouldn't let Vincent and Christina play in the backyard anymore. We all had to play in the living room. One day, when Mom asked me to keep the kids occupied, I decided duck duck goose would work. Christina learned very quickly to wait until she was almost completely past someone to say "Goose," so she had a good head start on them. She usually picked Vincent anyway since there was no chance he could reach over and grab her before even getting up like Michael or I could. Vincent loved being "it." He always had a big smile on his face when he'd say "Goose" to the first person he patted. I was trying to teach him how to duck duck first when Uncle Jim walked in.

I could tell from the way he stumbled past us that he was drunk. Mom stuck her head out of the kitchen. "Jimmy?"

He ignored her, walked into the bathroom, and started peeing without even shutting the door all the way. When he came out, he said, "What?"

Mom came over to us and waved her hands up. "Come on, come on. Gary, take these guys in the room."

I got so mad that I just blurted out, "Why? Because he's drunk again?"

Mom said, "Gary!"

Uncle Jim snarled to Mom, as he looked at me, "What did he say?"

"I don't care!" I yelled back. "You're a drunken alcoholic!"

Uncle Jim started toward me like he was going to hit me. He wasn't as strong or scary as Uncle Dan. I wanted him to hit me. I hated him. I'd always hated him, and I wanted Mom to see how crazy he was.

My body got tense, but then Mom stepped between us. "Jimmy! You are drunk!"

She turned to me. "Gary, go to your room – now!" Mom was so mad; I was more afraid of her than Uncle Jim. I was sure she was going to hit someone, and I didn't want it to be me. I ran to my room and slammed the door.

I didn't talk to Uncle Jim one time the whole week before he left. Even when he was leaving, Mom knew I didn't want to talk to him. I stayed in my room while everyone else said goodbye. When Dad got back from taking Uncle Jim to the bus, Mom told him, "Nick, maybe you're right. Maybe we should move somewhere else. New York is close to New Jersey."

Calvin Coolidge was the first school I'd ever gone to where most of the kids were nice. Even when Timmy realized I had a big head and said, "I need some head space," every time he walked by me, only a few of the kids would laugh. Tiffany was the smallest girl in our class, but she was never afraid to say something that everyone else didn't agree with.

One day, when Timmy had gotten two of Tiffany's friends to start saying that my head was too big, she said, "Well, I think you shouldn't talk about other people unless you're perfect yourself. Are you perfect, Timmy?"

When he said, "Yeah!" she asked him, "Then why do you need braces?" With that, she spun around and marched away. Her friends looked at each other and then ran after her. I had seen a *Phil Donahue* show where they talked about confidence. I wished I had confidence like Tiffany.

On my last day of school, my class threw me a party. They made cupcakes, and everyone signed a goodbye card. Bobby, who I always thought was a little weird, told me, "I signed your card 'Later, Ali-Gary.'" When I looked at him without saying anything back, he thought I didn't understand. "You know, Ali-Gary, instead of alligator."

I smiled. "Ok, I get it." He was happy I got it, and I thought, it's better to have a weird friend that's nice than a cool friend who's mean.

When I got home from school, Aunt Peggy was helping Mom pack up our kitchen. As she placed the dishes in the box, she said, "I'm going to miss you so much, Kath."

"I'm going to miss you, too, Peg."

I ran over. "Why don't you move, too, Aunt Peggy?"

She chuckled. "Then who'll be here with Aunt Doreen?"

Doreen? What did she mean? Mom cut in, "Peg, we didn't tell him yet," then bent down toward me. My throat started to get a choked feeling, but I held it. Mom didn't tell me Doreen wasn't moving with us because she thought I'd cry like a baby.

183

I held it tighter and forced my voice to sound normal. "Doreen's not coming?" It hurt like someone had punched me in the throat, but I wouldn't cry.

I waited in Doreen's room for her to get home. I was sure she hadn't closed her box of records yet so that she could listen to them while she packed. As I looked through Pink Floyd, Led Zeppelin, and Bruce Springsteen, I wondered why I always complained about her music. When she came in, my throat got tight again. She asked, "What're you doing, Gar?" I tried so hard, but I couldn't help it. The tears started running down my face.

She bent down. "Oh Gar, don't cry. I'll come visit." She hugged me, smiled, and hugged me again.

"Wh… Why do you have to… go… to school in Iowa?"

She hugged me while I cried. "It's ok, Buddy. It's ok."

A Blistering Offense

The whole name – Florida, New York – seemed funny. Whenever I'd seen New York on TV, it looked like the biggest city in the world, with cabs honking and tons of people walking around. When Michael asked if we would be able to see The Empire State Building from our house, Dad laughed. He explained that we were moving to Upstate New York, not New York City. I asked Dad if it was like New Jersey. He chuckled. "It's a lot more like New Jersey than Iowa."

I realized the town wasn't named Florida because it had palm trees and a beach littered with coconuts. There were patches of snow on the ground, and the grass on the hills was mostly flat and dead. The sun seemed a million miles away when we got out of the car into the freezing wind. Dad took Christina's hand. Mom said, "Gary, grab Michelle," as she picked up Vincent.

I wondered if Mom felt bad that Vincent had gotten burned and wanted to be sure he would never get hurt again. I'd rather hold Michelle, anyway. She didn't squirm and try to get down to run away like Vincent did. She was also cuter – dimples, perfect baby teeth smile and light hazel eyes – than any kid on TV or in real life and, at one and a half, her hair had begun growing in deep, shiny brown. I knew, just like Doreen and Christina, Mom was going to make her grow it down to her butt. She let Michelle have bangs, though, because Aunt Peggy had convinced her how beautifully they framed her little face.

Both Michael's and my hair had started darkening, and while Michael's "thickness" had evened out so that his body looked ordinary, I had begun the lanky pre-teen stage, with skinny arms, bony knees and hands and feet that looked too big. Christina and Vincent still had light brown hair. Christina even had a wispy blond streak, from the many hours she spent playing in the sun. Vincent, with his chubby cheeks and round face, and especially with his bouncy curls, – just like Dad had said – looked like he should be singing, "On the good ship lollipop," not chasing after Christina to play with a tennis ball. Christina didn't care how tangled her hair got when she was running with Vincent. As much confidence as she had playing baseball (or some other ball game she'd made up) with any kid, of any age, Christina was shy if an adult she didn't know spoke to her. She'd tilt her head, to allow her hair to hide the delicate features of her petite face, and offer a slight, closed-lip smile that they could barely see. When anyone spoke to Michelle, however, she would smile bright and laugh like she was the happiest little girl in the world.

As I pulled Michelle up, so her face was near mine, I could see that her cheeks were turning pink, and her breaths came out like tiny puffs of steam. She pointed with excitement, "How! How!" as she bounced in my arms.

I wasn't sure if she was trying to say house or home. I just smiled and said, "Yes." We walked up the frozen ground toward the house with wood siding that wasn't painted, and windows that were the tallest I'd ever seen.

The realtor had left the heat on for us, so it was toasty when Dad opened the front door. I took Michelle's puffy, pink coat off, then took my jacket off. Christina and Vincent ran right into the living room to look out the huge windows while Michael started climbing the stairs. From the railing above, he called out, "Hello, down there." As I got to the top of the steps, I looked down, too. I thought it was neat that you could see the entire living room and dining room from above, but I wanted to see the bedrooms.

Whenever we'd had enough bedrooms before, Doreen would get her own room. I used to ask Mom why Doreen didn't have to share while I did. She would tell me, "Doreen's older," and "Someday, Honey." I just figured I was going to have to share a peed-the-bed smelling room with Michael and Vincent forever.

Before we left the hotel in Indiana, Mom had whispered, "Gar, you're going to have your own room." When I looked up in disbelief, she smiled. "Are you excited?"

I was shocked. I didn't even think about the possibility of getting my own room after Doreen wasn't with us. As the realization settled in, the happiness grew until I was smiling as big as she was. "Yeah, I'm excited."

Even though my bedroom was the smallest, I didn't care. I was thrilled that I didn't have to share with Michael and Vincent. I'd decided where I was going to put my dresser and lamp. I was trying to figure out whether my Simon Says and Perfection should go in the closet or

187

under my bed when I heard Mom say, "Just bring in the mattresses tonight, Nick. Danny will be here tomorrow to help you unload the rest of the truck." The muscles in my stomach clenched and the happiness drained right out of my body.

I questioned how it could be real that Uncle Jim had finally left only to have Uncle Dan come back. I walked out of my room as Mom spoke to Dad. "He's bringing his new girlfriend, and Anthony's coming with him, too."

Dad asked, "Who's Anthony again?"

Mom answered, "I used to babysit him."

The next morning, Mom paced back and forth in front of the bright living room windows while she smoked a cigarette. She had started smoking again as soon as we left Iowa. At our first gas station stop, she'd told Dad, "Nick, get me a Diet Coke – and get me a pack of Kool's, too." I hated her smoking, but all of my thoughts about something I didn't like were focused on Uncle Dan. As I sat on the living room floor staring at *The Price is Right*, I kept thinking about how Uncle Dan's face contorted when he screamed, which pulled at the sick feeling already in my gut.

As their car turned into our long driveway, Mom whispered to Dad, "That must be his new girlfriend, Shari."

I got up and went to the window. There was definitely a girl with blond hair driving the car, and I could see the bald top of Uncle

188

Dan's head in the passenger seat. The guy in the back seat had a full head of wavy black hair.

When they came in the house, Mom squealed, "Dan!" and gave him a hug. She turned to the girl with the slender, freckled face and asked, "Shari?"

The girl smiled. "Kathleen? I've been dying to meet you. This is a beautiful house."

Mom said, "Oh, thank you, Hon. I haven't decided how I'm going to decorate yet – and call me Kathy."

Mom turned to the guy with the dark, beady eyes, who looked like he was about Doreen's age. "Anthony! I remember when you were this big. This is my husband, Nick, and these are our kids: Gary, Michael, Christina, Vincent, and Michelle."

Mom said, "Gary, take the kids to play so we can talk." I was curious about the new man and Uncle Dan's girlfriend, and I knew it would be easy to listen because the house was so open. I took the kids into the living room as the adults began gossiping in the kitchen. They talked about Uncle Jim being a bad alcoholic, Doreen dating an older guy, and Dad going to jail.

I heard Mom say, "When the police started chasing us, Nick sped up. I screamed at him to pull over."

Dad laughed. "Go to jail or deal with Kathy? I pulled over."

Mom chuckled. "I wasn't going to jail with four kids, and I didn't even know I was pregnant."

Anthony asked, "So, Vincent and Michelle are Nick's kids?"

It got quiet. From the corner of the sofa, where I was pretending to play peekaboo with Michelle, I could see Uncle Dan walking toward me. The memory of his deep, tough guy voice flooded back as he barked, "What do you think this is? The Eary Lackawanna? Go play!" He put his hand on my back and marched me to the far end of the living room as Anthony laughed.

I'd figured out that babies came from adults having sex when a boy in my third-grade class, Ricky, told one of the girls, "I'm gonna stick my dick in your pussy and give you a baby."

The teacher gasped and almost fell over, reaching for the chalkboard to hold herself up. She said, "My goodness!" as she held her chest. "Where did you hear language like that?"

I was *sure* he'd be in big trouble for cursing twice. When another boy had said, "Ewww, I stepped in dog shit on the playground," she made him stand in the corner for ten minutes. Ricky wasn't being put in a corner though. The teacher yanked his hand and pulled him right out of the classroom. As soon as the door shut, everyone started talking about "doing it" and what "fuck" really meant.

After Uncle Dan walked back to the kitchen, I thought about what Anthony had said and wondered why Mom didn't want me hearing it. As I tried to make sense of what the adults were hiding, I thought about Dad and how he and Mom must have had sex for her to get pregnant with Vincent and Michelle. I also wondered about Gary. Whenever I'd asked Mom about him, she'd get mad. "It doesn't matter. He left. Nick is all of your father." If that was true, then why did Anthony ask if Dad was only Vincent's and Michelle's father?

It was late by the time all our furniture and boxes were off the truck. I was in my room arranging my games under the bed when Uncle Dan opened the door. "Hey, me and Shari are gonna crash in here. Go sleep with your brothers."

I wanted to say, "But it's my room." Instead, I pushed Simon Says deep under my bed and got up. As I walked to Michael and Vincent's room, I looked down over the railing. Anthony already had a pillow and sheet on the couch. I knew that even if we had three sofas, Uncle Dan would have still made me leave.

Shari came out of my bedroom in the morning wearing pink sweatpants and a gray shirt that she'd cut in half so that you could see her flat stomach. She bent toward me. "Thank you for letting us sleep in your room, Gary."

I wanted to tell her that I didn't have a choice, but if I had, I'd let her and not Uncle Dan because at least she said thank you. I just said, "You're welcome."

The first couple of days, I could go in my room after Uncle Dan and Shari woke up, but then Uncle Dan started shutting the door like it was his bedroom. The last Saturday before we were going to start at our new school, Uncle Dan was outside throwing a football with Anthony. I snuck into my room to play Perfection. It made me feel good that I was playing a game that required intelligence while Anthony and Uncle Dan ran around throwing a stupid football. As the clock ticked, ticked, ticked, I picked up the little yellow pieces – X, star, oval, square – and placed them as quickly as I could as the timer ran down. I was almost done when my door opened.

Uncle Dan asked, "What're you doing in here?"

"I was just playing–"

POP!

"What is this? Get up and get your coat on. You're coming outside to throw the football."

"Ok, can I just–"

"Come on!"

I zippered up my coat and pulled my gray winter hat down over my head. "Come here!" Uncle Dan yanked the hat off like a sock. He folded the edge under three times and pulled it back down, so it only covered the tops of my ears. "You wear it like this. Only girls wear it the way you had it." I thought about telling him that only old men wear it the way he wanted, but I knew he'd say, "What are you, a wise guy?" or "Do you think you're funny?" I went outside wearing my hat like a thirty-year-old man.

Anthony ran farther and farther backward, holding the football near his head, with his other hand open, ready to block the phantom defensemen who were going to charge him. He threw straight up in the air, and the ball spun almost perfectly, with the white rings easy to see against the brown, grainy leather. Uncle Dan hollered, "Step back," as he jumped forward, then to the side. He held his arms open like he was about to catch a falling baby. The ball made a foop! sound as it crashed into his body.

Uncle Dan and Anthony impressed Vincent and Christina almost as much as they impressed themselves. Vincent yelled, "I wanna play!" Christina pushed herself in front to be sure she got a turn first since she was older.

Uncle Dan motioned with his hands and called out, "Ant, bring it in a little." Anthony took a couple of jog steps in. Uncle Dan yelled, "That's good!" but Anthony was still far enough away that Uncle Dan had to scream for Anthony to hear him. Oh great, I thought, as my heart started racing. This is where Uncle Dan wants me to catch that dumb ball.

Uncle Dan instructed me. "Let the football come to you and pull it into your body like this." I knew what he wanted me to do. I just wasn't sure if my body would do it when the ball, which was bigger than my chest, came flying at me.

The first time, I stood with my arms out as the ball flew through the air, Uncle Dan yelled, "Pull it in! Bend your knees! Spread your feet!" My mind raced as I hunched and scurried to obey his commands. The ball whapped on the frozen ground in front of me. The next time, when the brown leather bullet whizzed right at me, I jumped away in a panic before it hit. Uncle Dan yelled, "You look like a little girl!"

Anthony laughed and hollered out. "Maybe we should let Christina play!" Christina smiled big and hopeful, not realizing Anthony didn't really want her to play – he was only making fun of me.

After several fumbles and complete misses, the fear of Uncle Dan screaming (and making Anthony crack up) became stronger than the worry about getting hurt. Anthony hopped a couple spots back, raised the ball to the side of his head – clearly preparing to make his best throw. He shot the ball straight up. My heart pounded as the ball slowly hit its peak, high in the air, before beginning its plummet right toward me. I held my arms out and bent my knees. I didn't shut my eyes. I only squinted and turned my head a little. I took a deep breath and…

Foop!

I caught it? I caught it. I actually caught it! Uncle Dan ran over. "Good job! That's how you do it, Champ!" Christina squeezed her hands together and laughed. Vincent jumped up and down and clapped. The tightness in my stomach loosened into excitement. I imagined how cool I must have looked – easily catching the ball. I was still smiling about my feat when Uncle Dan got serious again. No time for celebration as far as he was concerned. It was on to the next order of business: throwing.

"Look," he said, as he took the football. He showed me how to place my fingers between the white laces, so the ball would spin and not wobble when I threw it. As we passed the ball back and forth, I thought, this isn't so bad.

I tried to figure out if we'd been out of school for three or four weeks as I got ready for my first day. I picked up my *Knight Rider* lunch box and wondered if the kids would think it's stupid. "Gar, what's the matter?" Mom asked.

"Nothing. I'm just a little nervous about starting a new school halfway through the year."

Mom put her hand on my shoulder and gave me a reassuring smile. "There's only a couple of months left, Honey, and then it'll be summer."

It was scary enough walking into my new fourth-grade classroom alone, but when the teacher made me stand in front of everyone and introduce myself, my heart beat so fast I was sure it was going to stop and give me a heart attack. When I walked to the empty desk in the middle of the room, the pounding in my chest slowed. After I'd taken my seat, the girl next to me asked, "Is your hair supposed to look like that?"

My heart raced again. "Yeah, it is."

She smirked like she already hated me, turned to her friend and said, "I guess his hair is supposed to look greasy."

When I got home, Shari was helping Mom hang curtains. Mom looked over. "Gar, how was your first day of school?" I wasn't going to tell her that everyone either ignored me or whispered to their friends and snickered at me.

I answered, "It was good," but I could tell from the look on Mom's face that she didn't believe me. I decided to add more detail to my lie. "One of the kids in my class told me their dad is an engineer. He said I could go for a ride on his train."

Mom gave a slight smile. I wasn't sure if she believed me, but Shari sure did.

"That's so cool," Shari said. "Does he work for Amtrak?"

I answered. "I think he works on a freight train."

I felt bad lying about my day at school, but there was no way I could tell Mom the truth. She'd give me a wounded look and then try to be helpful by saying, "Just try being really nice to them." I had tried that before when two boys in my second-grade class kept calling me Dumbo Ears. I smiled and told them that I liked their shirts. They looked at me like I was crazy, then burst out laughing.

After that, instead of just saying "Dumbo Ears" every time they walked by me, they'd say, "Hey, Dumbo Ears, I like your shirt" then crack up like it was the funniest thing they'd ever said.

"Shari!" Mom yelled. "Your boob!" then started laughing.

"Oh my God!" Shari yelped, as she crossed her arms and turned toward the wall. She was wearing the same half shirt she usually slept in. I realized her shirt must have pulled up higher than her boob when she reached up to hold the curtain rod. She must not have felt the air on her nipple as she walked around talking to me and Mom afterward. Her face turned red, "Did you see?"

I hadn't. "No," I said. "I swear."

I wondered what would happen when Uncle Dan and Anthony got home. What if Shari told them? I could just hear Uncle Dan. "Did Gary see your boob?"

Shari would think she was being nice by saying, "No, he didn't see anything!" not realizing Uncle Dan would wonder how a ten-year-old boy could not notice a boob right in front of his face. Anthony would call me a fag when no one was listening, the same way he called me "Ears" and "Headquarters."

I'd heard kids call boys they didn't like "fag" for as long as I could remember. When I was in first grade – the second time – Stephanie had told everyone in the class that Tommy was a gay fag because he talked like a girl and was really bad at kickball. I thought about the look on Tommy's face every time a kid told him he was gay or a fag, and it put an empty feeling in my stomach. I decided if Uncle Dan or Anthony asked me about what happened, I'd lie and tell them that I saw *all* of Shari's boob but that I didn't want to embarrass her.

Even though it meant I'd have to play football, I still couldn't wait for the school week to end. I'd rather deal with Uncle Dan and Anthony than the kids in my class. The first weekend after I started school, Uncle Dan got a small football that even Vincent could hold. He told Anthony, "Gimme a sec. I'm gonna get these two set up." First, he showed Christina how to hold and throw it. He said, "Now pass it to your little brother," as he stood behind Vincent to help him catch.

I heard Anthony from behind me. "Gar, think quick!" I turned. The football –

BAM!

I was on the ground. My right ear was ringing, and the side of my face felt hot. The sting made me want to cry. I put my hand on my ear. I heard Anthony. "I just lobbed it to him." "Lobbed" made it sound like a bouncy sponge. The ball felt like a high-speed cannonball trying to take my head off.

"Come on." I felt Uncle Dan's hands under my arms as he pulled me up. "You're alright." I looked around. Both Christina's and

Vincent's mouths were open, and the shocked look in their eyes told me I'd been hit as hard as I thought.

"Are you alright, Gar?" Christina asked as Vincent picked up my hat from the ground.

Anthony made a baby voice. "You ok?" then a sad face with his bottom lip stuck out, before running back out. "Dan, go deep!"

Shari left before Mom's friend, Laura Giordano, came to visit for Spring Break. I'd heard Mom tell Shari, "Yeah, they dated, but it was a long time ago."

For a couple of days after that, Shari kept telling Uncle Dan, "My mom has been asking when we're coming home. We should go see her." Uncle Dan didn't want to go. He told Shari to call him when she got back to Jersey.

Laura had her daughter, Laura Lynne, about the same time Mom had me. The last time I'd seen her, we were both probably three or four. Since then, Laura had two more kids, John and Joey. When they got to our house, Laura hugged Mom and then asked me, "How did you get so big?" I shrugged and grinned.

Mom said, "Gar, you remember Laura Lynne, right?"

Laura Lynne's dark hair was longer than I remembered, a little past her shoulders, and she was taller, almost as tall as her mom (actually we both were). But I remembered her.

I asked, "Do you want to go outside?"

She smiled. "Ok." Laura Lynne and I ran out to the backyard while Michael, Christina, and Vincent talked to John and Joey.

Laura Lynne brought her Cabbage Patch Kid outside with us. "I have her adoption papers," she said. "Every one is different like a real kid."

"Really?" I asked. "Can I hold her?" As Laura Lynne handed me the doll, I thought, there's no way this doll is the only one with green eyes and red, yarn hair.

Whether the doll really was the only one or not, Laura Lynne was excited to play with her. "We can pretend she's our daughter," she said.

As the week went on, Laura Lynne and I played house in the living room, explored the woods in the backyard – looking for squirrel holes and eagle's nests at the top of the tall narrow tree trunks – and we organized hide and go seek and tag for the younger kids. Laura Lynne was my favorite friend. When I told her that I wanted to marry her when we grew up, she said, "Me, too." We laughed. We knew it was such a great idea because we'd been friends since we were born. We decided that John should marry Christina, too, because they were also the same age. We went into the living room to tell them.

I started. "You two should get married when you grow up."

Laura Lynne followed with, "Yeah! We're gonna get married, too."

John was serious for a five-year-old. He pushed his glasses up his nose like a professor. "I'm not getting married, so I'm not marrying her."

Christina stood up. "I'm not marrying you, either!"

John shot back, "Good! I don't care because you're dumb," which made Christina mad. She tightened her lips and pushed him down.

As soon as he started crying, Mom came out of the kitchen. "What happened?"

John pointed at Christina. "She... pushed... me!" Mom grabbed Christina as she tried to shield her butt with her hand.

WHAP! WHAP! WHAP!

Christina started crying as Mom dragged her to the stairs.

WHAP! WHAP! WHAP!

"Go to your room," Mom yelled. "That's what you get for pushing."

My chest got tight as Mom shoved Christina up the stairs. I looked at John and wanted to smack him for getting her in trouble. When Michael had told John he was a nerd; I'd yelled, "That's not nice. Apologize to him, Michael," even though I agreed with him. If John

201

weren't such a nerd, I thought, he would have laughed and played along.

Laura Lynne grabbed John's arm and scolded. "John, there was no reason for you to be mean to Christina. It was a joke."

He screamed back, "I don't care!" and ran into the kitchen.

Since Shari left, Uncle Dan had been sleeping in my room alone. Laura and Laura Lynne were sleeping in Christina and Michelle's room, and John and Joey were piled up with me, Michael, and Vincent. It was the last night that they were all going to be there, and I didn't want to sleep. I lay in bed thinking about what I was going to do for fun after Laura Lynne was gone, and I got a knot in my stomach when I thought about going back to school. I pushed the thought out of my mind and began focusing on the sounds of the quiet house when I heard someone walking down the hall. I got up, stepped over John, and turned the door handle as slowly as possible. I opened it only an inch to peek out. At the other end of the hall, I saw Laura, wearing just a baggy, white tee-shirt opening the door to my bedroom. Uncle Dan's arm reached over her and shut the door with a click.

A few weeks after Laura left, Mom and Dad started talking about moving again. One day, when Mom was alone in the kitchen, I asked, "Mom, why do we move so much?"

"I know, Honey, we've moved a lot, but this is a great opportunity for your dad."

"What do you mean?"

"He's going to work on the new house, and we're going to buy it. And it has a pool."

"A pool? Really? Is anybody going to live with us?"

"Why do you say that, Gar?"

"I don't know. I just want to live normal."

She looked sad but smiled, "I know, Honey. We will live normal really soon. I promise."

When Shari came back, Uncle Dan grabbed her and dipped her over as she giggled. "What's that for?" she asked.

He said, "No reason. Just missed my girl." I knew the reason was because he had had sex with Laura when she was gone. Shari was pretty, smart and genuinely sweet. I remembered one time when she was talking to Mom, Shari had told Mom that Uncle Dan was sensitive deep down inside and was really a good guy. I wondered why Shari thought nice things about him.

The day before we were moving, Dad was at the new house meeting the owner. Mom picked up her keys and pocketbook from the counter. "Shari, do you want to take a ride to the store with me, Hon?"

Shari answered, "Yeah, I'll go."

I ran into the kitchen. "Can I go?"

Mom said, "Gar, we'll be right back, Honey. Stay here with Uncle Danny." Mom and Shari walked out and closed the door behind them.

I walked to the living room and flopped myself down on the couch. Uncle Dan gave me an angry look. "You better watch yourself." I felt so frustrated that I had to listen to him. *Why did he get out of jail? Why did he stay with us?* I sighed.

I jumped as soon as I saw him move. He came toward me as I grabbed the arm of the sofa and pulled myself up and behind, so the couch was between us. "I don't know who you think you are, but you better get over here," he said with so much hate that his lips got tight.

"I didn't do anything!" I yelled. He stepped to the right, and I went left. Then he darted toward the side of the couch I was on. I ran to the kitchen and stopped on the other side of the table. My heart raced. I wasn't going to let him get me. I screamed as he started around the table.

Christina and Vincent started crying in the living room. Michael begged, "Uncle Dan, please don't hit him, please." Uncle Dan didn't hear or see anything but me. I was sure he wanted to kill me. What should I do? What should I do?

CLICK

The door opened, and Mom ran back inside. She yelled, "What's going on in here!?"

Uncle Dan growled, "You better check your son!"

Shari came back in and ran to Uncle Dan. "Danny, why are you doing this? What happened? Leave him alone."

Uncle Dan stared at me and pointed. "Don't you forget. I won't."

Summer Cracked Swimming Pool

Mom told Dad to bring the kids outside while he, Anthony, and Uncle Dan loaded boxes on the truck. Michael, Christina, and Vincent stampeded through the front door screaming and giggling. They were excited to play in the front yard one last time. I waited a few minutes until the tone of Mom's voice let me know she was no longer frustrated.

I walked in the kitchen as Mom said, "Shari, Hon, put the glasses in this box." Mom was holding Michelle as she tried to write "kitchen" with a squeaky marker.

"Can I help pack the dishes?" I asked.

"Gary, no. Go outside and play."

I didn't want Mom to know I was afraid to be around Uncle Dan. As Shari took a stack of plates out of the cabinet, I begged. "Mom, please. I know how to wrap them in newspaper."

She snapped, "Gary, I'm not going to tell you again. Go outside." As I turned around to leave, Mom stopped me. "Here, take Michelle with you."

Christina and Vincent chased each other through the grass with a stick while Michael played near the car with his Gobot figure. He loved saying "Cy-Kill" in the deepest, robot voice a seven-year-old could muster. I thought about when my teacher had said, "This closet doesn't pass muster." She'd told everyone to hang their coats neatly over their book bags, but some were half hung while others were crumpled on the floor.

Donnie, whose dirty green coat was at the top of the pile, had asked, "Why would a closet pass mustard?" Everyone laughed before the teacher shushed to explain that "muster" was a military term for working hard. I knew it was a word Uncle Dan or Anthony would never use or even know what it meant, so I loved it.

When I saw Dad and Anthony turning the kitchen table on end to get through the front door, I knew the house was almost empty. The beds, dressers, couch, and most of the boxes were already on the truck. As Michael, Christina, and Vincent entertained themselves, I stayed focused on Michelle. I watched as she squatted to examine a ladybug she'd found in the grass. I was bending over to be sure it didn't end up in her mouth when I heard his voice – and froze.

"Hey!" Uncle Dan yelled. I looked up at him, but he looked past me like I wasn't there. "Michael, grab your brother and sisters and bring them inside." I turned to Michael, who gave me a confused look. He didn't understand why Uncle Dan was telling him and not me. A knot pulled deep into my gut as I realized Uncle Dan was speaking to Michael, like I wasn't even there, to let me know I didn't matter to him anymore.

Michael walked over to me, and I handed him Michelle's hand. Michelle looked up at me and reached with her other hand. "Ga-ga."

I smiled at her. "It's ok. Go with Michael." Christina and Vincent raced past us to get to the house first.

Once Michelle was inside, Michael turned back. "Gar, are you coming?"

I willed a smile. "It's ok. I'll be there in a minute." After Michael shut the door, I looked up toward the house and thought about when we had moved in. The bare, twiggy branch trees all over our yard had seemed dead in the icy cold. In only a few months, they were sprouting light green leaves that flickered in the sunlight. I remembered Shari saying, "What a shame you guys won't be here in the fall. The leaves will look beautiful." I questioned. *Why couldn't I be here?*

I wondered what my life would be like if I stayed and lived in the empty house alone. I could be in my bedroom whenever I wanted and for as long as I wanted. I could lean on my window sill and look out at the treetops that spread for miles. When I got tired, I could lie on a warm sunlit square on the carpet. No one would tell me to go play football or to go to Michael and Vincent's room. The thought made me sad but also peaceful because I'd never have to see Uncle Dan again.

Just like Mom had said, our new house had a pool, but it wasn't full of crystal clear water; it was empty except for a dirty, yellow puddle at the bottom of the deep end, and three of the concrete sections of the wall were cracked with dirt coming through. Some pool, I thought, as Michael blurted out, "The pool's broken!"

Mom said, "Dad's going to fix it," then directed me. "Gary, take the kids inside while we unload the truck."

The end of a move always meant pizza, and Mom decided the adults deserved more than a pie with extra cheese. I thought it was because it had been only six months since our last move, but Mom said it was because everyone had worked so hard. Other than writing on boxes as Shari packed the kitchen, the only thing Mom had worked hard at was telling everyone else what to do. She was still the first one, though, to give Dad her order. "Nick, I want a chicken parm dinner. Ant, tell Nick what you want. Dan, what do you and Shari want?"

Shari was quick and polite to answer. "It's ok, Kath. I don't mind eating pizza."

Mom told Dad, "Nick, get her a chicken parm, too."

I asked, "Can I get chicken parm?" which was quickly followed by Michael – "Me, too!" – and then Vincent's "Me, too!"

Mom snapped, "You guys are getting pizza. Gary, take the kids in the other room."

Dad got a sausage and pepper sub, which he unrolled and laid out on the greasy, white paper it came in. Mom pulled a silver container out of the bag and started pulling back the tiny edges that held a white cardboard cover in place. The steam from the melted cheese smelled delicious.

Mom knew I wanted a bite of her chicken parm, so she smiled at me. "You did a good job watching your brothers and sisters." She cut a small piece of chicken and placed it on my plate with her knife and fork. As I started blowing on it, Mom said, "Gar, hand this to your Uncle Danny, Honey." She held out another silver carton to me.

I took Uncle Dan's food and walked around the table. I didn't understand why Mom wanted me to give it when she could have easily shoved it across to him. As he reached for it, he smiled like he'd never been angry and said, "Thanks, Champ." I wondered if maybe he wasn't mad at me anymore.

When everyone was finished eating, Dad got up and began picking up paper plates and plastic forks. Mom followed him into the kitchen with her glass of Diet Coke. Uncle Dan walked downstairs to turn on the TV. Christina and Vincent ran downstairs after him. I wanted to be sure he really wasn't mad anymore, so I walked down, too.

I tried to figure out what I should say to Uncle Dan. Should I ask him if the Giants were on? Should I tell him I could move my stuff to Michael and Vincent's room, so he and Shari would have more space? I decided. "That chicken parm was good, wasn't it, Uncle Dan?" He stared at the TV with his arms folded and his feet on the coffee table without moving. Had he only talked to me upstairs because Mom was there? Maybe he hadn't heard me. "Uncle Dan?" I said again, a little louder. Christina, who was on his opposite side, looked over. She had heard me.

He blinked as the white light from the TV moved around his face. He said to Vincent, "Hey, Champ, go turn the TV up. Then come sit by your Uncle Dan." He patted the empty seat between him and where I was standing. My stomach felt empty even though it was full. I wished I hadn't eaten any chicken parm or pizza, as I left to go lie on the floor in Michael and Vincent's room by myself.

I only tried to tell Mom about Uncle Dan one time. I didn't want to sound like a crybaby with hurt feelings, so I just said, "I think Uncle Dan's mad at me, Mom." Of course, she looked shocked because he was always nice to me around her.

"Why would you say that? Your Uncle Danny's not mad at you."

I knew he had ignored me. I knew he had tried to make me feel bad by being extra nice to everyone else. I didn't know how to explain any of it without Mom thinking it hurt my feelings. *Shouldn't a mother instinctively know these things without a kid having to explain?* I gave up. "I don't know. Never mind."

I got used to Uncle Dan only speaking to me when Mom was around. The summer was almost over before he, Anthony, and Dad started working on the pool. Dad decided, since I had just turned eleven, I was old enough to start working with them. Mom had told Dad, "I don't care if you started working at that age. He's too young."

But eventually, she agreed that I could do little things to help, which meant running around for hammers or climbing in and out of the empty pool to pick up concrete pieces. Michael and Christina were still impressed as they watched me, which made me feel good. And I decided, even when I had to speak to Uncle Dan, I would pretend he was a stranger so that it wouldn't bother me when he'd answer without looking at me.

Uncle Dan was cold to me, but he still had fun with Anthony. One of their favorite ways to make themselves laugh was creating new bad words for boobs. The pool wasn't in the backyard, like most pools; it was on the side of the house next to the garage. As we worked, we were able to see people going by on the sidewalk. After a lady wearing sunglasses and listening to headphones jogged by, Anthony said, "Dan, check out the jugs on her!"

Michael gave a puzzled look and whispered to me, "Are jugs boobs?"

It didn't matter that I snapped at him. "No, they're… they're talking about her hands!" He and Christina both knew what they were talking about.

Fortunately, Christina wasn't interested in all the different words Anthony and Uncle Dan used to describe boobs. As many times as she had heard "bazooms," "knockers," or "tits," she never repeated any of them. She preferred the action curses that she could apply to herself. Uncle Dan and Anthony would announce, "I need to take a leak," or "I need to take a piss" every time they went to pee. It wasn't long before Christina was grabbing herself and saying it, too.

I had never wanted to curse, and Michael was smart enough to know that, if he did curse, not to do it around any adults – or me. But Christina was proud to be five years old and actively cursing. She'd say, "I have to shit," or "I need to take a piss," as serious as if she'd just recited The Pledge of Allegiance. She was careful not to curse around Mom, but she didn't think there was any reason she shouldn't curse around Vincent.

It was one of the last summer weekdays. Dad, Anthony, and Uncle Dan were working. Vincent walked into the kitchen, holding himself, and proclaimed, "I needa piss."

Mom stayed calm. She bent down and asked, "Vincent, where did you hear that, Honey? That's a bad word." He smiled and shrugged. He wasn't going to get Christina (who was a more fun older brother than either me or Michael) in trouble.

Michael immediately blurted out, "It wasn't me." Mom already knew it wasn't him.

Mom called out, "Christina!" When Christina walked into the kitchen, Mom asked, "Are you cursing? You better not lie to me."

"No."

"Then where did Vincent hear it?"

"I don't know."

Even though I knew Vincent was repeating Christina, I tried to put the blame where it rightfully belonged – where Christina had heard it. I wasn't about to use Uncle Dan's name. I said, "Mom, he probably heard it from Anthony."

Mom asked, "Did you hear that from Anthony?" Vincent shook his head no. It didn't really matter, anyway. Even if he'd said, "Yes," I knew Christina was still going to end up sitting on the kitchen counter with a bar of Ivory soap in her mouth.

When ladies in the grocery store or K-mart would tell Mom how polite and well-behaved Michael and I were, she'd beam a big smile like she'd just won a free chicken parm dinner. I knew she wasn't going to allow Christina to destroy her reputation as a great mother by teaching Vincent to say "shit," "damn," and "piss." She told Dad, "I think we should order The Disney Channel for the kids. I don't want them watching R-rated movies with cursing and boobs."

When Uncle Dan would go out with Shari, Anthony would watch Cinemax or HBO downstairs by himself. I knew he watched the same movies over and over because he'd call me. "Gar, come here. Watch! Watch!" like he knew exactly what was going to happen. If I didn't come, he'd make fun of me for saying, "Oh, man" too much or for still playing with toys.

I'd sigh and stare at the TV. Some stupid girl would get out of a pool and take her bikini top off to kiss a guy, or Chachi from *Happy*

Days would make girls tops fly off just by looking at them. Anthony would laugh so hard he could barely breathe. When he'd catch his breath, he'd ask, "What do you think of those titties? I loved titties when I was your age. Don't you like titties?"

What I liked was watching shows on *The Disney Channel* when all the adults were still asleep. Mom didn't like Anthony's being passed out and drooling on her tan sofa in the living room, but it was great for us. I'd get all the kids up and sneak them downstairs as Anthony snored upstairs. I knew we'd have at least two or three hours before Mom would wake up and find him in the living room. "Anthony, get up. You're sleeping on my good sofa!" Mom would say before he'd stumble downstairs, half asleep, with his pillow and sheet.

I'd toast all six blueberry Pop Tarts and take them downstairs on one plate with a roll of paper towels. Michelle would sit mesmerized in front of the TV where Kellyn would call out, "Hey kids! Are you ready to Mousercise?"

Michelle would yell, "Yeah!" and put her arms up.

Christina and Vincent were content as they ate their one Pop Tart each.

Only Michael would complain. "Why do you get two, and I only get one?"

The answer was because there were only six in a package, and I wanted two, but I told him, "Because I'm the oldest."

216

I didn't want Michael giving me sad eyes like he was starving after he'd scarfed down his one and only Pop Tart. I realized it was easy to convince Dad to buy two packs instead of one. I just had to be sure to ask when Mom wasn't around.

In addition to adding *The Disney Channel* to our cable channel line-up, Mom also decided we should go to Catholic school. I imagined she thought Christina's cursing would spiral out of control if she put her in a class full of public school kindergarteners.

"Gary, lift your chin." Mom clipped the plaid tie on my white shirt, then told me, "Don't let go of Christina's hand until you're on the bus."

"I won't."

Michael, Christina, and I piled into a big, green seat. As the school bus bumped along, I wondered what the school would be like. Even though my stomach felt tight, I told myself that the kids would have to be nice because the nuns would teach about Jesus and being a good person.

There were crucifixes hanging on the wall behind the teacher's desk in every classroom, and all the kids wore the exact same uniform, which gave me a relieved thought. *At least I won't get made fun of for what I'm wearing.* A boy with neat hair and a friendly grin who was sitting next to me leaned in. "Where did you go to fourth grade?"

I had actually gone to two schools, but I didn't want to mention the one in New York because those kids hated me, and this kid might know them. My heart beat fast as I answered, "I went to Calvin Coolidge in Iowa."

"Iowa? Was that a *public* school?"

The tone of the question made me realize any type of school other than Catholic was bad. I answered, "No."

He looked at me like I was stupid. "Really? Was it a Catholic school?" He laughed, then turned toward his friend, whispered, and pointed at me.

As the school days went by, I got used to the kids not talking to me. I tried to stay as quiet as possible and not look at them when they'd whisper to each other about me. One time a girl caught me looking at her when she was talking to her friends about me. She put her hand on her hip and asked, "What do you think you're looking at?"

"Nothing." I quickly looked away.

Recess was the worst because there weren't assigned desks, and kids could congregate together, making it obvious who was friendless and alone. The nuns didn't really pay attention to what the kids did either. As I walked outside, I noticed Michael on the other side of the playground where the first through third graders played. He was by himself, too.

As I stood near the fence, I noticed a bunch of kids from my class standing near the tetherball pole, looking at me, and laughing. Two of the boys put their hands in their pockets and started stepping in my direction.

"Dee Ode," one of them said as they walked around me then back to the other kids. *What did he say?* I tried to figure it out as they all cracked up. When we came in from recess, the kids in the desks in front of and next to me didn't look at me. They began hopping in their seats to scoot their desks away. Once they'd screeched their desks a couple of inches away, they giggled and whispered with each other.

Then, I heard the boy behind me ask, "Does anyone have Lysol?" Everyone around me started cracking up.

When I got home, I told Mom, "I need to talk to Dad."

"About what, Gar? What's the matter?" I knew talking about deodorant should be with a man. I imagined what the kids at school – or Anthony – would say if they knew my Mom had bought me deodorant.

"I just need to talk to him," I said, then went to my room.

A few minutes later, my door opened, and Uncle Dan walked in. "What's going on?" I wanted to die, but I wanted to kill Mom first for telling him.

I stuttered, "I… I… think I need deodorant."

Uncle Dan reached over and pulled my head in to sniff. "Whew! When was the last time you showered?" Actually, I showered at least every other day although I didn't always completely soap up. Sometimes I'd hop in, rinse off and wet my hair with my hands. I'd still let the shower run long enough so everyone would think I'd taken a complete shower, though. Uncle Dan didn't ask the question really expecting an answer. He said, "Come on," and marched me down the hall to the bathroom and turned the shower on. "Get in there, and when you get out, you rub this under your arms like this. You should be showering every morning before you go to school."

After I wrapped a towel around myself and turned the faucet off, I heard a knock on the door. "I'll be right out!" I yelled.

"It's just me." Uncle Dan's muffled voice sounded through the door. "Get your drawers on, and let me in." I rushed to get completely dressed before I opened the door.

"Did you use the washcloth?" he asked. "Listen, you need to wash under your arms – and your crotch, too."

I nodded. "Ok."

Uncle Dan tilted his head down and got serious. "Is anyone in your class making fun of you?"

"No."

He looked at me like he didn't believe me. "I'm gonna teach you how to fight." He gave me a quick smile and a wink then put his hand on the back of my neck. "Come on. Let's go eat first."

Immaterial Starscream

Uncle Dan couldn't wait to get started. He watched as I pulled small forkfuls from my clump of cheesy scalloped potatoes. He knew I was making the bites smaller and chewing longer so that I could postpone my boxing lesson.

"Come on. Hurry it up." I took my last bite and pushed myself back from the table.

Dad asked, "What are you guys doing?"

Uncle Dan put his hand on my shoulder. "I'm teaching Gary how to fight."

Vincent got excited. "Can I see?"

"Yeah," Uncle Dan said. "Come on. Michael. You come, too." I knew, even before she asked, Christina would want to watch, as well. She always looked fascinated when Uncle Dan and Anthony talked about whipping somebody's ass.

Christina started, "Can I–" but Uncle Dan stopped her.

"You stay inside with your sister. Fighting's for boys."

Christina crossed her arms and kicked under the table, which made Mom growl. "Christina, don't start!" We got up to walk downstairs.

I handed Vincent his jacket and told Michael to put his on, too, before I opened the door to the garage. The chilly air cooled my back as we stepped into the concrete room. Uncle Dan walked out behind us and clicked the red button next to the light switch which made the garage door whirr, whirr, whirr open. He flipped the switch, and the big bulb above the garage lit up the whole driveway.

Uncle Dan called me over. "Hold your arms up like this. Keep your fists closed and keep your face behind. They're gonna be going for your face."

I did exactly as Uncle Dan instructed. I smiled and pretended to believe the boxing lesson would help while I thought about the fights I'd seen in school. The kids never seemed concerned with how to hold their fists. They usually grabbed each other's shirts and tumbled to the ground. One kid would end up on top of the other, hitting him over and over as the other kid cried and screamed. The only part that seemed like a real boxing match was all the other kids yelling and cheering.

By the time we were done, Uncle Dan was sure he'd turned me into a tough guy, like the Fonz. I knew, in his mind, I'd hold my fist up and shout at every kid who made fun of me. "Say it one more time, and I'll knock your lights out!" The kids would trip over themselves trying to run away. And if a kid were too stupid not to know what was good for him, he'd throw a punch. I'd duck and then knock him out like Rocky.

But this wasn't like the movies, and I wasn't like Rocky or the Fonz. The closest thing to Arthur Fonzarelli in our house was Christina Mele. No one was telling her she smelled like B.O., and Uncle Dan wasn't teaching her to fight, either.

When Christmas break came, I was relieved that I didn't have to think about fighting or getting made fun of for two whole weeks. Michelle, being two years old, was just starting to understand how much fun Christmas was supposed to be. When Mom asked her what she wanted Santa to bring, Michelle smiled and shouted, "A doll!"

Christina didn't want dolls or Barbies, but she'd learned that's what she was going to get regardless of what she asked for. She made sure Vincent was the one asking for the things she was going to play with. When Mom asked Vincent, "Why do you want two baseball mitts?" he grinned and shrugged. "Because."

Michael would tell everyone that he liked GoBots better, but he still enjoyed Transformers just as much as I did. Every Saturday morning, we would both sit mesmerized in front of the TV as Autobots and Decepticons went all over the Earth fighting over energy they'd turned into cubes. Michael liked Soundwave because he had the most robot-sounding voice, and the cassettes in his chest turned into tiny robots that he could command. Starscream was my favorite. He was smarter than all the other Transformers, and he wasn't afraid to mouth off to anyone – including the leader, Megatron. He'd smirk and say,

"As you command, mighty Megatron" in a sarcastic voice so that all the other Decepticons knew he thought Megatron was a terrible leader.

For weeks leading up to Christmas, I'd tell Mom, "I only want Transformers, Megatron and Optimus Prime because they're the leaders, but I want Starscream the most. He's the gray jet."

Mom would say, "Make sure your brothers and sisters are being good."

Mom figured, at eleven, I didn't believe in Santa anymore, but I would make sure the other kids still did to earn my presents. I was sure to tell them, whenever Mom was listening, "If you're not good, Santa's going to bring you coal."

Mom usually slept until one or two in the afternoon because she was up all night drinking coffee and eating Entenmann's coffee cake with Anthony and Uncle Dan. Some days she wouldn't even change out of her nightgown. When she did get dressed, it wasn't until late in the afternoon. If she and Dad ever went anywhere, it was always in the evening, so I knew they hadn't gone Christmas shopping yet. As Christmas got closer, I worried that I might not get Starscream.

A few days before Christmas, I walked into the kitchen and said, "Mom, sometimes the stores sell out of popular toys. I saw it on TV."

She didn't want to hear it. "Gary, don't worry about it. Go see what Christina and Vincent are doing."

When Mom put on her silky red blouse and came out with lipstick and mascara on with her wig looking curly and perfect, I knew she and Dad were finally going Christmas shopping. It was Christmas Eve. As she put her cigarettes and keys in her purse, she said, "Ant, we should be back in a few hours. Danny and Shari are coming with us."

Once they were gone, Anthony asked me, "Gar, what's the difference between Transformers and GoBots?"

I knew it didn't matter what I said. Anthony was looking for a reason to make fun of me. I answered, "Transformers are more difficult. They're for older kids."

He questioned me further. "But they're still toys, right?"

I hated the way he squinted at me when he was making fun. "Yes, they're still toys."

It seemed like forever before Mom and Dad got home. When I heard the car doors close, I ran to the living room. When Mom walked in, she looked over at me. "Gar, is there anything else you want, Hon? We're having a hard time finding them."

I wanted to say, "Yeah, parents that actually care about my feelings." Most of the kids in my fifth-grade class already knew they had gotten what they wanted. They hadn't opened their presents, but they had found them and told all the kids what they were getting.

I asked, "Did you try Toys R Us?"

Mom gave a defeated smile. "We've tried everywhere, Honey."

I told myself that a store somewhere had to have at *least* Starscream. "What about K-mart?"

Mom turned to Dad. "Nick, let's drive up to Middletown." I could tell by the look Dad gave me that he knew it was hopeless, but he was going to try anyway.

"Ok, let's get going," Dad said, and gave a smile. I watched them get back in the car as tiny snowflakes whipped around in the darkness.

On Christmas morning, I got the three minicar Transformers that you could buy in the grocery store, including Bumblebee, who wasn't even the right color. He was red. They all transformed by pushing the arms and legs in like they were made for idiots. Even when Anthony said, "Wow, those look like they're hard to transform," I couldn't get annoyed at him. He was right. They were made for babies.

It wasn't long after we went back to school that the kids began making fun of me again, even though I showered and wore deodorant every day. One of the boys who rode our bus told his older brother, a seventh grader, about me. The first time they stopped next to our seat as they walked up from the back of the school bus, the kid who knew me asked, "Do you smell that body odor?"

His brother answered, "It smells like horse shit" before laughing and waving his hand in front of his face.

After a few days, the older brother got bored of trying to be funny. Instead of loudly stating that he couldn't breathe or coughing with his tongue out, he pushed his book bag into me as he walked by. It lunged my shoulder forward, but it didn't really hurt. I knew everyone else would think it was an accident if it only happened one time. I just needed to stiffen my body, so I wouldn't move when he did it again.

The next afternoon I counted the stops as the bus made its way through our neighborhood. I knew we were close to those boys' corner when the bus passed the house with the broken birdbath in the front yard. My ear tensed like an alert cat sensing danger as the bus came to a squeaky stop. When I heard their book bags rustling behind me, I knew they were getting closer to my seat. The hairs on the back of my neck stood up as my heart thumped in my chest. I wasn't going to turn around. I sat up straight and tensed the muscles in my back to be sure I would barely move when his book bag crashed into my shoulder. He's almost right behind me, I thought. I took a breath.

WHAP!

My chin hit my chest from the violent slap to the back of my head. I felt the sting on my scalp, and I knew my hair would be sticking up where he had whacked me with his hand. He stood next to me and waited to see if I would do anything. I sat motionless and looked forward with my hands in my lap. "Yeah, that's what I thought," he said, then continued to the front of the bus with his younger brother looking back at me, smirking.

I slowly lifted my hand and smoothed down my hair, as kids whispering around me.

"Did you see that?"

"He just sat there."

Next to me, Michael acted as if he hadn't heard or seen any of it. He rustled through his backpack for his science book, opened it and started telling Christina, "Saturn is a planet that has seven rings." Christina just stared at me with shocked eyes and open mouth.

I wondered if embarrassment was what was turning the knot in my stomach into a deep hole. When I had smashed my bare toe against the coffee table chasing after Michael, I felt stupid when Mom pointed and laughed. She cracked up at anyone who fell or got hurt in a way that made them look silly. Her screechy, loud "Haaa ha ha ha" had made me so mad that I wanted to throw the shiny, green ashtray I'd made for her at school. She calmed me down by saying, "Oh, you're ok. Just be careful where you're running." I was embarrassed, but I didn't want to die.

I had thought I wanted to die from embarrassment when the Boy Scouts delivered a Christmas tree decorated with construction paper and Popsicle sticks. I really had just wanted to disappear until they were gone.

I remembered other words I'd heard, like humiliation and shame, and wondered if those were the feelings I had from being afraid to fight or afraid even to say anything. I knew I'd feel them every time one of the kids on the bus looked at me. I'd feel them when kids whispered with other kids on the playground and told them that anyone could hit, punch, or kick me, and I wouldn't even fight back. The empty feeling in my stomach filled up my whole body until I really did want to die.

"Gar, Gar, it's our stop," Michael said as he patted my leg. I hadn't even realized that the bus had stopped. I pulled my book bag up from between my feet and started walking up the rubber walkway.

"Hey." My body tensed before I realized it was just the bus driver. She was holding the metal handle which was supposed to open the door, not about to let me out. "Did that boy hit you?"

"Uh… well… no." I wasn't prepared for an adult to ask me about it.

"Are you sure he didn't hit you?"

"No – I mean yes. I'm sure he didn't hit me."

"Ok." She pulled the handle, and the door squealed open.

As I stepped onto the curb, I thought about how stupid I thought Uncle Dan was for loving to fight. He was proud that he could take his top front teeth out the way a teenager could take out their retainer. He would tell people that he had lost his teeth in a fight, but they should see what he had done to the other guy. I was afraid to end up toothless. Maybe I'd worried too much about how embarrassed I'd be if I were missing teeth. I probably wouldn't want to die from that type of embarrassment.

As we walked around the corner to our house, I wondered whether I should say something to Michael and Christina about the hit. I didn't want them telling Mom because she would tell Uncle Dan. I was sure he'd say, "You let a kid whack you on the back of the head, and you just sat there? You're no nephew of mine" before walking away and ignoring me for the rest of my life.

I asked Michael, "Do you know what the bus driver was talking about?"

Michael answered like he'd been waiting to say it. "I didn't see anything."

But Christina asked, "Why did you let that boy hit you?"

I chuckled through my nervousness. "He didn't hit me. He was just playing." I knew she didn't believe me, but her sympathetic eyes assured that she wasn't going to say anything either.

When we walked in the front door, Christina yelled "Vince!" and ran downstairs looking for him.

The day after the seventh-grader hit me, the bus driver instructed me, Michael, and Christina to sit in the seat directly behind her. After that, when the seventh grader would get on or off the bus, he'd just talk really loud, laugh, and pretend he didn't see me. After a few weeks, the feeling of wanting to die either went away or I got used to it.

Saturday, before the adults got up, was my favorite time of the week. Even though I'd seen every episode, I still loved *Transformers*. Michael and I watched it every Saturday morning. As we waited for the episode to start, I watched the morning sunlight warm the swirling dust and thought about how it looked like a galaxy. I wondered if robots could really live for millions of years. My heart started racing as the song began. "The Transformers, more than meets the eye . . .." I smiled as I thought about how cool it would be if I were a twenty-foot-tall robot that turned into a jet. I'd transform and fly wherever I wanted. I'd say whatever I wanted. I'd find that stupid seventh grader and step on him, and I'd never want to die.

It was a few weeks before summer. Michael and I were playing on the stairs with my mini car Transformers – including red Bumblebee – when I heard Mom tell Dad, "As soon as the kids are out of school, we'll head back to New Jersey." I put my finger to my lip so that Michael knew to be quiet. I stepped up two stairs, so I could hear better.

Dad said, "Yeah, it's just a couple more weeks. Do you want me to get boxes?"

Mom rustled without talking, which usually meant she was lighting a cigarette. "Yeah, we should start packing."

Dad grabbed his keys from the counter and bent in to give Mom a kiss. I quickly finished my climb to the top of the stairs and walked around the railing. "Can I go, Dad?"

"Sure," Dad answered, before Michael, who was right behind me, butted in.

"Can I go too, Dad?"

Mom put her cigarette in her mouth and bent down to fix Michael's collar. She squinted from the smoke as she told him, "You can stay with me."

When we walked into K-mart, Dad went to the customer service counter to speak to one of the employees in blue vests. I scanned to figure out where the toy section was. It seemed like women's clothes and the jewelry counter full of watches and bracelets were always at the front of the store.

"Dad, is it ok if I look in the toy section?"

Dad was laughing with a blond girl who looked like one of the managers. I knew she had probably told him that he could pick up boxes out back. He answered. "Yeah, Gar." I took off running.

My heart almost stopped. Whenever I'd looked in a toy aisle before, I always found Skywarp and Thundercracker, the blue and purple jets, but never Starscream. There he was – the last one. The gray jet with a blue nose and red along the edge of the wings. I grabbed the box and turned to look.

234

"Dad! Dad! They have Starscream. Can I get him, please?"

Dad came over and looked down as he took the box. "Well, we didn't come to buy toys today." He looked at me. "Is this Starscream?"

I couldn't help but blurt out, "Yes! Please?"

I knew from his smile, before he even said, "Yeah, you can get him," that I would finally get Starscream.

Rocks in Snowballs

I watched Mom unwrap the crystal cigarette lighter which was supposed to look like a diamond but looked more like a glass door handle with a gold lighter switch at the top. She closed her eyes and waited for her favorite line of the song: "Those… were the best days of my life…" She mouthed the words as she set the lighter gently down on the coffee table: "Back in the summer of 69…" Mom didn't usually like popular songs, like the ones they played on MTV, but she loved that one, I figured because she was a kid in 69. I wondered if someone were to make a song called "Summer of '85" when I became an adult, would I want to shut my eyes and sing to it?

I looked out the living room window at the sidewalks running through the front lawns, under the summer trees that were thick with green leaves. I wondered for a moment why the town was called Old Bridge before thinking that New Jersey wasn't really that different from upstate New York.

One of our last days in New York State, Mom had told Shari, "I can't wait to get back to Jersey."

Shari asked, "It's ok now that Nick's parole is over, right?" I hadn't thought much about Dad going to jail since he had gotten out. When we were still in Iowa, I had asked Mom what he went to jail for.

"It was a mistake. He was falsely accused," Mom had told me.

Uncle Dan said the police were always after him, for no reason, and that's why they were assholes. Dad – I could believe was innocent. I was sure Uncle Dan deserved to be arrested every time he went to jail.

The best part about being back in New Jersey was that Uncle Dan and Anthony knew lots of people. When Uncle Dan got home from returning the U-Haul with Dad, he told Mom, "Kath, me, Ant, and Shari are going down the shore. We'll be back in a few days."

As I watched them pull out of the driveway, I wished they'd stay "down the shore," or wherever it was they were going.

It was the first time I'd ever remembered Mom unpacking alone. She turned the radio down and called, "Gar."

I walked into the living room. "Yeah?"

"Take this box upstairs to our bedroom. It shouldn't be too heavy."

Once at the top of the stairs, I walked into their bedroom and set the box down on the deep brown dresser that still needed the mirror attached. As I looked around Mom's bedroom, I smelled a faint, familiar scent, carpet shampoo, and it was quiet enough to hear kids playing kickball outside. I imagined how nice it would be if we could finally live normally. I trotted back downstairs and asked, "Mom, why do Uncle Dan and Anthony have to live with us?"

"Gar, they're helping your dad with work, Honey."

"I know, but can't they get their own house? We always have people living with us."

Mom gave the same wounded smile like she knew I was right, that she always gave when we talked about it. I thought about the times she had told people that her mother abused her and wondered if getting her to think about her childhood would make her want to have a more normal life for us. I asked, "Mom, what was it like when you were growing up?"

"Grandma and Grandpa were bad alcoholics, Honey. Grandma would throw parties. When I was a teenager, she'd come to my room, wake me up, and make me go downstairs and dance with her and her friends. "

The thought of Mom – a teenager – being woken by grandma and led downstairs to a room full of women speaking loudly over a blaring stereo and men, who stank like whiskey, staring as Mom clenched her pajama top closed, put a sick feeling in my stomach. I pushed the image out of my mind and continued.

"Did you have people living with you?"

"No, but. Grandma would get drunk and beat me with a belt."

I thought about how angry Mom got whenever Christina threw a tantrum. It seemed like she really wanted to kill her when she'd growl, "*Christina!*" I wondered if Grandma got just as mad when Mom upset her.

I looked at the side of Mom's face, as she unwrapped her favorite angel knick-knack, and thought about how pretty she was. I remembered Grandma and how, even as an adult, Mom was afraid of her. I imagined Mom being a little girl, terrified to be beaten with a belt by her mother – with no one to protect her.

"I love you, Mom."

She pulled me in and kissed my cheek. "I love you, too. You're my biggest and best. And Gar, we will live normal soon. I promise, Honey." She smiled sweetly.

Uncle Dan, Shari, and Anthony really were back in just a few days. A yellow car which Dad said was a Pinto, pulled up behind them. I recognized Anthony's ex-girlfriend, Laura Witham. She had visited with her son who was a year younger than Michelle when we lived in Florida, New York. Michael, once, had told Laura that he'd be sure her son, Anthony, didn't eat any yellow snow. She chuckled and told Michael how much she appreciated it. Laura had perfect teeth, dark eyes, and long, light brown hair. I had wondered why she would ever be with someone like Anthony. She, along with a man and a woman, got out of the other car. When they came inside, Mom hugged the stubby blond guy with the tight mustache the same way she had hugged Anthony when she first saw him.

"Joe Bianchi!" Mom squealed.

Bianchi? Oh God, I thought as the realization hit me. The short man, who arched his back to look tall, was Anthony's brother.

The other woman was tiny – short and thin – with black hair cut like Joan Jett and a pointy nose. "Hi," she smiled. "I'm Bonnie."

Uncle Dan said, "Hey Ant, help me get the beer out of the car."

That night, they all drank bottles of Budweiser and Michelob while music played so loud you could hear it through the whole house. I lay on my bed, listening to the party downstairs until the dark sky began lightening to blue. The party fired back up the next afternoon, then the afternoon after that again. It was three days before the new people left. Uncle Dan, Anthony, and Shari stayed.

It was a couple of weeks before the end of summer. Michael yelled, "Mom, can I go ride my bike?"

Mom got up and walked into the living room. Even before she asked, I said, "I'll go outside with him, Mom." I stepped down the front steps as Michael ran around the side of the house to get his bike. As he peddled away, I yelled, "Stay on the sidewalk, and don't cross any streets!"

About a half hour later, Michael rode back to our yard with two boys who looked like they were close to his age, about nine or ten. One had blond, almost white, hair and freckles all over his face. The other boy had brown hair and a big-toothed smile. They dropped their bikes in our yard, and the kid with the big teeth came right over to me.

"Hey, I'm Brad." He turned to Michael. "What's your name again?" After Michael answered, the boy continued, "Yeah, I was

241

telling your brother, Mike, that Arnie is great at kickball. Do you guys want to play – and what's your name?" This kid sure has a lot of energy, I thought.

"I'm Gary. Sure, we'll play."

For the first round, Brad and Arnie teamed up against me and Michael. Arnie got a super serious look on his face when it was his turn to kick. He raced up and – BONGK! – the rubber ball flew right past me and Michael and skidded down the street behind us.

I yelled, "Michael get it!" and he ran as fast as he could down the street after the ball. He hurled it to me with both hands as he panted back, but Arnie still made it all the way around the sewer grates and manholes that we'd designated as bases. Michael shook his asthma inhaler, sprayed twice and sucked in.

"Are you ok?" I asked.

Michael nodded before releasing his breath. "I'm fine."

Brad came over. "Alright," he said, "we should switch. Arnie, you and Mike will play against me and Gary." Brad whispered. "Mike should be on Arnie's team. That way he won't have to run as much."

I was impressed how Brad just took charge and Arnie did exactly what he said. In between catching Michael's kicks and chasing Arnie's down the street, we talked. I was excited to find out that Brad loved *Transformers*, too. He agreed that Megatron was a terrible leader, but he wouldn't admit Starscream should command. Brad said,

242

"Shockwave would be the best leader" before changing the subject to *G.I.Joe*. "You've got to watch. It's awesome. You should come over to my house tomorrow."

It was about a week later when I realized me and Brad had spent every day together. We played Transformers or G.I. Joe, watched TV and rode our bikes through different neighborhoods. Sometimes we would play with Arnie and Michael, too, but we had the most fun when it was just us. We were in his family room watching *Transformers* and eating a box of chocolate PoP'ems when Brad yelled, "Mom can Gary sleep over?"

"It's ok with me if it's ok with his mom."

Brad's mother walked out of the kitchen rubbing a hand towel. She asked, "Gary, your family lives around the block, across the street from Arnie?"

I sat up and answered, "Yes, Mrs. Greco."

Mom had always taught us to respect adults, which usually meant Anthony, Uncle Dan, and Uncle Jim. Unlike a drunk and two criminals, my new friend's mother was an adult I was happy to respect. She'd pop her head in to ask if we needed anything before wiping down the counters in her kitchen. And she didn't have any of her brothers – or their friends – living with her family.

Brad's mom asked me, "What does your dad do, and does your mom work?"

"He's a roofer, and my Mom stays home."

"Who are the other people at your house?"

"That's my Uncle Dan and his friend."

"Do they live with you?"

I couldn't tell her, "Yes, they live with us. They throw parties with friends for days and sleep in my and my brothers' and sisters' rooms."

I said exactly what Mom always told me. "They're just staying with us for a little while to help my dad start his business."

She paused then said, "Ok," in a way that made me wonder whether she actually believed me.

"Make sure you give your mom my number. Tell her to call me if she wants to talk. You can spend the night."

"Ok, I will. Thank you, Mrs. Greco."

When I asked Mom if I could spend the night, she gave a concerned look. "Gar, I don't know." Even though our house was crazy, she still wanted every one of her kids in it. I wanted to spend the night at Brad's house so bad, and I knew Mom trusted my judgment.

"Mom, Brad's family is really nice. His mom stays home just like you, and he's got three older brothers." I could tell she was considering letting me by the way she pressed her lips and looked at me. I quickly added, "They're just around the block. I'll call you if anything happens, and I'll come home first thing in the morning. Please."

Mom smiled. "Ok."

We lay in Brad's room and whispered after the rest of his house was quiet. We talked about which Voltron would win in a fight, the lion or the car, which Thundercat's power we'd choose to have, and how dumb we both thought He-Man was. Brad said, "It's for little kids," and I agreed.

We talked about how much it stunk that summer was over. When I told him that I wasn't going to public school, but was going to St. Ambros, Brad said, "I wish I could go to a Catholic school, too." I felt the same way, but I knew it wouldn't matter anyway because we were in different grades.

On the first day of school, the principal stopped in our classroom to tell us that Jesus expected us to love our neighbor and that she expected us to be nice to each other. As soon as she left, the kids in my sixth-grade class started snickering and whispering about how pudgy she was and how red her cheeks were. The girl sitting at the desk next to me was one of the first to speak up. She told her friend, "The principal looks like she's made of marshmallow. What does she weigh, like 200 pounds?"

I was surprised she said anything about weight because she was the fattest girl in the class. I thought about how Mom always said that "people in glass houses shouldn't throw stones."

I wanted to snicker, but I stayed quiet, hoping the girl wouldn't notice me. But in spite of sitting still and staring forward, the girl did notice that I wasn't participating in the conversation about the pudgy principal. She turned and asked me, "Do you like Madonna?"

Oh great, I thought. Why didn't she ask me about the Principal? I didn't even know who Madonna was. *Was she a singer?* I knew kids usually got made fun of more for what they did like than what they didn't. I made a disgusted face like Madonna was too stupid for me to like. "No."

The fat girl let out a shocked breath as she stared in disbelief. She turned to her friend. "He doesn't like Madonna." My stomach tightened as I realized I was going to be made fun of for not liking some dumb singer I'd never even heard about.

When I got home from school, I ran upstairs to change out of my uniform. I threw my blue shirt in the corner and laid my plaid tie on the dresser. I pulled my favorite striped shirt over till my head popped out, then turned to run back down. Ba dum, ba dum... halfway down the stairs, I caught Uncle Dan's eye. "Where are you going?

"To Brad's."

"Not today. You don't need to be playing GoBots with kids that are Michael's age. We're signing you up for football. Come on."

The knot I'd had in my stomach at school came back as I got in the car and pulled the door shut. Uncle Dan looked over. "You're gonna have fun, and I'll take you to McDonald's after your games."

As we pulled up to the field, which smelled like cut grass, I saw groups of kids with skinny arms sticking out of shoulder-pad-filled red jerseys. Some of the kids growled through their plastic mouthpieces. Others stood around with the same petrified look on their face I was sure I was going to have. We walked up to a man with blond hair and a visor. He had his lips pressed around a whistle and papers scrunched in his hand.

Uncle Dan called, "Coach Hawk!" The whistle dropped from the guy's mouth.

"Danny? Hey, come on inside."

As we walked into the small building, I saw all sorts of helmets and red jerseys on the wall. There were shoulder pads and equipment in bins. I knew there was no way I was getting out of playing, so I thought about McDonald's and tried to be interested. I reached into one of the big cardboard boxes and pulled out a hard-plastic piece. I wasn't sure what it was, so I put it on my elbow.

Uncle Dan turned. "What are you doing? Get that off your arm."

"What's it for?"

Uncle Dan snatched it and dropped it back in the bin. "It's for down there. It's a cup."

Once I realized what he was talking about, I felt my face turn red. I wondered if the coach would tell the other boys I had put a cup on my elbow.

But the coach hadn't been paying attention to what I had done. Coach Hawk had his finger on his mouth and a serious look on his face. He was sizing me up for something. "I think midget," he said.

"Nah, he's a pee wee," Uncle Dan answered back.

"Let's get his shoes off and get him on the scale." Coach Hawk picked up a helmet. Once I was on the scale, he looked concerned. "I don't know. It's close."

Uncle Dan motioned with his hand. "Come on. Get undressed."

I looked around the equipment store and realized the door wasn't even closed all the way. I asked, "Are you moving the scale into the bathroom?"

"It's just men," Uncle Dan said.

Coach Hawk added, "Don't worry. No one's coming in."

That didn't reassure me as I looked through the window at all the boys running on the field. Once I was down to my dirty brown socks and white underwear, I stepped back on the scale.

Coach Hawk nodded. "Yeah. Pee-wee – but you're gonna have to keep his weight down."

As we drove home, Uncle Dan said, "No more sweets, and you need to stop with the bread, too."

Great, I thought. The only reason I had to be happy about the whole football thing was getting McDonald's with a vanilla shake after every game.

A couple of months after school started, the big girl in my class, Brenda, decided she needed a better reason to make fun of me than my not liking Madonna. I heard her say to her friend, "If you take the 'r' out of his name, it spells 'gay.'" Her friend giggled and then whispered to Phillip.

Phillip was about my height, but skinnier with black hair and bulgy eyes, and I already knew he didn't like me from the way he squinted when he looked at me. He was quick to laugh when he heard the jibe and added, "Hey, Gay."

A bunch of kids between us laughed. "Gay? Gay? I'm talking to you."

For a quick second, the knot in my stomach released and the fear was gone. I turned and gave Phillip an angry look. He wasn't concerned that I was mad. He got excited and started telling kids, "He turned around. That's his name!"

When Uncle Dan first made me join football, he'd stay the whole time I had practice. Then he only dropped me off and picked me up, which wasn't so bad. A lot of the kids' parents did the same thing. If he couldn't pick me up, Mom would send Dad or Anthony. Most of the kids' parents were waiting for them when practice was over. Whoever was picking me up usually pulled in as the last cars were leaving. The first time they were late, Coach Hawk waited with me.

He looked at his watch. "It's ten past. Plus, we finished early. I'm sure they'll be here soon." The only thing I was sure of was that it wouldn't be the only time they were late.

When Dad finally pulled up, he said to Coach Hawk, "I'm sorry."

Coach Hawk waved as he got into his car. "It's no problem, but I have to get going."

The next time they were late, I lied. "Coach Hawk, I forgot to tell you. My uncle said you don't have to wait. He'll be here any minute."

He gave me a confused look. "Are you sure? I could give you a ride." The last thing I needed was Coach Hawk pulling into my driveway with four cars, a house full of people, and "money for nothing and your chicks for free" blasting through the windows.

I acted calm. "Yeah, he said you should go. Really."

He looked at me for a second, then got in his car. "Ok, stay near the clubhouse."

After he drove away, I leaned against the fence and looked back at the empty field with the woods behind. The sky turned from orange to purple. Even with a jacket on, the sweat on my back made me shiver. The big lights around the field clicked on as the sky finally turned completely black. I watched the road as tiny headlights in the distance grew brighter, hoping each time it would be the car to pull in. Dad finally got there. "I'm sorry, Gar. I just got off of work."

I didn't speak. I just crossed my arms and got in the car. I was so mad I wanted to cry.

When we got home, Mom was at the front door. I asked, "Mom, will you please make sure someone picks me up on time?"

"I'm sorry, Gar. Your dad had to work late." I could hear Uncle Dan telling Anthony and Shari some stupid story in the kitchen while they laughed.

I wanted to yell, "What about Uncle Dan? What about you?" but I stayed quiet. I knew, while I was waiting on the dark field alone, all Mom cared about was laughing with Uncle Dan and his friends. I took a breath and started to walk up the stairs.

Mom called, "Gar."

I turned and calmly stated, "I'm fine, Mom. Please just make sure someone picks me up next time."

The first time it snowed was overnight. When I woke, the sky out the window was gray, and flurries were still falling. I ran downstairs to the kitchen.

"School was canceled. It's a snow day," Dad said.

Michael asked, "Do you want to go outside, Gar?"

I told him, "I don't know what you're doing, but I'm going to play with Brad."

"Gary," Dad said, "don't be mean to your brother. Isn't Brad his friend, too?"

I wasn't going to say that even though Brad was Michael's age, Brad really wasn't his friend. He was mine. I said, "Yeah, come on." We both ran back upstairs to get dressed. I looked through our bedroom and all of the hall closets, but I couldn't find our gloves. We must have lost them in the move, I thought.

I walked back to the kitchen. "Dad, do you know where our gloves are?"

Dad finished pouring his coffee. "I don't know, Gar. Do you want to wear a pair of mine?"

Dad went out to his truck and came back in with his tan work gloves. They were so big that, when I put them on, they looked like flattened baseball mitts.

"What about Michael?"

"Those are the only ones I have, Gar. Maybe your mom knows."

I walked into Mom's room where she was snoring with her mouth open and one of her arms hanging off the side of the bed.

I whispered, "Mom... Mom," as I gently shook her shoulder.

Mom snorted, rolled over, and muffled, "What?" as she buried her face in her pillow.

"Michael needs gloves... Mom... Michael needs gloves." I waited a minute before shaking her again. She smothered the words through her pillow. "In my goat bockets." And she was snoring again.

When I handed Michael the black leather gloves out of Mom's coat, he whined. "I'm not wearing them. They're Mom's." He's such a stupid baby, I thought.

"Here, take Dad's! I'll wear Moms."

All the time we spent looking for gloves made it late morning before we finally got outside. Brad was already running through the snow with Arnie. He yelled at us. "Come on! We're having a snowball fight with some kids on the other side of my block."

Michael and I chased with them until Brad said, "Here. This is where we're building our fort. They're across the street."

Michael turned to me. "Gar, I think those kids are older than you."

I squinted to see through the falling snow. The kids were older, maybe fourteen or fifteen. I said, "Brad those kids are older."

He smirked. "Who cares? Come on. Let's get building."

By late afternoon the snow walls were done, and we had a pile of snowballs ready to fling. Brad was the first one up. He yelled, "Ahhhh!" like a sergeant riding into battle as he threw a snowball. That caused three snowballs to pshoo, pshoo, pshoo into the snow around us.

One of the kids on the other side yelled, "Pussies!" before another round of snowballs came hurling at us. We were taking turns standing, throwing, and falling back against the wall when WHAP! Michael got hit in the face and fell to the ground.

Michael screamed, "My eye!"

Brad and Arnie kept throwing. I leaned down to Michael. "What is it? What is it?" He wouldn't let go of his face as he screamed. I looked at the ground and saw rocks and dirt mixed in the snow.

Oh my God, I thought. My heart sank in my chest. "Brad, I have to get Michael home. They put rocks and dirt in the snowballs."

He looked at Michael, then hollered, "Those assholes! We'll take care of them."

Michael cried as I walked him home. I kept praying, please God, let him be ok, please. We turned the corner of our block, and I heard music in the distance which I knew was coming from our house. As we crunched through the snow up to our front door, I saw Uncle Dan, Anthony, and some of their friends, warm, in the living room window, laughing.

"Mom!" I yelled as we walked in. I didn't even stop to take off our snow boots. She was talking with Shari and one of her friends when she saw me.

"What's going on?" she asked. "Oh, my God! What happened?"

When Michael, Mom, and Dad came home from the hospital, Michael had a patch on his eye. Mom said, "The doctor had to rinse the sand out. He'll be ok, but he needs to wear a patch while it heals."

The next morning, it wasn't just Uncle Dan, Anthony, and Shari. Bonnie and Joe were in Christina and Michelle's room with the door locked. All five of us were piled up in Michael and Vincent's room. Christina and Michelle shared Vincent's bed, and I made Vincent sleep on the floor with me, so Michael could have his bed to himself to rest. I looked out the window at the dirty snow piles along the sides of the road where the street had been plowed and knew we weren't going to have another snow day. I only woke Christina. As we walked down, the stairs creaked. The house smelled like cigarette smoke, beer, and sweat. There was a guy I'd never seen before sleeping under a sheet on the living room floor. I stepped over him as I looked for cereal spoons that I could wash for me and Christina.

After school, I rode my bike to Brad's house. His mom answered the door and said he was grounded and wasn't allowed out for a week.

At the end of the week, Brad rang our doorbell. I ran down the stairs and opened the door as he was getting back on his bike. I asked him, "What were you grounded for?"

"I wasn't grounded. My mom just wanted me to spend more time with Arnie. She said since we became friends, I ignore him."

For a moment, I wasn't sure if I should say something. But I did. "I don't think your mom likes me, Brad." He shrugged. "I don't care."

It was a few days later. I put the kickstand down, left my bike at the edge of the driveway, and walked up to ring Brad's doorbell. I heard Brad's brother through the door. "It's for you, idiot," before running up their stairs.

Brad opened the door. "Hey, I want to show you the new G.I. Joe I got."

As we were walking to the family room, Brad's mom came out of the kitchen. "Gary, come here."

"Yes?"

"Brad told me you think I don't like you."

"Um... No. What I meant..."

"Listen, if I didn't like you, you wouldn't be allowed over," she said, followed by a stern smile.

Brad called, "Come here. I got Zartan. Look how he changes colors!"

Even though I was thinking about what Brad's mom had just said to me, I pretended to be excited, too. I smiled. "My dad got me Flint. I'll bring him over tomorrow."

The principal came on the intercom. "Students, there has been a tragedy. The Challenger space shuttle has exploded." Everyone in the room gasped. "Please prepare to pray for the souls of the astronauts. Hail Mary, full of grace, The Lord is with the . . .."

When I got home, Mom was watching the news in the living room. She put her hand on her mouth and whispered, "Oh my God." The TV replayed the explosion where the shuttle disappeared into a cloud of white smoke.

The talk about the Challenger disaster only slowed Brenda's and Phillip's efforts for a few days. They had gotten the whole class to start calling me "Gay" or "Gay Mele." Even Benny, whose shirts were so small the buttons on them pulled tight, started saying it. With his blond whiskers, he looked like he should be in high school, not the sixth grade. I had gotten left back because Mom was a terrible mother, who cared more about her criminal and alcoholic brothers than her own kids. I was sure Benny had gotten left back because he was stupid. I wasn't embarrassed or scared anymore. I was glad it was Friday. I just watched the black hand tick, tick until it was time to go home so that I could go over Brad's house.

When I rang the bell, Brad's Mom answered the door. I smiled. "Hi, Mrs. Greco. Is Brad here?"

"Brad's not allowed out today, Gary."

"Will he be allowed out tomorrow?"

"No, he's staying in all weekend."

"Ok," I said, then walked down to my bicycle.

As I rode around the block, I wondered if maybe Arnie was home. He wasn't as fun as Brad, but we could play kickball with Michael. I rang his doorbell. His five-year-old little sister answered the door.

"Is Arnie here?"

She blurted out, "Arnie's spending the night at Brad's house!"

Arnie's Mom ran over and pulled the little girl away. She said, "Arnie's not coming out today," then closed the door.

As I crossed the street to my house, I thought about how neither Brad's nor Arnie's moms wanted me around. My throat tightened, and I wanted to cry, which made me angry. I walked over to the side of the house where the moving boxes were that had been rained on and snowed on, that we had never thrown out. I leaned against the wall next to them and slid down. I looked up at the snow on the power lines and breathed in and out until the water in my eyes and the hurt in my throat went away.

The Outcome, Obviously

As we drove to our new home in Clark, New Jersey, I thought about Mom's lies. She said we were moving because the new house had a pool, a cabana, and beautiful gray marble steps. Michael, Christina, and Vincent believed it, but I knew it was because we were being evicted, the electric was being shut off, or both. When the last bill had come, I heard Uncle Dan say, "Just put the electric in my name, Kath," which meant they had stopped paying it, probably months earlier.

I also heard Mom tell Dad, "Nick, why would we pay three months' rent here? You know he's keeping our security deposit anyway."

Of course, he's keeping our deposit, I thought. Not because there were cigarette burns on the carpet, yellow sticky stains in the refrigerator, or dirty socks, soda cans, and garbage scattered throughout the house, He was keeping it because he was a "bastard," and our new landlord was a "real sweetheart." My thoughts made me chuckle, and I was happy to be too smart for Mom's lies.

We pulled up to the new house, and I refused to get excited. I knew we'd be moving again in six or seven months. The longest we'd stayed in any home was a year, and that house had had a ghost in it.

Michelle popped up behind me. "Is that the house?"

As Mom turned the wheel, pulling us into the driveway, she said to me, "Gary, make her sit down."

I turned. "Yes, this is our new house." I looked at Michelle's happy face, staring forward like she was looking at Cinderella's castle. I tried to remember when I was three and full of awe and hope. I looked at Christina, Michael, and Vincent. They were all excited, too. My anger melted, and I gave a small smile for them. I told myself that maybe this would be the house that we wouldn't move from.

Mom jingled the key and pushed the front door open to dark steps that split. Half went up to the living room, and half went down to the family room. Everyone ran upstairs first, and down the hall to find their bedrooms. Then they explored the cabinets in the kitchen before heading downstairs to the family room. I took in the new house smell then followed them down. Vincent ran right up and BOMMED his hands right on the glass door.

"Wow!" Vincent said as he looked out at the pool with a green cover on it.

I pulled him back. "Vincent, get your hands off the glass. You're gonna leave fingerprints."

Christina yelled, "Look! It's another house!"

"Awesome!" followed Michael.

I realized that was the cabana Mom was talking about. It was pretty neat. I opened the door.

"Stay away from the pool," I warned. All five of us ran over to the cabana.

After Uncle Dan, Anthony, and Dad maneuvered the living room couch through the front door, Mom said to Dad, "Nick, let's get McDonald's for the kids." She had him get a bag of cheeseburgers and small fries for our move in dinner. She even had him get me a vanilla milkshake like she got. She shushed and winked as she handed it to me. "Don't tell the other kids." As I sucked the sugary deliciousness, I couldn't help but smile a little.

It was late Thursday before we finished the move. I knew from listening to Mom talk with Dad and Uncle Dan in the kitchen that no one was getting up early to drive us to school the next day. I was glad I wouldn't have to see Phillip and Brenda for another three days. On Friday, after I'd unpacked, I sat at the kitchen table and watched Anthony lying on his back holding Vincent up with his knees.

"Go ahead. Hit me, hit me," Anthony said, as Vincent swung his fists in the air and giggled. I knew Anthony was only playing with Vincent, so Mom would think he liked him. It didn't fool me. I knew he didn't like any of us. I got up to go downstairs as Vincent ran through the living room.

I flopped myself down on the puffy brown couch that was supposed to look like leather. As the air squeezed out, I looked for the remote.

BOOM!

Vincent screamed. I darted upstairs. Vincent was on the ground holding his leg, crying.

Mom yelled, "What happened?"

Anthony said, "I kept telling him to stop, but he tried to jump over me."

Vincent pointed as he sobbed. "He... tripped... me!"

Mom yelled, "Nick!" Dad ran into the room to pick Vincent up.

When they came home from the hospital, Vincent had a cast on his leg.

"It's a double break," Dad said, "but he's a big boy. He'll have his cast off in six weeks."

Because we'd moved out of the school zone, Dad had to drive us the Monday we went back to school. It was still dark when we left home, but the sky had started to lighten by the time we pulled into the car line for drop-offs. I stretched my neck to see our bus on the other side of the parking lot. I imagined sneaking on it alone after last period and getting off near our house in Old Bridge. The windows would be dark, and the doors locked. I wondered what would happen if I walked around the block to Brad's house. Would his Mom answer the door? If she did, would she let me in?

I stopped thinking about our empty house and the streets where we had played kickball and where I'd ridden bikes with Brad. I knew Phillip and Brenda would be waiting for me to get back. I imagined all the things they had been saying while I wasn't in school and felt my stomach go empty. When Dad got to the front of the school, I hopped out and opened Christina's door as Michael walked around the car. I said, "Bye Dad, love you." We turned to walk up to the school.

I walked into my classroom and handed the teacher the usual note Dad had written for being absent – *To whom it may concern: Please excuse Gary's absence, as he was ill.*

As I walked to my desk, Phillip whispered, "Shhh, shhh," before giggling with Benny. I had forgotten about Benny. He didn't really care about making fun of me. He just wanted to see me and Phillip fight. I felt my stomach tighten, but it quickly turned to anger. *Why did Phillip have to be such a jerk?* I had never done anything mean to him. I took my seat and opened my social studies book.

We had to line up, single file, at the end of class before marching off to the next room. Two girls giggled as they kept switching places behind me. "I don't want to be behind him." "Neither do I."

Benny said, "Phillip will go behind him."

Phillip mumbled, "As long as you don't touch him, you won't catch his gayness," The kids in front started moving. As I began to take my first step, hands on my back shoved me forward.

My jaw clenched, and I whipped around. I met Phillip's eyes, grabbed his shirt, and yanked him out of the line. I knew it was Benny who had pushed me, but I didn't care. I clenched Phillip's shirt in my fists and pushed him to the wall.

Benny yelled. "Yeah!"

Everyone else in line started screaming. "Fight! Fight!"

My lips tightened as I pulled Phillip toward me. The fear in his face made me furious.

Gay Mele

That must be his name

I thought about every kid in our class who had laughed at me and hated me because of him. I was glad Benny was dumb enough to push me, expecting me to think it was Phillip.

I snarled, "Don't–" as I slammed him against the wall "you–" as I slammed him again "ever... touch... me... again!" SLAM! SLAM! SLAM!

"Gary! Gary, let him go! Let him go!" Our third-period nun was just as petrified as Phillip.

I breathed hard and felt alive. I wanted to kill him, and the nun knew it. She held her hand toward me as Phillip ran behind her. He looked like he was about to cry, and I was glad.

The nun made me, and Phillip stand on opposite sides of the classroom until the lady from the office came. Me, Phillip and (unsurprisingly) Benny were marched down to the office and directed to sit in the hard-plastic chairs of the waiting area. The office lady with short, gray hair, who usually smiled at everyone, kept her eyes down and her mouth tight as she stapled papers behind the counter like we weren't even there. I thought, so this is what it feels like to be in trouble at school. The principal called Benny into her office first. I wondered how they knew he was involved. He had pushed me, wanting me to think it was Phillip, but I didn't think anyone else knew that.

Benny walked out, and the principal called, "Mr. Mele, Mr. Marcello." After we sat down, she looked at us and shook her head slowly back and forth. I noticed the pink on her chubby face was a different pattern on each cheek. She didn't ask us what had happened. She told us that fighting is not how we handle conflicts in a Catholic school. She gave us each a week's detention, then pointed at the door. "Now, go back to class."

When I told Mom that I had to be picked up late because I got detention, her mouth dropped open. I thought she'd be happy that I was becoming a bully like Uncle Dan. Eventually, I'd be beating people up on the streets, flicking cigarettes, and calling cops "mother fuckers."

Mom asked, "Gar, what happened?" The disbelief in her eyes assured that she didn't think there was anything funny about me getting in trouble. I told her a kid pushed me, and we got in a fight. She put her hand on my shoulder and said, "Gar, that's not like you. You're always good. You don't fight."

I looked at her and tried to understand. If she didn't want me to be like Uncle Dan, if she wanted me to be normal, why didn't she try to be normal herself? I smiled sweetly. "Don't worry, Mom. It won't happen again."

After my fight with Phillip, he gave me his best phony smile every time he saw me. He'd ask me stupid questions like, "Do you know what they're serving for lunch today?" or "Will you show me how you cover your book so well?"

I would smile back and answer his dumb questions. It was better to have him being phony-nice than making fun of me. Benny had gotten what he wanted, so he moved his focus on to different squabbling boys. Fat Brenda never looked at me or spoke to me again, and none of the other kids in the class ever said anything mean after the fight. I still didn't have any friends, but at least everyone left me alone.

Most people needed a reason to throw a party, but not my family. I told myself that this party must be to celebrate the second weekend of summer.

Mom was on the phone. "Hold on a sec, Laur." She put her hand over the mouthpiece. "Vincent, please stop running, Honey. Your leg is not completely healed yet."

When Mom got off the phone, she walked over to me. "Gar, guess who's coming?"

She'd said, "Laur," but Mom knew a bunch of people named Laura. I tried to remember if she had said Uncle Jim's new girlfriend was named Laura. Oh God, I thought, please not Uncle Jim. I sighed. "I don't know. Who?"

"Laura Lynne!"

Mom's friend Laura, along with Laura Lynne, and her two brothers were on their way over. Mom wanted to be sure the house looked great. She did the dishes and wiped the counters while Uncle Dan and Anthony talked about The Jets at the kitchen table.

"They still suck," Uncle Dan said. Anthony laughed.

Mom pulled out the vacuum and called Christina. "Get in here and pick up these toys."

Christina said, "They're not mine."

Mom snapped at her. "I didn't ask if they were yours. Get in here and pick them up!"

When Mom finished vacuuming, she walked over to her brand-new stereo with a bottle of Windex. She squeaked the paper towel up and down the glass door, then turned the radio on.

As soon as I heard the song, I knew they were going to say something. "I just want your extra time and your... kiss!"

Uncle Dan got a disgusted look on his face. "Dancing around in makeup and high heels. He needs his ass beat."

Anthony added, "Prince is a fucking fag."

DING DONG!

Mom gave them both a dirty look as she walked to get the door. "You two are both assholes. Do you have to talk like that?"

Mom opened the front door. She and Laura both held their arms open and screamed, "Hey!" Laura Lynne came in, and we both smiled at each other.

Laura Lynne started telling me, "Oh, I love Prince, but 'Raspberry Beret' is my favorite."

Her mom turned to her. "Take John and Joey downstairs with the other kids. Keep them out of trouble."

Laura Lynne sighed. "I will."

Laura grabbed Laura Lynne's arm. "You better be listening to me, young lady."

Trying to distract, I turned to Laura Lynne and said, "Come on. Mom let us put the old stereo downstairs." I felt bad because Laura Lynne hadn't done anything wrong, and she was getting in trouble for watching her stupid brothers, which wasn't even her job, anyway. No wonder her mom and my mom were such good friends. They both expected us to be their built-in babysitters.

The kids knew the adults didn't care what they were doing as the party got louder upstairs. I heard Michael whisper to Vincent, "Go tell Shari that Mom said to give you the Little Debbie box to bring downstairs because you got your cast off." Vincent gave a serious nod, ready to execute the plan.

Christina turned to John, "Shut your eyes and hold out your hands. We're gonna play catch."

Michelle commanded, "Joey, come ere!" as she stood on the couch and pointed her finger down twice. He ran right over to her. I wondered whether Laura Lynne and I should behave like the adults we were expected to be or whether we should just have fun like everyone else.

Laura Lynne unzipped her backpack, dug through her folded tee-shirts, and pulled out a cassette. "I made it!" she said, with a bright smile. The tape had a white label with the songs neatly written in blue pen, which was kind of impressive. I hadn't really cared about music enough to make my own tapes. She clicked the deck closed, pressed play, and started singing. It wasn't like listening to Mom ruin a Sheena Easton song. Laura Lynne actually sounded like she was part of Bananarama as she sang, "I'm your Venus, I'm your fire, at your desire... Come on! Sing along!"

I certainly wasn't going to sing "Venus" and have Uncle Dan come down and tell me I was a "fag," but I did love the next song that came on. I looked around. Everyone was busy playing, and the music upstairs was so loud that no one would probably hear me, anyway. *Why should I care?* I inhaled a deep breath and began singing. "Kirie erie elay son down the road that I must travel! Kirie erie elay son there's a darkness in the night!"

Drinking for several days in a row sure made the adults look tired. I thought about how pretty Laura Lynn's Mom, Laura, usually looked when she came downstairs. The skin under her eyes was dark and puffy, and she had her dark hair pulled into a short ponytail at the back of her head.

Laura told Laura Lynne, "Get these guys ready. We're leaving soon."

As Laura walked back upstairs, Laura Lynne said, "Joey, put your underwear and shirt in your bag. John, make sure you have your glasses. We're not coming back if you leave them." Then she turned to Christina, "Christina, hand me John's socks."

Christina ignored Laura Lynne and kept clicking the doors on Michael's M.A.S.K Camaro toy. I knew she wasn't happy that I'd been spending all my time with Laura Lynne, so the last thing Christina was going to do was let Laura Lynne boss her around. Laura Lynne walked toward her, calling Christina's name again, then reached for her. Christina pulled away, ran to the other side of the room and threw Michelle's naked Barbie at Laura Lynn. Laura Lynne – in disbelief that Christina had actually thrown something at her – shouted, "Christina!"

Christina began reaching for anything around her. She threw Vincent's football, then Michael's Rock Lord figures, before grabbing Michelle's plastic baby-changing table and throwing it at Laura Lynne like a giant Frisbee. Laura Lynne screamed with shock. I ran over. "Stop, Christina, stop."

Laura came running down the stairs, followed by Uncle Dan. Laura yelled, "Laura Lynne, what are you doing?"

"Nothing! Christina threw a table at me."

Laura raised her hand like she was going to smack Laura Lynne. "Don't you take that tone with me!"

I jumped over to where they were. "She didn't do anything!"

Uncle Dan yelled, "Gary, stay out of it!"

"She didn't do anything! Christina threw a table at her! Mom!"

Mom ran down the stairs and barreled toward Christina as she fell to the floor with her hands up to shield herself. Mom grabbed Christina's hair. "Get up!" She growled at her, "What did you do?"

I yelled, "Stop!" and started toward Mom when Uncle Dan grabbed my shoulder and whipped me toward him.

"What do you think you're gonna do?"

I didn't know what to say. I froze as he screamed, "You a tough guy? What're you gonna do?" I felt his spit hitting my face and turned away, hoping Mom would defend me, but knowing she wouldn't.

"Danny! Leave him alone!"

Who?

What?

Mom yelled at him?

I was shocked and trying to believe that Mom had actually said something to Uncle Dan when he yelled back at her. "It's your fault he has an attitude. If he was my son, he'd have a foot up his ass!"

Mom screamed back, "Well, why don't you worry about it when *you* actually have a son!" She turned to me. "Gary, go upstairs – now!" I turned and ran.

Laura Lynne came upstairs to give me a hug goodbye. Once they were gone, I sat on the living room couch and waited. Mom came up first and went into the kitchen. I watched as Uncle Dan came up, to see if he'd look at me. He walked through the living room and didn't even turn his head. Good, I thought. I wasn't going to feel bad. I would ignore him just like he ignored me.

A couple of weeks after my thirteenth birthday, Uncle Dan left with Anthony and Shari for a few days. Mom told Dad it was because he didn't get along with Uncle Mike's wife, Aunt Lorraine. Mom also explained to Dad that she and Uncle Mike were so close because Grandma had abused him the same way she had abused her. Mom seemed proud that Uncle Mike, unlike Uncle Jim and Jack, who had become alcoholics, or Uncle Dan, who had become a criminal, had gone into the service, then married Aunt Lorraine and became a truck driver when he got out.

Uncle Mike was the only one of Mom's brothers who still had all of his black hair. Aunt Lorraine was as pretty as Christie Brinkley, with long, beautiful blond hair. When she and Uncle Mike came in the front door, Aunt Lorraine looked around. "Kath, I love the house. It's beautiful." Then Aunt Lorraine looked at me. "Hey, Gar, so you're thirteen now?" like I was one of the adults. I nodded and smiled. She asked me if I liked having a pool and what my favorite subject in school was before she said, "You should come spend a week with me. Your Uncle Mike will be on the road." She put her hand to her mouth, like she was telling me a secret, and whispered, "Plus, it'll give you a break from babysitting."

As I lay in Aunt Lorraine and Uncle Mike's guest bedroom, I thought about how quiet it was. I listened to crickets chirping and remembered my earliest memories of Aunt Lorraine, from when I was a little kid. I remembered telling her, "Aunt Lorraine, you're pretty." She smiled sweetly and said, "Thank you, and you're handsome." I also remembered Uncle Mike taking me to a bakery. He asked me if I wanted a cookie or a chocolate donut, but I didn't feel comfortable with him like I did with Aunt Lorraine. I was polite and answered, "No thanks." He insisted. "Come on. You know you want something." Once I finally agreed, he smirked, "Yeah, I bet you want something," then marched me out the door. I was glad he left at four in the morning, so I wouldn't have to get up and see his face.

The next morning Aunt Lorraine packed up towels and coconut smelling suntan lotion for a trip to the beach. She bought me sunglasses and showed me how to wear them on the top of my head. "You look like a real cool cat," she said, and we both laughed. We talked about movies. I told her *Goonies* was my favorite.

"Gar, you have to see *Aliens*. It's great."

We even talked about Uncle Dan. Aunt Lorraine asked, "Why does a grown man have to live with his sister?" I laughed, not because it was funny, but because she was the only adult who had ever asked the same question I'd wondered my whole life. She added, "And look at that head of his. He's a chrome dome." We both cracked up.

Before Aunt Lorraine took me back home, she told me, "I want to buy you a birthday present. What do you want? Clothes? A toy?" I told her Uncle Dan thought I was too old to be playing with toys, to which she said, "He needs to stop playing with Anthony and get a job instead of worrying about you playing with toys." She bought me the two biggest Transformers they had at Toys R Us. When we pulled into the driveway, I felt sad leaving her.

"Aunt Lorraine, I wish I could live with you."

"I wish you could live with me, too. I love you and try not to laugh when you see your Uncle Danny's chrome dome." She kissed me on the cheek and hugged me.

Uncle Dan came back a few days after I did. When he walked into the kitchen without looking at me, I remembered laughing about him with Aunt Lorraine and snickered to myself. Dad was sitting at the table drinking coffee and reading the paper. I knew it would bother Uncle Dan, so I asked, "Dad, The Transformers movie is coming out next month. Can we go see it?" I actually really did want to see it. The commercials said it was two years in the making and that Megatron and Optimus Prime fought to the death.

Dad answered, "Yeah, I'll take you, Michael, and Vincent the weekend it comes out."

I knew Dad felt bad that we didn't go the first weekend *The Transformers Movie* came out when he said "yes" to my asking for the soundtrack when we were at Pathmark. The music section in the grocery store had all the cassettes and records locked behind glass. As I waited for the employee to bring the key over, I scanned all the music until I found it. They had the record, with all the cool new Transformers on the cover shooting up at the sky.

When the boy slid the door open, I asked, "Do you have the cassette?"

He looked behind some records. "No, we're out. Just the album." I didn't want a record, but I wanted to hear the music so bad. Plus, I wasn't sure if we'd ever actually see the movie.

"Ok, I'll take the album."

By the time we went to see the movie, Michael, Vincent, and I had listened to the record probably a hundred times. I loved flying Starscream through the family room as the music played. I couldn't wait to hear Starscream's reaction when Optimus killed Megatron, finally making Starscream the leader of the Decepticons.

Dad bought me, Michael, and Vincent each a small popcorn and a Coke before we found our seats. As we munched handfuls of buttery popcorn, the lights went dark. The movie was like watching a new episode on a huge screen. The story began with Megatron killing a whole spaceship full of Autobots. I thought, wow, they had battles like that in every episode of the cartoon, but nobody ever died – this was going to be good! I was shocked when Megatron killed Optimus Prime, but he was badly damaged himself. Even though I thought Starscream should have finished Megatron off first, I still chuckled when he threw Megatron from the ship into space.

When Megatron came back as Galvatron, I thought there's no way he's going to kill Starscream, no way. Starscream was smarter than everyone else. He was meant to lead the Decepticons. Galvatron transformed and took one shot. Starscream didn't just die. He froze in place then crumbled to dust in slow motion, like the Kraken in *Clash of the Titans*.

Michael turned to me and whispered, "They killed Starscream," like I hadn't just seen it myself.

"I don't care. Shhh!"

Then Dad looked over. "Gar, was that Starscream?"

I smiled and acted like it didn't matter. "Yeah, I don't care. It's ok. I don't care."

Starscream wasn't the only character whose death I had a hard time accepting. *Dragonslayer* became one of my favorite movies after we watched it one Saturday afternoon downstairs. I couldn't stop thinking about the scene at the beginning though. The girl with long red hair who was being sacrificed to the dragon almost escapes by spitting on her wrists and pulling her hands out of the cuffs. Even though she runs away, the dragon finds her hiding behind a large rock, takes a deep breath, then burns her up as she screams. I wished she had found a better hiding place, so the dragon would have instead burned down her village and all the men who had chained her up.

Without any friends, the five of us created many games to pass the time downstairs. This included reenacting some of our favorite movies, like *Dragonslayer*. I would hold Christina's hands as Michael or Vincent pretended to be the dragon. Once Christina was free, she'd run faster than either one of them and escape. Christina didn't usually mind the game, but that day something on MTV caught her attention.

"Let me go." She ran over to turn the TV up.

A singer with short, blond hair was singing, "Papa, don't preach. I'm in trouble deep."

Christina was mesmerized. The singer was beautiful, and the song was catchy, too. I already wanted to sing along. As the video ended, the singer's name was shown. So that's Madonna? – the same stupid singer that girl in my class, Brenda, liked? I had thought Madonna had dark, wild hair and wore wedding dresses.

It was the last Tuesday of the summer pool party. Anthony and Uncle Dan had invited all of their friends from down the shore. Uncle Jim even came with his new girlfriend. Mom's friend Laura didn't come, so Laura Lynne wasn't there. Aunt Lorraine and Uncle Mike didn't come either. I didn't want to be around Uncle Dan's and Anthony's stupid, drunk friends, so I sat downstairs watching MTV by myself. Soaking wet strangers, carrying beer bottles and packs of cigarettes ran in and out through the open glass door. I tried to ignore them as I waited for Madonna videos.

The second time Uncle Jim walked by, he stopped. "Hey, Gar." Even though the music was loud enough to pretend I hadn't heard him, I figured that I should be polite.

I smiled. "Hi, Uncle Jim." I turned back to the TV, hoping he wouldn't keep talking.

Michael yelled from upstairs, "Mom! Someone's ringing the doorbell."

Of course, no one could hear it. The music was so loud I could barely hear the TV in front of me or Uncle Jim. Mom walked in drying herself off with a towel.

She screamed, "What?" as she tucked her black hair into her swim cap. The expression on her face got serious as she said, "Angela, hi, what are you doing here?" Mom hurried up the stairs and shut the music off.

Anthony jumped into the pool, popped up, and yelled, "Kath, turn the music back on!"

I got up, leaned toward the stairs, and listened. "I want you out, Kathleen! I want you out."

Mom begged. "Angela, it's just a party, please."

The lady's voice got louder and repeated. "I want you out. I want you out." I thought to myself, yup, we've lived here for six months. I dropped back down on the couch.

1 Castle Court

The carpets in the new house were dry and matted, not damp and spongy from being shampooed. I looked out the glass door in the family room to the backyard, which was completely shaded from huge oak trees. The tiny, fenced-in yard was full of soggy, black leaves. As we walked down the hall, where the bedrooms were, I wondered what dust smells like.

Michael asked, "What makes the house ranch style?" I knew he'd heard Mom tell Shari that.

Every time we moved, Mom talked about the new house like it was going to be the most amazing home we'd ever lived in.

"It's a split level," Mom would say, or "The countertops are real Formica." Some had pools, others had finished basements, while others had marble steps or a cabana. Mom had always talked up some aspect of the house we were moving to.

I wasn't sure what I should tell Michael. I wanted to say, "Ranch style means it's a dump," but I knew he was trying to see the best in our new home. I thought about what I'd believe if I were ten and said, "It's because we don't have a basement." I didn't feel bad about my made-up fact. It wasn't like he was going to be explaining ranch style to his new fourth-grade class.

Michael quickly moved on to his next question anyway. "Do we own the house?"

He'd also heard Mom talk about that, but what she had said confused him. Mom had told Uncle Dan that we bought the house with Josie, some old woman that Dad had met through his roofing company. She'd put the money down, and Dad was going to paint and put a new roof on the house, so we could all sell it together. I wasn't sure if that was all true, but still, I answered, "Yeah, we own it."

From my, Michael, and Vincent's room, I looked out the window at the other side of our, dingy, L-shaped, white house and thought about our address, 1 Castle Ct. I tried to count how many addresses and phone numbers I'd memorized in my life. Ten? Fifteen? We'd never lived on a court or been number one before. If we really did own the house, at least it had a neat address.

I contemplated last names as Mom and Dad drove me, Michael, Christina, and Vincent to our new school, St. Paul the Apostle. Whenever Mom talked about Anthony's ex-girlfriend, she almost always said Laura Witham. I knew it was so people wouldn't confuse her with Laura Giordano, Laura Lynne's mom. I wondered if Mom was going to feel uncomfortable telling the nuns that Vincent's last name was Moore. She liked to pretend that Dad was really all our father like Gary had never existed.

I had already given a lot of thought to what I'd say. I knew my heart would race if someone questioned me, but regardless of who Vincent's father was, he was as much my brother as Michael. If anyone asked why he had a different last name, I was prepared to tell them, "He's my brother. It's none of your business, so don't worry about it."

When we got to the school, the nun who came out of the office was short and skinny with a serious face. She looked at Mom. "Hi, Kathleen, I'm Sister Francis."

Mom turned toward us. "Guys, Sister Francis is the principal." She introduced us. "This is Gary, Michael, Christina, and Vincent."

Sister Francis looked at each of us. "So, we've got all four Mele kids in our school."

I immediately realized that Mom had lied and told Sister Francis that Vincent's last name was Mele. I smiled and felt relief as I looked at Vincent. Then I thought about Michelle. I knew we probably wouldn't be in the school more than a year, but still, I wanted Sister Francis to know that Michelle was a Mele, too.

I piped up, "There's actually five of us, Sister Francis. We've got a younger sister at home." I don't know why I expected her to say, "I'm glad you told me. I'll remember that when she starts kindergarten next year!" She gave me a stern look to let me know it didn't matter how many sisters I had at home – I shouldn't be correcting a nun, a nun who was also the principal. Sister Francis turned and said, "Your brothers and sister are on this side of the school. Let's go."

After we walked Vincent, Christina, and Michael to their classrooms, Sister Francis clicked her shoes in a marching step until we got to the far end of the school where my seventh-grade classroom was.

After school, the teachers directed us to the line for our bus. As we stepped up, the bus driver said, "Oh, we've got some new students." She told an enthusiastic eight-grade girl to show us where to sit. The girl explained that the seating arrangement on the bus was youngest to oldest. Vincent stepped closer to me because he didn't want to sit where she told him to.

The eighth-grade seating officer bent down and cooed, "Oh, you're so cute. Look at those curls!" I knew, in Vincent's mind, being thought of as cute meant he was a baby – and he hated that. Vincent scrunched his eyebrows and brushed the curls from his face.

"Ok, I understand," the girl continued. "You're a big boy. You pick which side of the seat you want to sit on." She smiled to let me know she knew how to handle him. Christina sat in the middle rows, and Michael sat a couple of seats in front of me, next to the only black girl on the bus.

Next to me was a Chinese boy, who sat two desks away in our class. His hair lay completely flat against his round head. I hated that I had to part my hair and brush it into a style that never stayed in place. There was always a puff somewhere on my head that wouldn't stay down no matter how long I pressed my hand on it. Mom called them "cowlicks." When I was younger, she'd lick her fingers and try to smooth them flat. I looked up at Michael talking to the black girl. Every time he turned his head forward, I could see the two hooks of hair that stuck out over his ears. Anthony would say to him, "Hey Mike, you gonna take off with those wings?" but Michael didn't care. I wished I didn't care what my hair looked like.

As I was wondering if Chinese people realized how lucky they were to have straight, black hair that never stuck up, the kid turned toward me. "I'm Thomas."

"Hi, um, I'm Gary."

Thomas looked down at his book bag. "Do you like Dungeons & Dragons?"

I usually wondered if kids were looking for a reason to make fun when they started talking, but Thomas seemed too serious. When I told him I'd never heard of it, he said, "It's really cool" and pulled out a red book with a Viking fighting an orange dragon. He handed me some multi-colored, funny shaped dice. As he explained that the game is entirely in your mind, I rolled the different shaped dice around in my fingers.

"I never knew there was a dice that went up to twenty," I said.

Thomas answered, "If you're talking about one, it's a die. Dice is for more than one." I imagined the look I'd get from Uncle Dan if I said that the next time he, Mom, and Shari were playing Monopoly.

Even though I'd just been corrected, I wanted Thomas to know I understood bigger, more important things about the real world, like where he was from. "Were you born in China?"

"I'm not Chinese. I'm Korean."

"Korean? Oh yeah... Korean."

How could I be so stupid? I needed to change the subject – fast! I knew the smiley, loud Chinese... er... Korean girl, in Christina's section, was his sister because I'd heard him shush her as they were getting on the bus.

"I think your sister and my sister are in the same class."

Thomas leaned up and looked toward the front of the bus where his sister was standing up, explaining something, obviously, very important to the boy next to her. Thomas said, "That's Annie. She's a brat and doesn't listen."

I had never told anyone at school that my brothers and sisters were brats, probably because that would kind of be like making fun of them, and I was always being made fun of myself. I appreciated that Thomas shared something so personal, which made me want to share back.

"All of my brothers and sisters are brats, too, especially Christina. She throws tantrums and kicks things when she doesn't get her way."

288

He gave a quick smile before changing the subject back to Dungeons & Dragons. He explained the reason for a twenty-sided die before we got to my stop. As I grabbed my book bag and stood up, he said, "I'll see you tomorrow morning."

I smiled. "Yeah, I'll see you in the morning."

The bus door squealed open. Vincent hopped off and began running. Christina jumped down and took off after him. They raced to be the first one across the huge front lawn. Michael and I flung our book bags over our shoulders and walked. As we stepped through the grass, Michael asked, "Gar, are you gonna be friends with that Chinese kid?"

"He's not Chinese," I snapped. "He's Korean. Sheesh!" I added, "Are you gonna marry that black girl you sat next to?"

One time, Anthony had said "nigger" in front of Mom. She'd yelled, "Don't use that word in my house!"

Anthony had laughed. "Do you want us to call them spooks or jigaboos instead?"

Mom's lips curled in. "You ignorant bastard. It's not funny!"

Even with all the things Mom did wrong, she never said anything mean about black people or any other race. I started feeling bad, so I told Michael, "If you ever want to marry a black girl, it'd be ok. You know, I was just kidding."

Michael looked at me. "I don't care if Aisha's black. I would never marry her because she bosses everyone around."

"No, I'm not gonna stop!" Shari was yelling from the kitchen as we opened the door.

Uncle Dan's voice was loud and deep. "You better watch yourself!"

I heard Mom's footsteps as she hurried Christina and Vincent out of the kitchen. She yelled, "Gary, take them to their room!"

"Come on!" I hollered and pressed my hands on their backs until they were in the bedroom. I shut the door behind me and walked back out to get Michelle.

Mom screamed, "Danny! Danny! Let her go! Let her go!" I heard a BOOM BOOM BOOM near the front of the house as Shari screamed.

Uncle Dan yelled, "You fucking bitch! I'll fucking kill you!"

As I crept to the edge of the hall, I could see Michelle crying in the family room, which was next to the kitchen. I took a few steps, picked her up, and hurried back to the bedroom as Mom started screaming, "Get out! Danny, Get out!" I had never heard Mom scream so loud. The front door slammed and shook the whole house. Through the window, I could see Uncle Dan walking across the front yard.

He screamed back toward the house. "You better watch yourself! You fucking bitch!"

Christina and Michelle were both crying. I tried to calm my voice. "It's ok. It's ok."

Shari sobbed while Uncle Dan walked out to his car. After he slammed the door and drove away, she grabbed her purse. "I have to go, Kath. I have to go."

Mom hugged her. "I'm sorry, Shari."

As I watched Shari's car drive away, I thought about one of the last conversations we'd had. When I told her, we had to read *The Outsiders*; she had said: "I love that book!" I told her how our teacher explained the difference between obvious and subtle storytelling. Shari smiled, "Subtle storytelling is better because you have to think about it."

Christina stood at the window, quiet, with tears running down her cheeks. I thought about when Laura had said, "Michelle is so beautiful."

Mom had smiled. "Thank you. Isn't she?"

Shari, who didn't usually interrupt, had added, "I think Christina's beautiful, too."

"Oh," Mom said, "Christina's naturally pretty."

Christina knew that Mom thought Michelle was prettier and that Shari really believed Christina was beautiful. I walked over to Christina, put my hand on her shoulder, and pulled her toward me. I whispered, "Christina, it's ok. She'll be back," even though I didn't believe it.

The next day, as we waited for our bus, I thought about how grateful I was that Thomas' house wasn't one of the six in our court. I was pretty sure his mother didn't know any of our neighbors, so there wouldn't be any secret phone conversations to end our friendship.

I also thought how funny it was that our address was number one. What were we the number one of? We were the number one crazy family our neighbors would probably ever see. I was sure of that.

The bus squealed to a stop. Vincent got on, followed by Christina, Michael, then me. I smelled the dark green seats, wondering if they were really leather, as I walked to the back of the bus.

Thomas gave a smile. "Hey."

I grabbed the back of the seat and plopped down. "Hi."

At recess, Thomas asked, "Do you like *X-men*?"

"I've never heard of them. Is it a comic book?"

"Yeah. It's awesome. There's a new one called *X-Factor*. It's the original team back together. You want to come over to read them?"

"Yeah, I think that'd be cool. I'll ask my Dad if he'll take me after school."

As we pulled up, I noticed that Thomas' house looked newer than ours. Thomas' Mom opened the door and gave me a big smile. She said "hi" like a Korean woman trying to speak English. I wondered what a Korean house would look like as I stepped inside.

There was a couch, a love seat and their TV was on, with Annie watching *She Ra*. She turned and giggled. "Are you guys going to Thomas' room?"

Thomas ignored her. "Come on up," he said. "I'll show you my comic books."

Thomas' comics were upright in a box, each one in a clear plastic sleeve that fit perfectly. Thomas lifted the flap and carefully pulled the comic straight out and laid it on the carpet. I heard a muffled BOM BOM BOM and knew his sister was running up the stairs. Thomas caught the door with his hand as it flung open. "Get out, Annie! Mom!"

Annie's happy smile turned to a frown when her Mom called from downstairs. "Fine!" she yelled and slammed the door as she left.

"She's such a brat." Thomas plopped down onto the carpet. He slid the comic over. "Be careful turning the pages. If you crease the edge, it loses its value."

I scanned the page. I didn't know those superheroes, except Iceman. I asked, "Is that the same Iceman from the *Spider-Man* cartoon, and is the woman with red hair, Firestar?"

Thomas tightened his lips and shook his head. "I don't think so. He's boring, anyway." He pointed at the redhead. "That's Marvel Girl. She was the Phoenix and died. She always comes back when she dies."

Really? I was interested in that, so I began asking questions. By the time Thomas finished explaining, I really couldn't wait to read for myself.

"You can borrow them," Thomas told me. "Just don't let your brothers and sisters touch them, especially Christina."

"Don't worry. I won't."

Dad picked me up, and as we pulled into our long driveway with its six different cars parked in it, I could hear the stereo blaring, "I didn't mean to turn you on… Oh, I didn't mean to turn you on…" I sighed as I remembered getting evicted for having loud pool parties with soaking wet people running through the house.

When we walked into the kitchen, I thought, of course. Shari's gone, and Uncle Dan is back. He was probably proud that he'd beaten her up. Anthony was there, too. He had his arm around Laura Witham.

Bonnie Perrett was telling Mom, Uncle Dan, and Anthony's stupid, short brother, Joe Bianchi, that Cherry Hill is actually a suburb of Philly. She tried to make it sound like a really big deal. I didn't care if Cherry Hill was a suburb of Paris, France. If it was so great, why was she at our house? I thought about Thomas' parents, both sitting on their couch, alone, watching a Korean TV show when I had left. Why did we have to have so many parties and people over all the time?

As I walked to my room, Mom called, "Gar, come here."

"Yeah?"

"Your new friend – is he Korean?"

I'd already told her before. She knew he was Korean. "Yes, Mom. He's Korean."

Uncle Dan decided he was talking to me again. "Orientals aren't bad people."

I remembered Thomas explaining that you don't call people Oriental. That's for carpets and lamps. I said, "Actually, they're Asian. Oriental is only when you're describing things, not people."

Joe piped up, "Well, they're in our country. They're lucky we don't call them chinks."

Anthony laughed, which made me mad. I wanted to say, "I don't know what you're laughing about. They've done more work in this country than you have!" Instead, I went to my room.

After Anthony and Laura were back together, she began spending more time at our house. The first time we got home from school, and our bedroom door was closed, Michael asked, "Why is the door shut?"

Vincent ran in after Michael. He scrunched his face, waved his hand, and said, "P.U." then asked, "What's that smell?" Michael looked at me as we both sniffed. It smelled like sweat and something I'd never smelled before.

A few days later, I heard Uncle Dan ask Anthony, "So, you're hittin' that again?"

Anthony laughed. "Sometimes we like to nap in the boys' room. You know what I mean, Dan."

Gross! I thought. I knew they weren't doing it on Michael and Vincent's bunk beds. I wanted to gag, thinking about Anthony and Laura rolling all over my bed, naked and sweating.

Michael didn't mind the stench of Laura and Anthony's sex, because the days they did it, Laura would walk around wearing sweatpants and a black half shirt without a bra.

Michael whispered to me, "Gar, sometimes when she lifts her arms, you can see the bottom of her boobs." I scolded him, "You shouldn't be looking at her boobs, Michael." But then I thought that maybe if I told Laura that Michael was looking at her boobs, it would embarrass her, and they'd stop having sex.

I walked into the kitchen where Laura was talking with Mom and Bonnie. I told her, "Michael's telling everyone he can see your boobs, Laura." It was quiet for a moment until Bonnie piped in, "I wish I had boobs," then laughed like a ferret.

Mom looked shocked. "Michael!"

When Michael walked into the kitchen, Mom said to him, "Michael, you shouldn't be trying to look under woman's shirts."

Michael's face turned hot red, and he began stuttering. "I... I... uh... uh..."

Telling her was a waste for me and Michael. They still had sex in our room – and Laura always put on a bra afterward.

Talking with Laura and Bonnie was more fun than watching MTV. I waited for a day when Uncle Dan and Anthony were actually working. Laura, Bonnie, and Mom were sitting at the tiny kitchen table pressed up against the window with the afternoon sun. I walked in to pour myself a glass of Coca-Cola. I asked Laura and Bonnie if they wanted anything. I wondered if Mom was going to say, "Gary, go play. We're talking," but she didn't shoo me away.

Laura said, "I'm good. Thanks, Gar." Bonnie said she'd take a glass of Diet Coke.

After I handed Bonnie her soda, I leaned against the counter. She started telling Mom and Laura, "My mom is gonna kill me when she finds out I'm pregnant."

"What about Joe?" Laura asked

"He's an asshole," Bonnie snapped. "He said I don't even know if that baby's mine."

Mom put her hand on Bonnie's shoulder. "He *is* an asshole. I don't care how long I've known him. Bon, you can stay here if you need to, Hon."

I was proud of Mom for taking Bonnie's side, even though she'd known Joseph and Anthony since they were kids. I'd found out that Laura's son, little Anthony, was Anthony's son. He didn't care about him when they were broken up, and even after they got back together, he still made fun of him just like he did us. When Little Anthony fell down and scraped his hand, Anthony had turned his crying into a joke. For days he'd walk around going, "Mommy owe owe, Mommy owe owe," like an idiot.

I thought, who makes fun of a two-year-old, who's also his son? Yeah, I was sure Joseph was an asshole, just like his brother, Anthony. I said, "Bonnie if you need help with the baby, I'll help you."

She smiled. "Aw, thanks, Gar."

Mom smiled like she was as proud of me as I was of her.

As I lay in bed, I remembered how angry Mom had gotten when Uncle Dan hit Shari. That night she had come to my room. "Gar, you know you never put your hands on a woman, right?"

"I know, Mom."

Thinking about Uncle Dan and Shari breaking up made me sad because we'd probably never see her again. At least she was smart enough to not have a baby with him.

I thought about Laura and Bonnie and how they were both attached to Anthony and Joseph forever because they'd gotten pregnant. Laura had broken up with Anthony before. She knew he was a jerk, but he would always be little Anthony's father. I was sure that was why she tried to get back together with him. I wondered if Bonnie would have the same feelings after she had her baby.

As my eyelids began feeling tired, I thought about how Mom had left Gary. I always believed he would try to find us, but it had been almost ten years. Maybe he didn't care like Mom had always said. Maybe he was happy that Mom took us. I got a lump in my throat, turned over, and fell asleep.

When Christmas break came, Christina asked Dad if she could get Madonna's tape again, because I'd pretty much stolen hers.

Dad said, "I thought I got you Madonna's True Blue tape?"

Christina responded, "I told Gary he could have it."

I appreciated Christina's effort to keep me out of trouble, but I had been spending so much time with Mom and her friends that I was like an adult. I wasn't going to get in trouble for taking something from one of the kids.

Michael asked for a Nintendo, and Vincent gave a big smile. "I want red boxing gloves, so I can fight with Uncle Dan!" I remembered how much fun I had thought Uncle Dan was when I was five. I looked at Vincent. He won't think Uncle Dan's so much fun when he gets his butt beaten for talking back to an adult.

I already had the Dungeons and Dragons books I wanted, and I knew Thomas would lend me any I didn't have, so I decided on a pet. I thought dogs were stupid, and Mom hated cats. I wanted something different, anyway. I told Mom, "I want a hand fed cockatiel. They're really smart, and you can teach them to talk."

Vincent got his ridiculous boxing gloves. Uncle Dan told him, "Look, Santa brought me a pair, too." He bopped Vincent on the top of the head as Vincent ran around Uncle Dan's legs, laughing and trying to punch him. When Vincent swung at his crotch, Uncle Dan said, "Woah! You almost nailed me in the family jewels."

I named my cockatiel Cijay. I explained to everyone that she wouldn't bite because she was hand fed by a person from the time she had hatched so she didn't know she was a bird – she thought she was human. Everyone was impressed when she nibbled on my bottom lip without biting me. I would say, "She's giving me kisses," then put her on my shoulder and walk around the house.

Michael played Super Mario Bros. for days straight in a row. He would only break for eating, going to the bathroom, and getting the mail when he heard the truck outside. I knew he wasn't supposed to be going through adult things, so I'd chase after when I caught him.

One day, when I realized Michael was outside getting the mail, I bolted for the door. As I ran up to him, he'd already opened the mailbox and pulled the letters out. He mumbled "Mom, Mom," then asked, "Who's Margaret Whiting?"

That was Aunt Peggy, but why would we be getting her mail? I was about to tell Michael to show the letter to me when he started opening one. I yelled at him. "What are you doing?"

As I grabbed for it, Michael yelled back, "It's mine! See? It has my name on it."

It was a bill for a car, and it did have his name on it. When we got inside, I handed it to Mom. "Michael opened this, but it has his name on it."

"That's your Dad's work name."

Michael gave me a funny smile. It made sense for Dad to change his last name to Mele because of Vincent in school, but I had no idea why he would use Michael's name. I shrugged, then asked Mom "Why are we getting Aunt Peggy's mail?"

"She's coming back to New Jersey. She's going to stay with us."

When I heard Mom talking on the phone with Aunt Peggy, I knew it wouldn't be long.

"How's the drive going, Peg?"

"Great! Can't wait to see you!"

When Aunt Peggy pulled into the driveway, I could see the little head looking up in the seat next to her. Billy looked like he was younger than Michelle, maybe three, and I wondered how Aunt Peggy felt, losing custody of Josh to Uncle Bruce. Regardless if she only had one of her kids, she still seemed excited to be back in New Jersey. She looked great, too. She was still thin, and her black hair had grown out long and wild, like a rocker chick from a Bon Jovi video.

After Aunt Peggy hugged Mom, she yelled, "Gar! You've gotten so big and handsome. How old are you now?"

I smiled. "Thirteen." Then she hugged Michael, Christina, and Vincent.

Mom picked up Michelle. "Peg, isn't Michelle beautiful?"

Aunt Peggy answered, "Oh, my God! She is!" Michelle beamed.

I looked over at Christina and smiled. Aunt Peggy caught my look and turned back to Christina, too. She ran her fingers through Christina's light brown hair and said, "Your hair is so long and pretty, and you've got beautiful skin. I bet you have a lot of boyfriends at school."

Christina gave a shy smile. "I don't have any boyfriends."

Aunt Peggy got a job at Wawa, the convenient store up the street from our house. When she came home with her whole hand wrapped in a white bandage, she laughed so hard she could barely talk. She said between laughs, "I cut… my hand… on the meat slicer." I could tell Mom didn't think it was funny, but she couldn't help laughing because Aunt Peggy was cracking up.

"Peg, are you nuts? You sliced your hand, and you're laughing about it?"

"Well, I guess I'm not doing anybody's hair anytime soon." Aunt Peggy answered then laughed so hard she had to hold her stomach with her good hand.

Aunt Peggy didn't just entertain us. She quickly made friends at Wawa and brought them home. Bernadette was as tall as Uncle Dan – and big. After Uncle Dan met her, he made a face and whispered to Anthony. "Woo! Imagine getting stuck under that?" They both laughed.

Bernadette wasn't just fat. Mom said she was big boned. She had a curly blond perm that was short on the top and sides and down to her shoulders in the back.

Aunt Peggy told Bernadette, "Bern, you should let me do your hair. That style makes your face look enormous." Bernadette brought her friend that she'd just graduated high school with – Julie – to come over, too. She had dry blond hair that went straight down her back. She wasn't as big as Bernadette.

Mom said, "Julie's just hippy."

Spring came, and the weather started getting warmer. I decided I could take Cijay outside for a few minutes at a time. The first time I did it, Julie had asked, "Will she fly away?"

"No, she won't leave me."

Bonnie said to Mom, "You shouldn't let him bring her outside. She's gonna fly away."

I wanted to tell her that she shouldn't be worried about me and my bird. She should worry about the baby she was about to give birth to.

It was a couple of days later. I had Cijay on my shoulder. I was walking around the side of the house in front of all the big windows, acting like picking up papers from the grass was the most important thing I had to do. As I thought about how impressed everyone would be when I went back inside, a flutter of birds took off from our neighbor's tree. Before I realized what happened, I saw Cijay, with her white wings spread, coasting down, then up into the woods where she disappeared.

My breath was gone. I looked toward the house, toward the woods, and then ran inside. Everyone was talking and laughing. No one had even been paying attention to me. I ran over to Mom. "Cijay flew away!" Mom asked, "What?!"

Within minutes everyone was walking through the woods, crunching branches and calling, "Ci-Jay! Ci-Jay!"

Aunt Peggy said, "Gar, don't worry. We'll find her. I had a cockatiel. They never go more than twenty yards from home."

I asked, "Really?" even though I didn't believe it.

As it got darker, one by one, everyone told me, "We'll find her" before heading back inside. Dad helped me write out lost bird signs and drove me around the neighborhood to tape them to light poles, but no one called.

A couple of weeks after I'd lost Cijay, Mom and Dad told me they wanted to talk to me alone. As Dad shut the bedroom door, I wondered if they were going to buy me a new bird. I didn't want a new bird. I wanted them to offer a reward for Cijay. Mom took a breath, smiled, and then started. "Gar, do you want to visit Gary?"

Altering Indemnification

As I lay in bed, I wondered if I'd said the right thing. I didn't understand why Mom pretended like it was suddenly all right for me to want to see Gary. Throughout my whole life, whenever anybody asked about him, Mom would snarl. "He left me homeless with two babies and pregnant. He's a rotten bastard!"

I used to get so mad that she made it seem like he had left for no reason. I wanted to add to her story: "Before my father left, he worked every day. While he was building stairs and decks in the hot sun, my Uncle Jim and Jack were at our house drinking beer in our kitchen. They took turns sleeping on our couch, based on whoever passed out first. Grandma had Uncle Dan stay with us because juvenile delinquents who stole cars and beat people up had to have a permanent address. They weren't allowed to live at The Holiday Inn. Oh – and Grandma left Doreen with us because the Irish pubs she went to during the day were strict and wouldn't allow twelve-year old's to sit at the bar. My father, the rotten bastard, got tired of fighting with Mom about her family, so he left."

I snickered as I imagined the look of shock on Mom's face if I had ever actually said that. I wasn't sure when I had stopped being angry at her. Maybe she was right, I thought. Maybe all the craziness wasn't an excuse for Gary to leave. I was Michelle's age when he had stormed out and driven away for the last time. Mom, Doreen, Michael, and I went from living in a car to (what I didn't realize at the time was) a boarding house full of transients and vagabonds. Even with her round, pregnant belly, Mom had still gotten the men to smile and talk to her for hours while she sat on the front porch drinking orange juice. I remembered running out to tell her about the man I had met who had worked on a train, which was, at that time, the most exciting moment of my life. Before I could finish explaining how excited I was, Mom pulled me close to whisper, "Gary, this is Nick."

I was embarrassed when Mom had coaxed me into calling Nick "Dad," but eventually it became comfortable, just like our relationship. Dad had always made me cereal before leaving for work, and he had always answered my questions – no matter how many – and he knew how much I loved trains. He'd pull over and wait so I could watch as the locomotive and passenger cars barreled by. One time, he'd asked me, "You want to see something neat, Gar?"

He placed a penny on the track. "Wait till you see what the engine does to it."

Dad was right. I stepped back onto the tracks after the last silver passenger car flew by. The rails were still warm, and a burning diesel smell hung in the air. I picked up the flattened copper piece from the gray rocks and smiled. "Wow, that's so cool, Dad."

My relationship with Dad was different because we both knew the truth. I thought about how he acted with Michael and Christina. When he'd go to the store, he'd come home with a Kit Kat for Christina, and he'd smile when he handed it to her. She'd smile back,

"Thanks, Dad!" and hug his waist. He would buy Michael a bag of Starburst or Skittles and tell him that he was in charge of them, but he had to share with everybody. He had also told Michael he had to save his allowance for the Kung Fu Nintendo game he wanted. After only two weeks, Dad asked, "How much have you saved, Mike?" Michael was eager to give Dad the three dollars and fifty cents he had saved up – a fraction of what the game cost. Still, Dad came home with the game for him. Michael and Christina would have no reason to believe he wasn't their father.

Mom knew I would want to see Gary even before she asked me. I thought about how Dad had been such a good father to all of us and got quiet. Dad smiled. "Gar, its ok if you want to see him."

I was so curious about Gary. *Was he normal?* Did he regret never coming to find us? I had so many questions. I felt like I should have said, "No, I don't want to see him. You're my dad. You're all our dad." Instead, I shrugged and said, "Ok" like I didn't really care one way or the other.

Mom told me that Gary had moved to Georgia, and we were going to visit him when we went on vacation to Florida with Aunt Lorraine and Uncle Mike at the end of the summer. She said we were going to say he was an uncle.

"Your Aunt Susie is coming to visit in a couple of weeks, too."

"Who's Aunt Susie?"

Mom explained that Aunt Susie was Gary's sister, but because the other kids didn't know about Gary, we were going to pretend she was Dad's sister. She also said that Uncle Jim was actually the father of Aunt Susie's oldest son, but no one knew that either. I chuckled to myself and thought, "Of course no one would know that."

"Does her son even know?" I asked.

"No, he doesn't. Don't say anything, Gar," Mom said.

I thought about my cousin, Michael. His mother got pregnant when she was seventeen and had to move to North Carolina and marry some man she didn't know so that Michael would have a nice, normal father. He thought his mom had just divorced his dad, not knowing that his father was really a drunk named Jimmy from New Jersey.

Is this for real? I wondered. Could the Mele's be just as crazy as the Canaley's? I had hoped for as long as I could remember that Gary had been normal and that was why the way we lived seemed so crazy to me. The moment Mom said that Aunt Susie, Gary's sister, was coming to visit, I assumed it was to see her long-lost nephews and niece. After I'd heard the whole story, I knew she was coming to see Uncle Jim.

I had been thinking so much about Gary, Aunt Susie, Uncle Jim, and how crazy everyone was, that I didn't even care when Mom said Doreen was coming to stay for the summer. It wasn't until the car turned into our driveway, and I saw Mom and Doreen cracking up, that I smiled. Doreen got out and pulled her big, leather duffle bag from the back seat. Her black hair still streamed straight down her back, the same way Mom had always made her keep it.

When she smiled and said, "Hey, Gar, how's it going?" I remembered all the craziness we'd experienced together and how sad I had been that she had stayed in Iowa, alone, to go to school.

I smiled back. "Good. How're you, Dor?"

When we walked inside, Aunt Peggy was dancing in the living room, snapped her fingers as she mouthed words. "I knew you were waiting… I knew you were waiting for me…"

Uncle Jim hugged Doreen. Uncle Dan asked, "Hey, Diddle Dumpling, how's Iowa?"

Doreen smiled. "Hey, Dan. Hey, Jim."

Mom said, "Bern, Julie, this is my sister, Doreen." Then Mom turned toward the living room. "Peg, turn that up. I love George Michael. He's a doll."

Doreen added, "Oh, he's a fox."

Uncle Dan made his usual face of disgust whenever anyone said they liked a male singer. "He's a fag."

Of course, he's a fag, I thought. Real men, like Uncle Dan, would have beaten Aretha Franklin up, not sang a duet with her.

I'd barely finished my thought when Bernadette's voice boomed from across the room. "Yeah, you wish he was a fag!" Bernadette winked at Mom and smiled at me. As everyone laughed, I wondered why I was the one she smiled at.

The party went on long after it had gotten dark. Aunt Peggy hollered over the music. "Kath, I'm gonna go get ribs and chicken."

Mom reached toward her purse. "Hand me my pockabook, Peg. I'll give you some money." Mom handed Aunt Peggy a couple of folded bills then went back to singing with Doreen. They both closed their eyes and sang along like Bono's backup singers. "I have climbed the highest mountains . . . I have run through the fields . . . Only to be with you . . . Only to be with you . . ." They laughed when they finished and walked into the kitchen to get Diet Cokes.

As everyone chattered in the kitchen, I took the opportunity to pop my Madonna tape in. I liked singing along to her the way Mom liked singing to Stevie Nicks. I figured as long as I changed the pronouns, Uncle Dan would have no reason to call me a fag. "Daddy, Daddy if you could only seeee. . . just how good *she's* been treating meeee . . . you'd give us your blessing right now . . . cause we are in loooove . . ."

The front door opened, and Aunt Peggy walked in with a stapled, brown paper bag and two plastic bags full of Styrofoam containers. Michael and Vincent ran to the kitchen. After every adult got their plates of sticky ribs and potato salad, Aunt Peggy started handing plates of barbecued chicken and coleslaw to the kids. I got two

312

ribs along with my chicken. After I'd licked the sweet, red sauce from my fingers, I ran back to the living room to turn Madonna back on.

As I sang, "Tropical the island breeze . . . All of nature wild and free . . . This is where I long to be . . . La ki slah foenitah!" Doreen stuck her head out of the kitchen. "What did you say?"

I huffed. "I'm singing." Sheesh, I thought, I didn't say anything when she was belting out U2.

"What's the name of the song?" she asked. I paused, then answered, "La ki slah foenitah."

Doreen laughed. "It's La Isla Bonita."

Blood rushed to my face as the music blared. Christina plopped down in front of the stereo and pulled the cassette sleeve from the plastic case. She unfolded to read as Michelle danced in a circle and bobbed her head back and forth. When Christina folded the sleeve back up without saying anything, I knew Doreen was right. It was La Isla Bonita.

Michelle pulled my hand. "Gar, keep singing."

But I didn't want to anymore. I smiled at her. "You sing. You sound more like Madonna than I do."

As I contemplated what I could say to embarrass Doreen back, I realized no one was paying attention, anyway. Julie was all ears as Dad and Uncle Jim told her about the ghost house.

Uncle Jim said, "I swear to Christ, there was a trench coat floating with nothing in it." I wanted to tell Julie that Uncle Jim added things to make it sound like a scary movie – if she wanted the truth, she should only listen to Dad.

Aunt Peggy had been trying to convince Mom to let her cut Doreen's hair. "Kath, she needs some layers. This is so heavy."

But Mom was more interested in the ghost house discussion. She got serious. "Jule, I swear. I felt it when I was alone in that house. I get goosebumps to this day talking about it."

Mom swearing to God and Uncle Jim making the house sound like *The Shining* held everyone's attention except Bernadette's. Uncle Dan was way more appealing to her than some unbelievable haunted house. When Uncle Dan told Bernadette, the Jets wanted to recruit him because he could kick a thirty-yard field goal, she smirked. "Yeah, right. I'll believe it when I see it."

He laughed. "If my knee wasn't busted up, I'd show you right now."

I wasn't sure if Bernadette's flirting with Uncle Dan was because she really liked him, or if it was her way of becoming part of our family. She seemed to love the parties at our house, and she didn't care when Bonnie whispered, "Be careful. He hits his girlfriends." Bernadette waited until she wasn't around to remind everyone how stupid Bonnie was.

Bonnie did say stupid things – like right after she had had her baby. She squealed as she walked out of the bathroom with a white towel on her head. "Holy shit! Are they going to stay like this?" She pulled her shirt tight against her chest, so everyone could see the outline of her bra and her boobs plumping out at the top. "They started growing when I turned the shower on!"

Mom had laughed. "Bon, Hon, it's because you just gave birth, and they're producing milk. It'll stop after a couple of days."

Bernadette had realized if she wanted to discredit Bonnie's unasked-for opinion about Uncle Dan, she needed to focus on the things Bonnie said that people would find gross rather than funny. Julie and I were both shocked when Bernadette had said, "She's an idiot. Who talks about stuff oozing out of their snatch?" Mom quickly scoffed. "Even if that were true I wouldn't be telling people." But then, Mom got sweet. "I told her she doesn't need to announce things like that to the whole world." Bernadette turned away and rolled her eyes at Julie. Doreen had seen the whole exchange and added, "Bern, you shouldn't talk about stupid. You're the one trying to get with my brother, Danny." Everyone laughed.

I knew they had gotten together when Uncle Dan told me what Bernadette was like in bed. It was late at night, and I was in the family room watching *Aliens*. Uncle Dan came in, flopped down on the couch, and pulled a pillow behind his head. "Whatcha watchin?"

I turned toward him. "Aliens. It's really good." I knew he was going to tell me to put a game on unless I convinced him it was a manly movie. As I explained that Ripley was the only one who wasn't a Marine, the phone rang.

"Hello? Hey, hang on, Bern…"

Mom walked around the corner with the phone pressed to her chest so that Bernadette couldn't hear and whispered, "Dan, its Bern."

He made a face like he'd just licked a lemon. "I'm not here."

"*Danny*, she knows you're here."

He waved his hand above his head and shooed her away.

Mom walked back into the kitchen. "I think he's outside, Bern. I'll tell him to call you."

Once Mom was out of the room, Uncle Dan whispered, "Whew, I never should have hit that." He chuckled. I wasn't sure what to say, so I offered, "Uh, I really liked Shari. I never thought you'd get with Bernadette."

Uncle Dan got a serious look. "Listen, pussy's pussy. The problem with Bern is she just lays there like a dead whale, and now she's up my ass constantly. Shari had nice titties, but she just laid there, too." I knew he expected me to be engaged, so my mind raced with all the women I knew he'd slept with.

"What about Laura?" I asked.

316

"Wooo, her titties were shot, but she could suck the chrome off a tailpipe." He cracked up, and I forced a laugh, too, like I thought it was as funny as he did. There was no way I was going to tell him I felt uncomfortable hearing about anyone's titties.

Bernadette was louder and quicker to make Uncle Dan angry than Shari ever was. During one of their fights about him going out with Anthony, Bernadette yelled, "You think you're so hot. I can get any guy I want!"

Uncle Dan – *hot?* No one thought he was hot except her. I started wondering why she didn't just go get another guy, like she said she could, when I noticed that Uncle Dan was clenching his lips. I knew it wouldn't be long before he pushed her or knocked her out completely.

I hurried. "Michael, Vincent – come on. Christina, grab Michelle." As we scurried into the bedrooms, there was a thud, followed by Uncle Dan yelling, "Ow! Fuck!"

As I peeked back into the kitchen, Uncle Dan was holding his hand and wincing. Bernadette tried to comfort him. "Oh, my God. We need to call an ambulance. I think he broke his thumb."

Michael looked puzzled as he whispered behind me, "Is she helping Uncle Dan after he tried to punch her?"

I shushed him. "Go back to the room!" but thought, he's right. It didn't matter how many stupid things Bonnie said, Bernadette was the real idiot of 1 Castle Court.

"Gar, it's Thomas," Mom called from the kitchen. I had been lying in my bed reading *Alpha Flight*, the only comic they sold at the Wawa up the street where Bernadette and Aunt Peggy worked. I pulled myself up to walk down the hall and pick up the phone.

"Hello?"

Thomas told me his mom and dad had said I could come over. I told him I would bring the *Aliens* video.

"Did you rent it again?"

I thought about the lies I told to hide how crazy my family was. Every time I started a new school, I pretended it was the first time we'd moved. When anybody asked, I said we moved because of dad's job. When the eighth-grader who sat behind me and Thomas asked why I had so many cars in my driveway, I said they were my dad's workers. I didn't think about him living in the neighborhood up the street from us. When he said, "I drove by your house last night, and all the cars were still there," I felt my face turn hot.

"Uh…Well…" I frantically put together a story that would cover my lie. "It was late. My dad's truck broke down. They didn't get home until seven."

"It was nine o'clock when we drove by."

"It was actually closer to eight o'clock. Are you sure it was nine?"

There was also the time Michael debated with the kid on our bus about us owning our house. The kid next to him said, "Nuh-uh, my aunt's a real estate agent. She said you're renting that house."

I knew the fourth-grade busybody was probably right. I wasn't even sure if we owned it, but I still said, "We bought it with someone. Your aunt wouldn't know that."

Thomas even added, "Is your aunt going to look up my house and tell me we don't own it either? Does she want everyone's address on the whole bus? Why does she care?"

The kid huffed. "No, she doesn't care, and neither do I." He crossed his arms and turned toward the window.

Dad had rented the *Aliens* video four or five weeks earlier. Uncle Dan, Anthony, and even Bernadette filled out applications, rented movies, and never returned them. I knew when Dad told the man that his name was Mike Mele, we probably weren't going to return *Aliens* either. All I thought about was when Aunt Lorraine had said, "Gar, you're going to love the movie. Ripley's awesome. Let me know when you watch it."

I smiled at the man behind the counter when he'd handed me the video, feeling guilty, knowing he'd probably never get it back.

319

I didn't realize how expensive the videos were until I saw the bill for thirty-four dollars. When the bill for seventy-eight dollars came, I got a knot in my stomach. No one in my family cared, but I was the one who had asked Dad to rent the movie.

I contemplated Thomas' question "Did you rent it again?" and wondered what he would say if I told him the truth. Would he go quiet? Would he ask why my family hadn't returned it? Would he say he realized he had stuff to do and that I shouldn't come over?

"Yeah, we rented it again. It's really good. You're gonna love it."

Doreen got a job at Cumberland Farms, the convenient store across the street from Wawa. I wanted to walk up and ask her what it was like living in Iowa all by herself, but I wouldn't go there, because it was next to the video store where Dad had rented *Aliens* for me. I was sure the owner of the video store would recognize me and come out yelling, "Where's my video and my seventy-eight dollars?"

Whenever I wanted a pint of chocolate chocolate chip ice cream, I'd walk up to Wawa. I asked, "Mom can I walk up to the store?" Uncle Dan answered for her, "Where are you going, Wawa?" I wanted to say, "No, I'm going to see Doreen," but I didn't want to risk lying to him. So, I told him I was.

He said, "Come on. I'll drive you. Bern's working."

When we pulled up, I could see Bernadette inside, behind the counter alone. I looked to see if they had a new *Alpha Flight* or any new Madonna magazines. Everything was the same as the week before, so I grabbed my ice cream and walked up to the register. Bernadette asked, "Is that all you want?"

"They don't have any new Madonna magazines. Do you have any behind the counter?"

Bernadette had bought me one the month before. She told me she had pulled it out of the box the day before they were supposed to put them out. "No, we haven't gotten any more, but grab some other stuff." She laughed. "Your Uncle Dan's paying for everything."

As I thought about what she said, I watched Uncle Dan place two six packs of beer on the counter. He hustled back down the aisle and started grabbing bags of potato chips and pretzels. He looked at me. "Grab some stuff. Get some candy for your brothers and sisters."

Steal? They were stealing. My stomach sank as I looked across the street at the Cumberland Farms sign, almost white in the bright sun. I thought about Doreen. I was sure she wasn't acting as an accomplice to some two-bit criminal stealing cigarettes and booze from her store. I should have walked there and risked getting yelled at by the video store owner.

Uncle Dan reached past me and started pulling sunglasses off the white rack. He pulled dark shades from each side. He opened a pair that looked like something Don Johnson would wear on *Miami Vice* and placed them on my face. He turned my cheek. "What do ya think, Bern?"

She pointed. "He'll look better with those."

Uncle Dan switched them out. "These?" My stomach tightened as I wondered if stealing sunglasses was enough to get you locked up in juvenile detention.

I didn't even want my ice cream anymore. I wanted to throw up as Uncle Dan and Bernadette loaded Snickers, pretzels, and about twenty packs of Marlboros in plastic bags. Uncle Dan put on his stolen shades and commanded, "Get those on, and grab that bag." We walked out the door, and I hustled to get in the car. I pushed the sunglasses close to my face and sank down in the seat as Uncle Dan turned the radio on.

As we drove home, Uncle Dan let out the laugh he'd held in. "Wooo!" I gave my best fake smile as Bon Jovi blared from the radio. "I'm a cowboy. On a steel horse, I ride..."

The day Aunt Susie was supposed to arrive, I sat at the kitchen table turning the pages of my Madonna magazine, wondering why she had cut her blond hair so short. I could hear Vincent behind me in the family room running around giggling hysterically while Uncle Jim lay on the couch reading his paperback book. Uncle Jim's careful whispers, "Please stop running, Vincent. Please stop" put a smirk on my face. I knew he was annoyed, but he wouldn't dare raise his voice to baby Vincent.

As I examined two different pictures, trying to figure out which was more recent, Christina walked by me. Whatever made Vincent so giddy got Christina, too. As soon as she stepped into the room, she tore after Vincent which made him squeal. Uncle Jim screamed. "Kath, these kids are running, and they won't listen!"

I stared at the photo of Madonna with white hair and bright red lipstick as my thoughts followed the angry knot in my stomach. I remembered the beginning of summer. Uncle Dan didn't even give a reason when he had bought Vincent a battery operated Bigfoot truck that he could ride in – five months after his birthday. Vincent jumped up and down, ran right over, and climbed up into the seat of the blue truck. He jerked forward and laughed. Uncle Dan laughed, too, and said, "Woah, easy on the pedal, Champ." Michael watched and probably wondered why Uncle Dan had never bought him a gift that nice. The only time Uncle Dad even paid attention to him was when he'd yell, "Stop sitting in front of the Nintendo. Get your ass outside and get some fresh air."

I also remembered how proud Bonnie was when she trotted in with her Toys R Us bag. She reached in and handed Michelle a Strawberry Shortcake doll as Christina looked on. Michelle sniffed the red hair, scrunched her nose, and smiled. "She smells like strawberries!" Then she got serious. "The next time you go to the store,

Bonnie, get me Blueberry Muffin." Bonnie got excited about Michelle's specific request like it was a command from the princess of the castle. I wanted to tell her that my four-year-old sister would have been giving orders to everyone in the house if they'd listen to her. It didn't mean she was in the royal family's good graces. It meant she was an imbecile.

Whenever I tried to bring up to Mom how some adults treated Vincent and Michelle differently than Michael and Christina, she'd snap at me. "They're not being nicer to them. They're the babies. Everyone treats you guys the same." Only Aunt Peggy and Shari, when Shari was still around, made an effort to make Christina feel as special as Michelle. Doreen would yell just as loudly at Vincent as she would Michael, and she never bought anyone presents trying to impress Mom or Dad. They were the exceptions. I wanted to tell Mom what I knew for sure, that most adults treated Vincent and Michelle better because they were Dad's real children, but I had to be careful bringing up anything about Dad not being my, Michael, and Christina's real father. Even though some adults viewed us as the children of Nick, who was still there, or Gary, who was gone, Mom had convinced herself that there was no difference between the five of us.

The anger I felt about the unfair treatment clenched at my gut. Why would an adult treat two children differently based on the presence of an adult blood relative? I thought about Uncle Jim's history with Aunt Susie – *Christina's* Aunt Susie, *Christina's* blood relative. I stood. "Christina, come in here. Aren't you excited to meet your Aunt Susie?"

I knew Uncle Jim was nervous as he put the tip of the cigarette he'd smoked down to the filter up to the one he was about to light. As both tips burned orange, I thought about how different he was when he didn't drink. His voice was soft when he spoke, and he didn't slam cabinets or ask, "You have a problem with that?" He never had a girlfriend for very long. His last one, Kelly, watched like she was waiting for him to get drunk. When Mom said she couldn't deal with his drinking, I wondered if he drank on purpose to make her break up with him. I also wondered if losing Aunt Susie and his son was the reason he had become an alcoholic.

When the doorbell rang, I followed Mom and Uncle Jim to the living room. Aunt Susie had wavy brown hair, down to her shoulders. She smiled brightly, like a new kid in school. She looked at me and put her hand on her mouth. "Oh, my God! Gary, you were a baby the last time I saw you. How old are you? Thirteen? Can I have a hug?"

I answered in a serious, adult-like tone. "I'll be fourteen in two weeks." As I put my arms around her back, I forgot about Uncle Jim. All I could think was that this was Gary's sister. Through the faint smell of Tide and Ivory soap, her skin smelled familiar. I shut my eyes, breathed in, and wondered if that was what Gary had smelled like. I squeezed her as tightly as she squeezed me.

As the adults mingled in the kitchen, Aunt Susie's kids, my cousins – Michael, Michelle, and Josh – ran out the front door with Michael, Christina, Vincent, and Michelle. Aunt Susie was explaining how things didn't work out with her ex-husband, Michael, when I piped up. "Well, you're better off without him if he didn't appreciate you, Aunt Susie." When she got quiet, I tried to figure out what I'd said wrong. Bonnie, Julie, even Bernadette loved when I said things like that.

Aunt Susie tilted her head down, like a teacher, and said, "You should go outside and throw a ball with your cousin. This is an adult conversation."

I looked at Mom, but she just gave me a sheepish grin to let me know I should listen to Aunt Susie and go.

I smiled and said, "Uh, yeah, I think I'll go outside. That's a good idea. Yeah."

By the third night of their visit, I realized, even though Aunt Susie had made mistakes with men, she took being a mother very seriously. She stepped out the front door and called, "Michael, Michelle, Josh – you have a half hour. I want you in this house, not a minute after 8 o'clock."

My cousin Michelle, who was a year younger than me, looked over at me. "I wish my mom was like your mom. She never tells you what time you have to be in."

I thought about how Mom did tell us when to come in, sometimes. She usually just did it through me. It depended on how involved she was in a conversation with Bernadette, Julie, or another adult. I would be in the kitchen, mostly just listening, when Mom would say, "Gar, tell the kids to come in."

Sometimes I'd volunteer. "It's almost 9:30. I'm going to tell the kids it's time to come in."

I figured it must be 8 o'clock when the front door clicked open again. Michael, Michelle, and Josh ran across the yard leaving the five of us alone in the warm dark. As crickets chirped, Michael, Christina, and Vincent darted around the yard cupping lightening bugs in their hands. I thought about Aunt Susie inside, probably wondering how late we'd stay out past 8 o'clock. I knew Mom wouldn't worry, knowing I was outside, too, but I imagined the disappointing look I'd get from Aunt Susie if we stayed out much longer. I clapped my hands. "Come on, guys. It's time to go in."

A couple of weeks after Aunt Susie left, Mom asked me what I wanted for my birthday. I thought about Cijay and knew we were never going to find her. I had read in *Bird Talk* magazine about different kinds of parrots. Some were as intelligent as people and could understand and answer questions. I imagined a little companion that was only mine that I'd never lose.

"Do you think I can get a parrot?"

Mom asked, "How much are they?"

I knew it would be too much. "Like two hundred dollars, but I wouldn't want anything else, and you don't have to give me allowance."

"Wow! She's huge," Michael said.

"Does she bite like Cijay?" Vincent asked.

I was focused on my new bird; whose dark metal cage was as big as our desk. "Her name is Margie. Cijay didn't bite, but she will. Don't put your fingers in her cage, Vincent." Christina and Michelle knew they weren't allowed in our room without knocking, so they stood at the door, watching, mesmerized by the huge green bird. Once I was sure the door and feed cups were locked tight, I turned toward Christina and Michelle

"You guys can come in, but don't put your fingers in the cage."

When we picked Margie up from the breeder, Mom had said, "I didn't realize an Amazon parrot would be so big."

The lady with the short, black hair and bird poop streaked down the back of her shirt answered, "I know you have younger kids. Don't let them poke at her and tease her. She'll be very loyal to one person."

I knew that person was going to be me. I also knew Mom wasn't worried about anyone teasing the bird. She'd looked at my parrot's solid black, hooked beak and probably imagined Vincent's little pinky getting popped off, as Dad set the cage in the back seat next to me.

Mom looked back and smiled. "You like her, Gar? Just be careful with the other kids, ok?"

I didn't take Margie outside. I spent most of my time with her in my room. I talked to her in a soft baby voice, sure that she understood what I was saying. "Are you a good girl? Are you? Do you want a peanut?"

Dad bought me dried, unsalted peanuts in the shell. When I would take one out of the bag, Margie would KACK and dilate her orangey, gold eyes. She used her foot like a hand and held it as she peeled the shell and crumbled up the peanut. She mumbled to herself when we turned the light off for bed.

Vincent asked, "What's she saying, Gar?"

I whispered, "She's talking to herself."

He giggled. "Really?"

I was in my room talking to Margie when I heard Mom and Bernadette yelling from the kitchen. I could tell from Mom's tone she was annoyed by something stupid Bernadette had said. I opened the door to listen when I heard a small crash and a BING. Did somebody just throw the phone? I wondered.

Doreen yelled, "There's a baby in here, you fucking idiot!"

There was a scuffle, and Mom screamed, "Doreen! Bernadette!" I heard a BOM BOM as someone ran for the front door.

I darted to my window and saw Bernadette walking out and slamming the front door behind her. She started walking toward the driveway when Doreen swung the door open.

"Get back here, you fat bitch!"

Bernadette screamed back, "Fuck you!" and held up her middle finger. I saw Doreen's teeth as she took off after her. I ran out to the kitchen. Bonnie was holding Joseph.

I asked, "What happened?"

Bonnie stuttered, "I… I… I don't know. Bernadette threw the phone at your Mom, and Doreen went after her."

The front door opened and Doreen's voice was angry. "She's lucky I didn't kill her."

I walked down the hall toward her. "Is everything ok?"

Doreen ignored me.

Mom said, "Gar, everything's fine. Don't worry about it."

A couple of days after Doreen and Bernadette's fight, Aunt Peggy asked, "Did she really beat the shit out of her, Kath?"

"Yeah, she knocked her flat on her ass, Peg."

Aunt Peggy put her hand over her mouth. "Oh, my God. She shouldn't have thrown the phone at you." "Well, when she comes over, don't say anything about it, Peg. I don't want her to feel uncomfortable."

Bernadette came over after work. "Hey, Kath, I brought some stuff for the kids." She dumped out a bag of Reese's and Milky Way's on the table. Christina and Vincent ran right over. Bernadette looked at me. "Gar, I got a new Madonna magazine for you."

I took it and flipped through. There were all sorts of pictures of her new movie, *Who's that Girl.* "This is so cool. Thanks, Bernadette!"

She turned to Mom. "We're going to see her in concert. I want to take Gary."

Madonna? In person? Before Mom could answer, I blurted out, "Mom, please! Please!"

She looked concerned. "Bern, I don't think so. I don't want him seeing her. She shows her boobs." I knew Mom was thinking of *Penthouse* magazine. I had read that those pictures were taken when Madonna was a model in New York.

I panicked. "Mom, she doesn't show her boobs. The pictures were from when she modeled."

She started to lose her patience. "Gary, no! I don't care! You're not going to see her. She's a pig! Madonna? She should change her name to Ma-Pigga or Ma-Whora! No, you're not going."

I ran to my room and slammed the door. Uncle Dan could talk about everyone's titties, jugs, bazooms, and flapjacks, but Madonna showed her boobs one time, and she was called a whore and a pig. I threw myself on my bed and screamed into my pillow. I hated Mom. She was so unfair. I sat up and whispered, "Hey Margie, I can't wait to get us out of this place. I'll see Madonna whenever I want, and I'll take you with me."

I didn't understand why Doreen would rather stay and work at Cumberland Farms than go with us to Florida. I even tried to convince her. "Dor, I'll help with the kids. Plus, it'll be fun."

"Thanks, Gar, but I've only got a few more weeks before I go back home. I don't want to quit yet."

Once Mom accepted that Doreen wasn't going to join our road trip, she turned her focus to Julie. "Jule, Hon, you should come with us. We're paying for the condo and everything. You can help me with the kids, and it'll be a great vacation."

As we packed into the Station Wagon, Christina and Michelle between me and Julie, and Michael and Vincent in the far back, I got excited. After I shushed Michael and Vincent and told Michelle to sit back, I asked, "How many days will it take to get there, Dad?"

He finished explaining to Mom, "I don't need the map to get to 95, Kath," then answered, "like three days, Gar."

"Are we stopping anywhere on the way to Florida?"

"Not on the way down, Gar."

I figured we must be stopping to see Gary on the way back. I turned to Christina as we backed out of the driveway. "It's going to be a fun vacation."

When we crossed the bridge to Fort Meyers Beach, Michael told Vincent, "That's the ocean."

Julie corrected him. "That's the Gulf of Mexico, Michael."

Michael gave her a funny look. "It looks like the ocean."

"Well, it's connected to the ocean, but it's considered a separate body of water."

Bvvvvvvvvt

I didn't care if it was the Red Sea. The water looked beautiful, and I wanted to smell the salty air.

As we turned onto the street where Dad said the condo was, Vincent asked, "Are there palm trees at the condo? Can I get a coconut?"

Everyone laughed, and Dad looked in the mirror. "We'll get you a coconut, Vince. Don't worry."

The tall white building had a big "S" on it that must have spanned three floors. After we shut the car doors, we walked up to the building. There was a bridge over a pond full of fat yellow, orange and white goldfish.

Michael looked down. "Neat! Gar, look at how huge they are." When we walked inside, it smelled like suntan lotion. Everyone behind the counter was wearing white shirts and smiling.

Dad said, "We're here to check in. It's under Kathleen Mele."

From our room, we could see the beach and hear the ocean waves.

Christina ran to the railing. "Dad, are we going swimming in the ocean?"

"Yeah, tomorrow. Then we're going out on a boat."

Mom said, "Gar, make sure everyone's bags are in their rooms. We're going up to see Aunt Lorraine and Uncle Mike."

Aunt Lorraine answered the door and gave each of us a hug. Once everyone was inside, she whispered, "How'd it feel driving down, smashed in like sardines, Gar?"

I started giggling. "It was crazy." She began cracking up.

"Did Julie help you take care of the kids, Gar?" I laughed so hard I lost my breath.

Aunt Lorraine said, "Ok, ok we have to stop" as she wiped tears from her eyes.

When we went out on the boat the next day, Dad and Uncle Mike took turns waterskiing. After several passes, they tried to get the women in the water. Mom said, "I don't want to get my hair wet," which meant she didn't want her wig flying into the Gulf of Mexico.

Julie was polite. "No, it's ok. I'll stay in the boat with the kids." Aunt Lorraine was the only other one. She bobbed in the water with her orange life vest and her skis sticking out in front of her.

Uncle Mike yelled, "Ya ready?" He revved the engine and jerked everyone in the boat. Aunt Lorraine quickly rose up and for a couple of seconds looked like a real water skier. Then her feet started to separate until she did a split and splashed down in the water.

Mom howled, "Aaaaaah ha ha ha ha! You looked like Olive Oil, Lorraine!"

Mom's laughing usually made people mad. When Uncle Dan had stepped in a hole that Michael and Vincent dug near the sidewalk, they ran to the bedroom when they saw him limping to the front door, cursing. Mom cracked up as she opened the front door to Uncle Dan's – "Fuck! Shit! Mother fucker! It's not funny, Kath!"

I wasn't sure how Aunt Lorraine would react to Mom's laughing at her, but she smirked as Uncle Mike and Dad pulled her into the boat. I knew she was being sarcastic as she dried her hair, "You sure you don't want to try, Gar? It's loads of fun."

I laughed. "No thanks, Aunt Lorraine."

Mom didn't say anything about seeing Gary during the whole vacation. We drove up I-75 to I-4 when we left to go home. I knew the next road, I-95, was the one that went through Georgia. When we stopped at McDonald's for lunch, I asked, "Mom can I talk to you for a second?" We walked over to the counter with the napkins and ketchup.

"What is it, Gar?"

"Uh, um, I was just wondering when we're going to stop and see Gary."

"Oh Gar, I don't know if we're gonna be able to stop, and he never called."

I felt my chest tighten. She put her hand on my shoulder and smiled sweetly. "Gar, you didn't really want to see him, did you?"

I forced a quick smile. "No, no, I was just wondering. This vacation was so much fun, Mom. We really should do it again next year."

Saint Paul

The upper grades at Saint Paul the Apostle switched classrooms for different subjects, I assumed, to make it feel like high school. When the bell rang, the students scooped up their books and popped out of their desks to head off to social studies or religion, which were being taught across the hall. But unlike high school, every homeroom class, like a traveling caravan of students, stayed together as the class changes progressed throughout the day. When I was in seventh grade, I'd heard stories about kids who were best friends in sixth grade, but once they were assigned to different homerooms, they developed new friendships and barely spoke the next year.

When Thomas called and asked, "Did you get your homeroom assignment yet?" I felt my stomach go empty. I was so happy about going to the same school two years in a row that I didn't think about the possibility of Thomas and I being in different classes.

"No, did you?"

"I'm in Sister Luke Kathryn's class."

Sister Luke Kathryn was one of the only nuns left at the school. I wasn't sure if that was why Mom liked her, or if it was because she was black. Sister Luke Kathryn would stand next to Sister Francis in the hall, straight up, with her hands behind her back and her lips tight. Sister Luke Kathryn was known for being super strict. There was a rumor that she made a kid lay his hand on her desk, where she whapped his fingers with a ruler in front of the entire class. Thomas and I didn't understand why several of the eighth-grade girls had sobbed as they hugged her goodbye on the last day of school. Regardless, I still wanted to be in the same class as Thomas.

"Hold on a sec." I ran out the front door to the mailbox. When I saw the envelope with the St. Paul emblem, I took a breath and pushed my finger under the flap to tear it open. Gary Mele, eighth grade homeroom: Sister Luke Kathryn. I ran back inside, picked up the phone and panted. "I'm… in her class, too."

"Awesome!"

Uncle Dan walked into the kitchen. "Gar, you wanna take a ride? I'm gonna pick up some wings for the game."

I was so happy about being in the same class as Thomas that I didn't care that Uncle Dan just wanted me along for company. "Yeah, I'll go."

Uncle Dan parked the car. "I'm just gonna run in. I'll be right back." I watched as shopping carts clanged against light poles, and people jogged in different directions across the parking lot. Some were going into the grocery store, others the record store. As Uncle Dan walked into the bar, I wondered who would be sitting in a dark, smoky bar on a sunny afternoon.

After a few minutes, Uncle Dan stepped back out with his brown, stapled paper bag. A tall man whose tee-shirt was stretched tight across his muscled chest hustled out after him. He grabbed Uncle Dan's collar and yanked him backward. As Uncle Dan turned around, the guy swatted, and the bag of wings exploded onto the sidewalk. The guy clenched Uncle Dan's shirt by his shoulder as he threw a punch with his other hand. Uncle Dan's arms and fists popped up, just like a boxer, to cover his face.

A lady screamed as she ran with her carriage of groceries. A man hollered, "Call the cops!" Uncle Dan stumbled to get his balance and then threw a punch back at the guy. He threw another, hit the man in the face, and yanked himself out of the guy's grip.

Uncle Dan pulled his shirt down and yelled, "Come on mother fucker!" Other men came out of the bar and stood between the two. My heart raced as I got out of the car.

BWOOP BWOOP

Two police cars pulled in as a crowd of people formed on the walkway and in the parking lot. The man being held back by his friends hollered, "I'll kill you, Danny!" His cheek was red where Uncle Dan had punched him. I pushed through the crowd to where Uncle Dan was. He wiped his face with his shirt, then motioned for me with his hand.

"Come here."

He pulled my head so close his mouth was touching my ear. He panted. "My name's Daniel Kelly, Daniel Kelly." He pushed me back and looked in my eyes. "You got that, right?"

I nodded my head. "Yeah."

Two officers walked over to the man, and two walked over to Uncle Dan. I stepped back. My chest pounded. The man begged with the officers. "That's Danny Canaley. I know it. He's Jimmy Canaley's brother."

One of the officers with Uncle Dan responded. "He said his name's Daniel Kelly."

Uncle Dan sounded shocked and angry. "I don't know who this man is, but I want to press charges."

The man's face started drawing in like he just realized he'd made a huge mistake. He cried out, "Man, I'm sorry! I thought you were someone else."

Uncle Dan folded his arms and repeated, "I want to press charges." After one set of officers handcuffed the other guy and drove away, one of the two who had been talking to Uncle Dan walked back from his police car and whispered something to the other officer. Most of the crowd had begun leaving, but I was still standing in the parking lot.

The officer who had been talking to Uncle Dan motioned for me to follow him to the sidewalk, away from Uncle Dan. My heart raced as he looked at me. "Is that your uncle?"

I swallowed. "Yes, Sir."

"What's his name?"

"Daniel Kelly."

"Are you sure about that? Are you sure his name isn't Daniel Canaley?"

I felt the palms of my hands getting cold and wet. I debated in my mind whether I should tell the officer the truth. Could I get in trouble for lying to a cop? He probably knew who Uncle Dan was, anyway. What would it matter?

I answered, "I've always known him as Daniel Kelly." The officer squinted as I stood there motionless, only barely moving my fingers in my palms.

The policeman turned to his partner. "We need to take him to the station." He looked back at me. "We'll call your parents when we get there."

The officer opened the door to the police car. "When we get to the station, I'll let you out." My heart pounded again as I ducked into the back seat. After he slammed the door, I looked at Uncle Dan. He was staring forward with his hands cuffed behind him.

I knew Uncle Dan wasn't going to talk. He had always said, "Don't say anything in front of cops." As he stared at the black grate between the officers and us, I wondered how many times he'd been in the back of a police car. My stomach dropped. What if a kid from school was in that crowd and had seen everything? Uncle Dan being put in handcuffs? Me being put into a police car? I slouched away from the door and put my hand on the side of my head, so no one could see my face.

When we got to the police station, the officer opened my door. I watched as his partner took Uncle Dan through a door that slammed with a loud bang. The officer with me said, "I need you to tell me again what your uncle's name is."

I felt my heart beating as I answered. "Daniel... Kelly." He led me to the cold waiting area. "We've called your parents. Wait in here."

When we got home, I walked down the hall to my room. Michael asked, "Gar, what happened?" I ignored him and flopped down on my bed. "Gar?" he said in a soft voice. I got up and put my finger against one of the thin black bars of Margie's cage. Her tiny gray talons made metal echoes as she climbed over to my finger. She turned her head as I rubbed her neck.

I finally answered. "Nothing happened, Michael. Uncle Dan got into a fight and got arrested. That's all."

After I snapped at him, I felt bad. I was thinking about something nice to say when the front door opened to the muffled sound of Uncle Dan's excited voice. When I heard, "Where's Gary?" I knew I needed to walk out. Uncle Dan grabbed the back of my neck and pulled me close. "Good job, Champ! Good job."

I wasn't sure if the excitement was because we were going to the same school, actually starting on the first day of school, or because all five of us were going to school. Michelle's face beamed when she ran out wearing the same gray, plaid smock as Christina.

Mom began brushing Michelle's hair into a ponytail. "Michelle, hold still, Honey."

Bernadette asked, "Kath, do you want me to do Christina's hair?"

"Yeah, thanks Bern." Mom answered as she looked in their direction. "Christina, what have you got on your uniform?"

Christina whined. "I didn't do anything." The truth was she'd been running around the house with Vincent while Mom was getting Michelle dressed.

Mom walked over and grabbed Christina's arm. "Get over here!" She took a blue rag from the corner of the sink and started scratching at the smudge on Christina's chest.

We stepped onto the bus and Michelle plopped right down in the first seat. She turned to the boy next to her. "What grade are you in? My brother said these seats are for kindergarteners."

Vincent and Christina took their seats where they were supposed to. Michael stopped and gave me a defeated grin as he sat next to the new fourth graders. I felt horrible for him. At least when I was left back, I repeated the first grade in a different school. I gave him the same sad smile Mom had given me whenever I asked her when we were going to live normal. As I made my way to the back of the bus, I got excited when I saw Thomas in the very last seat. I dropped down next to him, looked out the windows of the back door at the street and cars behind us, and thought how cool it was.

Sister Luke Kathryn sat at her desk with a pencil in her hand. She scanned the room with her eyes, without moving her head. I looked around, too. Mario, the boy with black hairs on his upper lip, who sometimes hung out with Thomas and me at recess, was in the other class. The tall, thin, blond girl, Angela, was in our class, but her best friend, Kathy, was in the other class, too. It was split, almost in half, the number of kids that had been in my and Thomas' seventh-grade class but were now in the other homeroom. In addition to noticing the kids who were gone, I scanned the faces of the kids that were new. Colleen O'Brien was in our class.

The year before, the entire seventh-grade class had taken a vote for class President. It was between Erin Murphy and Colleen. The day before the vote, Colleen had come over to me and Thomas at recess and smiled. "Gary? Thomas? I'll remember if you two vote for me." She giggled, flipped her blond hair, and proceeded to the next set of kids to talk to. Even though Erin seemed more genuine, we both voted for Colleen because she made a point to talk to us. I wasn't surprised when she won. I wondered what it was going to be like being in the same class as her.

It was the first time in my life that the reasons I didn't like school were the same as every other kid's. Sitting through an hour of pre-algebra made the fact that I'd stayed up in bed thinking for almost two hours excruciating. Some of the kids were able to sleep with their fists pressed in their cheeks, but I was afraid of the look I'd get after a desk drawer slammed to wake me up. I held my sleep for the weekends.

There was a distant sounding bum bum bum . . . bum bum bum. I blinked and rubbed my eyes as I realized I wasn't dreaming. Someone was knocking at the front door. I yawned and looked out the window. The lady we got Margie from was there with her husband. In one breath I was completely awake. Why was she at our house? I got a terrible knot in my stomach as I looked at Margie. She tilted her head at me and garbled. I heard the front door open. I pressed my ear to our bedroom door. I could tell, even though muffled, what the woman was saying. "Where is she? Where is the bird?"

My heart sunk further as I looked at Margie. "Shhh… shhh." When I heard the talking get louder, I wondered what I should do. I sat back down on my bed and put my hands in my lap.

The bedroom door opened. Mom followed the two people in. "Please, it was a mistake. The money's in the bank now."

The woman ignored Mom's pleading. She scanned Margie's cage with her eyes. "This is filthy." She turned to her husband like they were the only two people in the room, and I was invisible. "Grab the cage. We're going."

I imagined standing up and screaming, "You're not taking my bird anywhere!" but I would have only done that if I was shocked it was happening. I wasn't shocked or upset. I was embarrassed that it had been over a week since I had cleaned Margie's cage. I wished I had scraped the dried, white poop from the grate on the bottom and put fresh newspaper in the night before. Maybe then the woman would have felt guilty taking Margie from someone who took such good care of her, even though his parents wrote her bad checks. The man picked up the cage and followed his wife out of the room.

I sat and stared at the wall until I heard their car drive away. I blinked and forced my eyes to move away from the section of the wall that'd turned blurry. I got up and looked at the square outline of seed shells left on the empty desk. I picked up one of the soft, baby-down feathers that had grown underneath Margie's sleek, green feathers. I felt my throat tighten but stopped it by thinking; *I don't care.* I said it over and over in my mind.

Mom appeared at my door. "Gar, we're going to get her back. I promise. Don't worry."

I thought about the year before at school when Sister Francis had called me to the office. Everyone had watched as I walked out of the classroom.

Sister Francis had told me, "Gary, we need to speak to your parents about the last tuition check. I need you to tell them to call."

"Uh, uh, yes Sister Francis." I tried to explain. "Our phone … my uncle… Maybe they didn't get the –"

She spoke over me. "Just have them call." She motioned. "You can go back to class."

On the bus, Thomas whispered, "Why'd you have to go to the office?"

"Oh, Sister Francis was asking about Michelle. I don't know why she was asking me instead of my mom and dad."

I could tell by the look on Thomas' face that he didn't totally believe me, but he still replied, "They think my parents don't speak English. Nuns are weird."

When I got home, I told Mom what Sister Francis had said.

"Gar, your dad just got paid for the last job. I'm sorry, Honey. Don't worry about it."

I looked at Mom's face and knew she felt terrible about Margie. Was it her fault? Was it Dad's? Who wrote the bad checks? I was sure they never expected the woman to show up at our house.

I said, "Ok, Mom. I know you're going to get her back. I'm going to call Thomas."

As I walked past her, she touched my arm. "Gar, I'm really sorry, Honey." I thought about the stolen videos, candy, Madonna magazines, and now Margie.

I put on my best fake smile. "Mom, I know" then walked to the kitchen and picked up the telephone.

A few minutes after I got to Thomas' house, he pulled out his newest *Dungeons & Dragons* book. "It has information about the ethereal plane that I told you about." I had been excited when Thomas had told me about it on the bus ride home on Friday. That was before Margie was taken. I lifted the cover to look at the crazy one-eyed monster.

As I imagined what it would be like if I went to the ethereal plane, Thomas asked, "Are you ok? You seem like you're upset."

I turned on the fake smile again. "I'm fine." My eyes moved to the glass door.

I stared at the sunlight flickering off the water in his swimming pool. It was September, and too cold to swim. I imagined holding my arms out and sinking below the frigid water, breathing in and drowning.

"Are you sure you're alright?" Thomas asked again.

I turned and looked at him. "Thomas, I need to tell you something."

"What?"

"Well… my family is kind of… crazy."

"What do you mean?"

348

"Um, well, my Uncle Jim is an alcoholic. My Uncle Dan is a criminal. I was even with him when he got arrested. All those people that are always at my house – well, most of them live with us."

"So what?"

I gave a nervous laugh as relief coursed through my body. Thomas laughed, too. "It's not you."

"It's crazy," I said. "I can't talk about my family because they're so crazy."

Thomas paused for a couple of seconds, then told me, "My mom hits me with a two by four if I get bad grades."

I was so shocked by what he'd said I went quiet. Then, as I thought about how crazy it was, I started to smile. I wasn't happy that he got beat for getting bad grades. I was happy to know I wasn't the only one with a ridiculous secret.

"Really?"

"Yeah, she gets really mad. You're not the only one with a crazy family." After a couple of seconds, we both started laughing. We laughed so hard we lost our breath and cried.

As we pulled ourselves together, between chuckles, Thomas said, "Don't say anything, ok?"

"I won't. You won't say anything either, right?"

"Never."

When I got home from Thomas' house, I swept the seeds and dust from the desk into my hand. Christina walked in. "Gar, are you sad about Margie?" I could see that she was sad for me.

"A little." I brushed the handful of tiny, dried shells into the garbage.

Christina smiled and reached to give me a hug. I smiled back and hugged her tight. "It's ok, Christina."

On the day we got our first quarterly report card, most of the kids in class compared grades with their friends and talked about which teachers were unfair. Thomas slid his into his book bag and kept quiet, which was fine with me. I didn't want to talk about my grades. It wasn't until we'd taken our seats on the bus that he whispered, "Be sure no one sees me." He placed his science book between us, then pulled the tan card out and laid it down.

I asked, "What are you doing?"

He shushed me. "If you're careful, you can scrape the grade off with a razor and then change it."

It seemed risky to me. I whispered, "But after your parents sign it, you have to give it back to Sister Luke Kathryn. She'll see that you changed the grade."

"I'll change it back again." Thomas began to scrape. Once he was done, I looked. He was right. There were clean, empty boxes where the Cs and Ds had been. He neatly wrote A's in the boxes, then asked me if I wanted him to do mine.

I laughed. "My parents don't care about my grades. Plus, I don't want to risk Sister Luke Kathryn. You better hope you don't get caught."

When I walked in the front door, Mom was telling Bernadette, "The morning sickness will go away in a few weeks, Bern."

Bernadette huffed. "Danny's being a jerk off. I never should have gotten pregnant."

She's the jerk off, I thought, for letting him get her pregnant. I handed Mom my report card.

"Gar, you can do better than this, but at least you got an A in religion."

Mom signed the card, handed it back to me, and continued, "Bern, he doesn't know how to show emotion, so he's being an asshole. Don't let it get to you."

I walked into my bedroom and dropped my book bag on the desk. Michael and Vincent walked in after me.

As Vincent struggled with the clip on his tie, he asked, "How does Bernadette know she's pregnant?"

"She looks like she's pregnant all the time," Michael said, which made Vincent giggle.

I knew Bernadette's being fat wasn't something they were supposed to be making fun of. I told both of them, "She went to the doctor, and he told her." I left the room and walked down the hall.

I flipped the light on in the bathroom and thought about how light bulbs made rooms look dingy and yellow. I liked the way fluorescent lights made everything bright, bluish white, like at Pathmark. I looked at myself in the mirror and wondered if everyone in the whole world felt like they were too thin or too fat. No matter how much chocolate, chocolate chip ice cream and Snickers I ate, I still stayed skinny. Dad called me "Stretch" because I was thin and because I'd grown a couple of inches taller than him. I leaned in and smiled. More than being tall and thin, I hated my teeth.

Mom had said, "It's not that bad," but I didn't like the space between my two front teeth. As I turned my cheek, I was glad at least I didn't have acne. I knew Julie thought it was a compliment, but it still felt weird when she told me I had nice skin. It seemed like something Anthony or Uncle Dan would say that only fags cared about.

The next day in science class, I wondered why some of the kids called our teacher Mr. Drabface. His eyes were set deep, and by late afternoon he looked like he needed to shave. I wasn't sure if that was the reason for the nickname or if it was because he wore his tie loosely and his pants pulled up too high. He was definitely the most boring teacher. He would try to get the kids engaged, but it always felt phony, like he didn't really care. Even when Sister Luke Kathryn explained the difference between past and present participles, it was obvious how much she loved English.

Everyone sat up and paid attention when Drabface began explaining how all creatures had jobs – ants, honeybees, even elephants. He seemed genuinely excited when he asked, "Angela, what does your father do for a living?" After she answered, Drabface started popping around the room asking everyone.

Some kids were proud to answer. "My father is a defense attorney," or, "My dad is a doctor."

When he got to Megan, she looked uncomfortable but still answered. "My father's a carpenter."

I felt my face get warm as I answered, "Uh, my dad's a roofer."

Thomas said, "My parents own a dry cleaner."

It was Colleen's turn. She sat straight up in her desk, folded her hands, and stated, "It's none of your business what my father does."

The whole class gasped. Thomas and I were thinking the same thing as we looked at each other. Woah! Could she get away with saying that? I looked at Colleen as she stared at Drabface, defiantly.

"Fine! Fine, Colleen," he said, not quite loud enough to be yelling, but still obviously angry. He slammed his book open. "Turn to page 23."

The next morning in homeroom, the kids whispered with excitement. "I can't believe you said that to him," and, "he got so mad."

Colleen said proudly, "Well, it was none of his business, and I told him so."

I didn't usually talk to anyone but Thomas, but even I felt compelled to tell her, "It was really awesome." She gave the same fake smile she had given when I said I'd vote for her.

On the bus ride home, I asked Thomas, "Did your mom and dad say I could spend the night on Friday?" When Thomas' parents spoke to me, they'd usually just say "yes," "no," or "ok," but speak their full sentences in Korean to Thomas.

Even though his parents didn't talk much to me, I knew they liked me because I was respectful. I always said, "thank you" and was the first to get up to clear the dishes when they made dinner.

Thomas told me, "I did ask them... if I could spend the night at your house."

I had never had a friend sleep over my house. When I did have friends, like Brad, we would ask his mom, but she always said "no." When I finally understood why she always said "no," I stopped asking or hoping ever to have a friend spend the night at my house.

"What did they say?"

Thomas grinned. "Of course, they said yes."

Michael, Christina, Vincent, and Michelle were more excited than me that we were having someone sleep over. When Thomas got off at our stop with his book bag and his duffle bag, they all started chattering, asking questions, and offering their toys and beds.

"Guys," I said, "we're sleeping on the floor in my room. I don't want you bothering us the whole time."

Mom opened the front door with a big smile. "Hi, Thomas!"

Oh my God, I thought, Thomas knew my family was crazy. I didn't tell him they were weird, too. He said, "hi" to Mom, and then looked at me. "Where's your room?"

We walked past the kitchen, where Uncle Dan and Anthony were talking, and down the hall to my bedroom. Thomas put his bags on the desk and looked around. "You share this with Michael and Vincent?"

"Yeah, they sleep in the bunk beds. Do you want something to drink?"

When I came back with a cup of Coke, Thomas pulled out his D&D books. "Do you want to play with your brother? It'd be cool to have an extra person. I can be the dungeon master."

I shrugged. "Sure." I called, "Michael!"

Once Michael understood the idea that the game was completely in your imagination, he asked, "Am I going to cast spells?"

"Not at first," I said. "You have to gain experience."

Michael picked up the die. "Oh, ok."

After we'd played for about an hour, I heard someone's voice getting louder from the kitchen. I opened the bedroom door just as Anthony screamed into the phone, "You're a cunt, and you can suck my cock!"

I cringed as Anthony smashed and ground the handset until it clicked, and the bell from inside the phone clanged.

I turned and gave Thomas a nervous smile just as Uncle Dan started in. "Fuck her and that other dumb bitch, Bonnie. She's been fillin' her head with shit because you're Joe's brother."

I looked at Thomas. "I'll be right back. Sorry."

I clicked the door behind me and snuck down the hall. "Mom!" She only had to look at me, and she knew.

She turned to the kitchen. "Danny! Anthony! Gary has a friend over." I walked back to my room with a knot in my gut. It was one thing for Thomas to say he understood my crazy family. It was another thing for him to actually experience it. When I opened the bedroom door, he was explaining the different levels to Michael.

Again, I said, "Sorry about that," as I squatted on the floor.

356

The door opened behind me, and Uncle Dan stuck his head in. "Sorry about that, guys."

Thomas looked up, shrugged, and smiled. "It's ok."

As Thomas and I lay on the floor in the dark, I whispered, "Now, do you see how crazy my family is?"

"That was it? That wasn't anything." Then he said, "Your brother's actually pretty good. He catches on fast."

I rolled onto my back, stared at the dark blue shadows on the ceiling and thought that Thomas was the best friend I could ever have before falling asleep.

The first day back to school after Christmas break was depressing but exciting at the same time. The entire class was talking about what they got for Christmas and where they had gone on vacation. I didn't notice the lady from the office whispering in Sister Luke Kathryn's ear until Sister Luke Kathryn called, "Gary."

She told me that the principal needed to see me, and my stomach dropped. When I walked into the school office, Sister Francis motioned for me to go into her private office. After she closed the door, she sat down and began, "Gary, we're having a difficult time reaching your parents, and we need to speak to them." The energy drained from my body.

When I got home from school, Mom was listening to the stereo in the living room. She looked at me and mouthed the words, "Tell me lies, tell me sweet little lies…." I had no interest in watching her pretend she was part of Fleetwood Mac.

I interrupted. "Mom, I need to talk to you."

"What is it, Gar?"

"Sister Francis called me out of class, in front of everyone, to her office. She's been trying to call you and Dad about our tuition. Mom, I don't want to change schools. Will you please call her and make sure the tuition is paid?"

"Gar, we're gonna pay the tuition, Honey."

"Mom, I'm serious. Please make sure."

It was a couple of months later when the lady from the principal's office asked to speak to Sister Luke Kathryn out in the hall. I knew it couldn't be about our tuition again. Mom had yelled not just at Dad but at Anthony and Uncle Dan about finishing the jobs they had started and making sure they had new jobs lined up. She showed me when she wrote out the check. "This is for all five of you, and we're all caught up."

Mom smiled when I smiled. "I love you, Gar. You're going to graduate eighth grade, and we're gonna throw a big party. I promise."

Sister Luke Kathryn opened the door, and the whole class held their breath. She said, "Thomas, I need to speak to you out here please." My heart dropped as Thomas walked out of the room. I thought about our third quarter report card which we had just turned back in. I remembered being on the bus as Thomas changed grades. He had changed the first and second quarter grades again, too. All the scraping with the razor had started to wear on those boxes.

I had even warned him. "Thomas, you can kind of tell, especially with the first quarter."

"No, there's no way to tell. They're not even going to look at it."

When Thomas denied it – "No, there's no way to tell. They're not even going to look at it" – I felt bad. I didn't want to make him worry, so I gave a reassuring smile. "Yeah, I'm sure you're right."

When Sister Luke Kathryn opened the door again, I could hear Thomas' voice. It sounded like he'd been crying. I wanted to get up and tell her she couldn't tell his mom because she'd beat him, but I sat in my seat and didn't move. I felt terrible. I watched as Thomas came back into the room and walked to his desk. He sat and looked down. Sister Luke Kathryn walked in behind him.

"Does everyone have their assignment ready?" The whole class scrambled for their books.

As soon as we took our seats on the bus, I asked Thomas what had happened.

"Sister Luke Kathryn told me she has to call my parents, but she's going to give me extra credit work to help with some of the grades. She was really nice."

I thought about how Thomas got punished but didn't get beaten as he hugged Sister Luke Kathryn on the last day of school. His mom was way nicer than he expected her to be. Whatever Sister Luke Kathryn said to her must have kept her calm.

When Sister Luke Kathryn hugged me, she looked into my eyes and smiled. "Gary, you're very smart. I expect you to work hard in high school."

"I will, Sister Luke Kathryn."

It felt like a movie when they had us throw our graduation caps. All the students laughed and hugged each other goodbye. Everyone had their own graduation party to go to. Mom had all sorts of relatives I'd never met coming to my party. She hired a DJ to set up on the front lawn, and she told me I could have him play as much Madonna as I wanted. I hugged Thomas last before we left for my celebration.

He smiled. "Don't eat too much food, and don't let your family get too crazy at the party."

I laughed. "I won't. You either. And I'll call you tomorrow."

Marlboro

When Mom opened the front door and shook her head no, Uncle Dan looked surprised. "What? You've got to be kidding me."

Uncle Jim was shocked, too. "The judge gave them the house?"

Mom nodded.

"We didn't have a contract," Dad said. "It was a verbal agreement with Jodie."

It didn't matter how much time Mom had spent putting on eyeshadow, puckering in the mirror, and adjusting her cream pantsuit. I knew when she'd said that Jodie had died, and her kids wanted to take Mom and Dad to court; we might lose the house.

It had been just less than two years since the last time we had moved, but it felt like forever. As I walked through the hallway, I looked into Mom and Dad's bedroom. The heavy gold drapes that I thought made their room look depressing were still hung. I could smell Mom's Obsession, which I got for her thirty-third birthday the summer before. I placed my hand on the clean spot in the dust where it used to sit on the dark brown dresser. I pulled open an empty drawer. Mom's bras and pantyhose were packed in a box sitting on the bare mattress.

I walked into our bedroom where Michael and Vincent were stuffing shirts and toys into boxes that looked like they were taped together by little kids. Michael asked, "Gar, are you excited you're gonna have your own room again?"

"I want my own room," Vincent piped up.

I opened the dresser to be sure they hadn't touched any of my clothes, especially the tee-shirt of Madonna arching her back with a leather jacket sliding off her bare shoulders. Bernadette had bought it for me at her concert. "Yeah, I'm excited. It's going to be years before you get your own room, Vincent."

As we pulled up to the new house, I thought about Uncle Dan rubbing his fingers together and saying, "Whew, Marlboro's where the money is." I remembered when he'd looked at Anthony and said, "Murph is living the high life now!" They both laughed like two kids whose father had gotten a fat Christmas bonus.

Michael had asked, "What's Murph mean?"

Uncle Dan said, "Your mom is like Murphy's Law. Anything that can go wrong will go wrong."

Nothing about the new house seemed like Murphy's Law. It had an upstairs, a freshly painted and carpeted basement, and a maid's bedroom right off the kitchen, next to the laundry room. When Vincent asked why the maid's bedroom was next to the washer and dryer, Michael answered, "So she can wash Christina's underwear in the middle of the night when she pees the bed." Vincent cracked up, which put a scowl on Christina's face.

362

I interjected before Vincent got pushed for laughing. "I wouldn't be talking, Michael. You were older than Christina when you stopped peeing the bed."

Christina smiled, Michelle giggled, and Michael blurted out, "Well, you poop the bed!"

I knew I should have acted like an adult and ignored Michael, but it was just the five of us, and I wanted to get him back for starting with Christina. I smirked. "Pee the bed! Michael pees the bed!"

Michael was barely able to hold his anger. "Poop the bed! Gary poops the bed!"

When Mom and Dad walked in with Yvonne, I'm pretty sure all five of us we were expecting Alice from *The Brady Bunch*, not an older black lady with short auburn hair. She stood proper-postured with a shiny leather bag at her side. She turned and walked into the living room where the new white furniture was still covered in clear plastic. Yvonne looked around and asked, "Thees eese da room?"

Mom smiled as she tried to act like a rich lady. "Yes, Yvonne. I don't want anyone in this room." We followed as Mom showed the rest of the house before Yvonne nodded and closed the door to her bedroom.

Michael asked, "Is she from England?"

"She's from Guyana," Mom stated.

Christina asked, "Does she live with us?" followed by Vincent, "Does she have to do what I tell her?"

Mom turned on the sink, squeezed a drop of Palmolive, and started washing her hands. "Vincent, you can ask her to get you a cup of milk or a snack, but you still need to say please and thank you, Honey."

I looked at Christina. "She lives with us during the week but goes home on the weekends."

After dinner, Yvonne stood and began clearing dishes from the table. Uncle Dan leaned back, put his hands behind his head and began talking about Doreen. "I don't know why she has to bring the fag with her."

Of course, Anthony laughed. He added, "He better not try anything with me."

Mom snapped at them. "Will you two not talk like that? He's her friend." She picked up her plate and some forks. "Yvonne, I'm sorry about the way these two are speaking."

Yvonne wiped her hands on her apron. "A'hm not listenen."

Vincent leaned in and whispered. "Why is Mom picking up dishes if we have a maid?"

Michael smirked. "Maybe she got a maid so she'd have a reason to clean now." Christina and Michelle both laughed.

A few days later, Yvonne sat at the kitchen table folding clothes as she watched Ronald Reagan talk about the Soviet Union, farmers, and how much he'd done as President. As the audience laughed or clapped at everything he said, I wondered if he would be jealous if his Vice President really did become President.

Vincent walked in. "Yvonne, can I have some chocolate milk?" She got up, walked over to the cabinet, and took out a tall glass. As she opened the refrigerator, Vincent turned and gave me a mischievous grin. It was his second glass in less than an hour. He was asking her to do things because he thought it was funny. She clinked the spoon around, turning the glass of milk light brown, then handed it to him. He turned to walk out.

Yvonne stepped in front of Vincent. "Uh-uh, seet und drink eet all. Ah don't want you to be thirsty now." As she smiled, he knew she'd caught onto his game. He furrowed his brow as he sipped from the huge glass.

I whispered, "That's what you get for making people do things because you think it's funny." He huffed and turned away.

DING DONG

As everyone ran, the front door was opening. Behind Doreen was a really tall, skinny guy wearing whitewashed jeans that flared out at the hips. His brown hair was parted in the middle, and even though it was short in the back, it was longer everywhere else, even covering his ears. It looked like a shorter version of a lady hairdo.

Oh God, I thought, he really does look like a fag. I imagined Uncle Dan and Anthony talking about beating the shit out of him. I hugged Doreen. "Hi, Dor."

After Doreen introduced J.D., he told Mom, "Oh, I love the living room, especially the end tables."

Mom was nonchalant like we'd always had plastic covered furniture. "Those are black lacquer, Hon."

Anthony stayed out with one of the guys who had begun working with him, Uncle Dan and Dad – Ted Maloney. I assumed it was because he didn't want to be around Doreen's gay friend. Uncle Dan came home, though. He asked J.D. questions and even joked as he held his hands open in front of him like he was holding invisible cantaloupes.

"So seriously, when you look at Jessica Hahn's tits, they do nothing for you?"

J.D. scrunched his nose like he'd just sipped raw grapefruit juice. "No, nothing."

Uncle Dan laughed. "You don't know what you're missing."

Even though Uncle Dan was nice to J.D., he still didn't want to hang out with him. He spent a lot of time with Anthony and Ted. I would have preferred spending time with Doreen regardless, but I was drawn to talk to J.D., too.

J.D. told me, "You should let me cut your hair. That part on the side is really not in style anymore, and you're starting high school in the fall." Just like Aunt Peggy, he carried his hair cutting supplies with him everywhere. After he washed my hair in the kitchen sink, he wrapped a white towel around my head. As I stood up, looking like a woman who'd just gotten out of the shower, I thought, thank God Anthony and Uncle Dan aren't home.

"It's just to keep your hair wet until we get downstairs," J.D said. I put my hand on the towel and hurried after him to the basement.

Doreen came down and sat on our old couch as J.D. snip, snipped my dark, wet hair. She tried to convince him how wonderful New Jersey was by pointing out that it's close to New York City and the beach. As he rebutted everything she said with "yeah..." and "well..." I knew there was no way she was going to convince him that New Jersey was better than Iowa.

J.D. stood back to examine his master style. "Ok, we're done." He held up the mirror. "What do you think?"

I tried to hold my gasp as I realized he'd given me the same long, down to my ears, lady-do that he had. "I like it. I really like it!" I exclaimed as I imagined how ridiculous it would still look even after I parted it on the side and brushed the long hair behind my ears.

Sharon Maloney started coming over because her husband, Ted, was working for Dad. She wasn't like the other young girls that congregated around Mom, seeking motherly guidance. She was married when she had had her baby, and she seemed to know exactly what she, and especially Ted, should be doing. She was very bold about giving other people advice, too. I figured that someone must have told her I had no interest in hanging out with Ted and Uncle Dan. Instead, I was spending my time with Doreen and J.D.

Sharon gave a stiff smile. "Gary, my apartment complex has a beautiful pool. You should come hang out with me by it." I tried to figure out what about her face looked manly. Her dirty blond hair was straight to her shoulders. She had perfect teeth. Was it her chin? I'd seen black and white movies where a woman was referred to as handsome. I couldn't figure out exactly what made it that way, but I decided that Sharon had a handsome face.

I reluctantly said, "Ok," which was followed by Michael's enthusiastic, "Can I go, too?"

As Michael held his nose and tried to touch the bottom of the shallow end, Sharon held Elizabeth Grace at her side and made baby surprise faces.

I remembered when Uncle Dan had told me that he could get Pamela, the married woman he was having an affair with, to give me a blow job. "She loves giving head. Sometimes she sucks me off three times in a row."

I had tried to act happy while I expressed a logical concern. "Yeah, but I'm only fourteen. Would she want to?"

Uncle Dan had laughed. "Are you kidding? She'd be excited to do it to a fourteen-year-old." Most of the girls who had been around – Laura, Bonnie, Julie, Bernadette – I never got the feeling they would try anything weird, but Sharon made me uneasy. She was comfortable talking about how *big* Ted was, and when she popped her nipple out to feed Elizabeth Grace, I noticed she'd always move her eyes to any man in the room. They would quickly look away, but she'd smirk like she was happy they'd seen her boob. I wouldn't be surprised if she was just like Pamela.

I kept my body under the water and bounced in place. I looked around at the different people in the pool as I waited for Sharon to say she was ready to go in. Once Elizabeth Grace stopped splashing and turned her focus to a floaty ball, Sharon called, "Gary, come here." Michael, of course, not wanting to be left out, splashed over to listen, too.

Sharon ducked, so her big chin touched the water. "See that woman over there?"

I turned. There was a woman with her arms outstretched along the edge of the pool, with her head back, letting the sun warm her face. "You should play blind man's bluff," Sharon said.

As soon as she said it, I knew what she meant, but I still played stupid. "What's blind man's bluff?"

Sharon's eyes got bright. "Swim underwater with your hands in front of you, like you can't see. Cop a feel."

I turned to Michael. He loved boobs, but even at eleven, he knew that was a dangerous plan. He gave me a quick look as if mentally asking if Sharon was nuts. I didn't want Sharon to think we were making fun of her, and I really didn't want her thinking I wasn't interested in copping a feel of some strange lady's boobs.

"Oh, that sounds like fun," I said.

Sharon gestured with her eyes and then turned back to Elizabeth Grace. I was sure she wanted it to look like she had nothing to do with it if I carried out her plan.

I inhaled a deep breath and sunk below the surface. I pushed off in the direction of the lady. Even though everything was blurry, I had no problem opening my eyes under water. I swam about five feet from the woman, popped up, and looked back toward Sharon. She gave a commanding eyebrow raise, letting me know to keep going, then smiled at Elizabeth Grace. I took another breath, then dipped below again. I debated what to do. Should I grab the woman's leg? She'd jump for sure, and I could pretend I had grabbed her boobs. How would

Sharon know the difference? No, I couldn't bring myself to do that, even though it was much less inappropriate. I popped up, inhaled a huge breath, and swam back over to Sharon. I thought about how ridiculous the whole idea was as I shook my head.

"She knew I was up to something, Sharon. I don't think it's a good idea." I got out of the pool. I didn't care if she believed me or not.

As I lay in bed, I thought about the panic I had felt when I realized I would rather see men naked than women. I was probably twelve. I had snuck Anthony's *Hustler* magazine, which he kept under the family room couch, into the bathroom. I quietly turned the pages and examined the different women. They were all beautiful with perfect makeup. It was interesting looking at all the different types of boobs. Some had really big nipples and hung low, while others were tight and round like grapefruit halves on their chest. None of the pictures excited me, though, and it seemed like every one of the women was sitting on a chair or lying in a bed with their legs wide open. As I stared, I tried to understand why looking at the inside of their vaginas was supposed to turn men on. It looked kind of gross to me.

The tiny ads in the back of the magazine sometimes had pictures of naked men. Those excited me more than twenty pages of boobs. I had so many questions about being gay. Other than being girly, J.D. seemed pretty normal. I wondered if I should talk to him.

It was early in the evening. Mom, Doreen, and J.D. were in the kitchen talking about the man Doreen was dating, Gene. Doreen told Mom how Gene said he was fine with J.D. as long as he didn't try anything on him.

J.D. interjected, "I told him don't flatter yourself," which made Doreen crack up.

Mom said, "I need cigarettes. Do you want to go to the store, Dor?"

Doreen sighed. "Kath, I don't feel like it."

J.D. smiled. "I'll go for you, Kathy."

As J.D. grabbed his keys, I asked, "Do you mind if I go, J.D?"

As we drove, my heart raced. I imagined several different ways of saying what I wanted to say before just telling him, "J.D., I think I'm gay."

He asked me, "Have you ever been with a man?"

"No, but I'm pretty sure I am."

He told me about how he had known by the time he was my age and how hard it was for his mother at first, but she was fine now. "You have to tell your aunt," J.D. said. "She is wonderful."

A few hours after we came back from the store, J.D. whispered to Doreen. She told Mom that we were going to take a ride, and the three of us left. After we slammed the doors to J.D.'s car, Doreen turned around, "What is it, Gar?"

My heart began pounding. "I'm gay, Dor."

Doreen spoke in the nicest voice I'd ever heard from her. "Are you sure, Gar?"

"Yeah, I'm sure."

"Gar, you have to tell Mommy."

When I said I didn't feel comfortable telling Mom, Doreen and J.D. spent over two hours trying to convince me as we drove past the same Shoprite and Dunkin' Donuts about ten times. When I finally agreed, Doreen reassured me, "Gar, it'll be fine. I promise."

Uncle Dan and Anthony were out. Uncle Jim was in the kitchen watching TV with Yvonne, and the kids were in bed. I felt safe with Doreen and J.D. as we climbed the stairs to Mom and Dad's bedroom. I could hear their voices softly through the door as Doreen knocked.

"Come in." Mom's muffled voice came through the door.

Mom was sitting on the bed with a cigarette, looking up at the ceiling. I could tell from her red eyes and wet cheeks that she'd been crying. Doreen, J.D., and I sat on the floor. Dad walked around the side of the bed to examine a paper that had been in his pocket, like none of it was a big deal at all. Mom looked at me, and I felt a lump form in my throat. She sobbed. "What?"

"I'm gay."

Mom looked up at the ceiling again and took a long drag from her cigarette. After a moment, she looked back at me. "You can't be gay. I've seen you look at boobs. You like boobs."

Seeing her cry, like it hurt her so much, made me begin crying. "I am, Mom. I'm sorry."

Doreen said, "Kath if he's gay, you can't change it. You have to accept it."

Mom snapped, "I know my son, Doreen," which caused me to cry even harder.

As Mom and I sat quiet with tears streaming down our cheeks, I wondered why I had said anything. Because, I tried to convince myself, I was being honest, and it was the right thing to do.

After, an hour of discussion, Mom finally resided. "Well, I want to take you to a counselor, Gar, just to be sure. Ok?"

I was still crying. "Ok." I stood up and reached for the door handle. As the door clicked, I heard a BUM BUM BUM on the stairs.

Uncle Jim was almost to the bottom when we stepped out. He looked up. "Oh hey, I was gonna use the bathroom, but I didn't know if you guys were done."

I didn't even care that he'd been listening. I went to my room, shut the door, and sobbed into my pillow.

After a few minutes, my door opened. The light from the hallway warmed the room as Mom stepped in. She sat on the side of my bed and put her hand on my back. "Gar, you know I love you, right? I just don't want you to have a hard life."

I didn't even lift my head. My voice was muffled through my pillow. "I know, Mom."

She leaned down and hugged me tight. I felt a little better, lifted my head, and said, "I can feel your boobs on my back, Mom." We both laughed, cried, then laughed again.

I wasn't sure if J.D. went back to Iowa because he really missed his mom or because the pressure of my being gay and having to go to counseling was too much for him. Mom wanted Doreen to go with me, I figured, because there was no way I was going to become straight with her telling everyone there was nothing wrong with me being gay.

I knew Doreen thought that going to counseling was ridiculous, as we sat on the leather couch, which we both sank down into. She crossed her arms and her legs and stared defiantly forward. The psychologist opened the door to her office gingerly as if she were entering our home. "Hello."

The psychologist was older, thin with blond hair, and a perfectly pressed ivory suit. She said to Doreen, "Tell me how you feel about Gary saying he's gay."

I could tell by Doreen's sigh that she had probably rolled her eyes. "I don't feel anything about it. I don't care if he's gay." After several questions that Doreen answered with an attitude, the lady gave a phony smile and asked Doreen if she could speak with me alone for a few minutes.

The psychologist asked if I felt comfortable telling her about my fantasies when I masturbated. I almost laughed. I wondered how many sexually confused teenagers she'd asked that question to. Did she really think there was a possibility I'd say yes? I was polite. "No, I don't feel comfortable but thank you for asking."

She gave me a nice smile and stood. "Ok, our half hour is almost up. Wait out here with Doreen. I'm going to speak with your parents." She opened the door. "Kathleen, Nick."

By the time we had moved from Castle Ct., most of the people who had slept on our couches and in the kids' beds during the day, had found their own place to live. Laura spoke to Mom only on the phone since Anthony started bringing his new girlfriend, Joy, around. Bonnie moved back near her parents in Cherry Hill, so she only popped in from time to time. Bernadette would bring the baby, Jack. If she stayed, it was usually only for a day or two. Aunt Peggy had her own apartment, so Uncle Dan and Uncle Jim would spend time at her place, in addition to ours. Because Ted worked with Dad, he'd come by, sometimes with Sharon, but they never stayed the night.

Even though Mom was proud that no one lived with us, the house was still full of people talking and laughing. Mom's white, Lincoln Town car became the only place we could speak privately. Mom, Doreen, and I took a lot of rides with just the three of us. We had many conversations about being gay. I felt strongly that, as terrible as it was to be gay, I was doing the right thing by acknowledging and accepting it.

As the weeks passed, I began thinking about the desperate look in Mom's eyes. At the end of every conversation, as stubborn as I was about being gay, she still told me, "I love you, Gar, so much." I realized she was never going to accept it like J.D.'s mother did. She couldn't.

I imagined her trying to explain to Uncle Dan, Anthony, Ted and Sharon, knowing they were whispering to everyone, "Kathleen's son is a fag." Anthony would move away, Ted would quit working for Dad, and Uncle Dan would be getting into fistfights in grocery store parking lots all the time. It would all be my fault. I knew, as crazy and sometimes terrible of a mother Mom had been, she was trying to protect me.

The final conversation was about how I'd never actually done anything sexually. Mom said, "Gary, it's penis to butt and penis to mouth. Do you understand that? Is that what you want?"

I wasn't sure about the butt part, but I'd certainly imagined having a penis in my mouth. Still, I waited a minute, like I was really thinking about it before answering, "No, I don't."

"He doesn't even understand what gay is," Doreen said.

I knew she was tired of talking about it, too.

Doreen left to go back to Iowa a couple of weeks later. She hugged me and nodded to let me know she knew the truth, and it was still ok with her. I thought about how different she was from Mom. Doreen had no problem arguing with people. Even walking through the parking lot at the grocery store, she'd slam someone's hood with her hands. "Pedestrians have the right of way, asshole!" I imagined her yelling, "Yeah, that's right. He's gay. If you don't like it, you can kiss my ass!"

I hugged her back. "I love you, Dor."

Near the end of summer, Aunt Peggy had everyone over her apartment for a party. I liked Aunt Peggy's home because it was clean, and her furniture was sleek and modern. Her puffy couch went around the corner of her living room, like an L. Unlike our kitchen table, which was dark, heavy wood, Aunt Peggy's had four gold legs and a round glass top.

As they ran around the kitchen table, Michelle yelled, "Billy! If you don't share, I'm telling your Mom."

Aunt Peggy said in a soothing tone, "Billy, please share, Honey, and please stop running around the table."

Billy yelled defiantly, "No!"

What a brat! I knew Aunt Peggy had spoiled him because she'd lost custody of Josh, but Billy just thought he was the little prince who answered to no one – not even his own mother.

Other than Billy's brattiness, the party was a lot of fun. Aunt Peggy took her air singing, "Pour some sugar on me" so seriously that it was hard not to smile.

Mom laughed with Dad. "Oh, yeah, you wish I had it easy during the day. All Yvonne does is cook and do the laundry." It wasn't until Uncle Jim walked in and stumbled that the atmosphere tensed.

Mom approached him. "Jimmy, you can't be here drunk. You have to leave."

Uncle Jim waved her off. "Fuck you. I'm not drunk." He stumbled to the kitchen.

CRASH!

The sound was so loud and shocking that everyone froze. Uncle Jim was on his back. There were hundreds of broken glass pieces under him, scattered throughout the kitchen. Aunt Peggy's face turned from sweet to insane. "Jimmy! Billy! Michelle! Out of the kitchen! Out of the kitchen!"

Mom ran over. "Peg, we'll clean it up." Then, Mom turned to Uncle Jim, who was trying to sit up. As he pulled himself forward, red drops appeared on the floor. He looked at the blood on his hand and stammered, "I… I…"

Mom grabbed a towel and put it on his hand. "Jimmy, you have to leave."

Aunt Peggy stared at the floor, where her beautiful glass table had been. She took a breath. "I'm leaving. We're moving to Florida. I'm not raising Billy with this family."

We had Aunt Peggy's going away party in our finished basement. Mom wore a sleek taupe pantsuit. Dad wore tan slacks and a brown Alligator shirt. And they both had on their indoor sunglasses to look as cool as possible. The stereo, which Mom had brought downstairs, blasted, "I don't wanna go on with you like that," as the kids ran around the card table set up to hold all the booze. Christina looked around, smiled, and snuck one of the many half-drank, plastic cups of booze from the edge. Mom took a sip of her wine cooler and gave a sad smile. "Peg, I can't believe you're really leaving."

Aunt Peggy was happier than I'd ever seen her. She practically cooed. "Kath, don't be sad. Florida's not that far. Maybe you should move there."

The air was chilly as I waited for the bus on the first day of school. It wasn't like my last year at St. Paul where all five of us were in the same school. Even though we were in different grades, it had been reassuring to know that we were all in the same building. The worst part about beginning high school was that Thomas wouldn't be there. I wasn't sure if the tuition for his school was too expensive, or if I didn't have the grades to get in, but Mom had tried hard to convince me that Saint John Vienni was going to be great.

When the bus squealed to a stop, I stepped up and looked around. The five students on the bus all sat several seats away from each other and stared out at the gray sky as Guns and Roses blared, "She's got a child... it seems to me... reminds me of childhood memories..." Even with the radio playing, everything felt sad. I took an empty seat at the back of the bus.

As I walked from class to class, I thought, this is what high school feels like. Every classroom, full of a different group of teenagers, seemed like a different world. Even if I never made any friends, at least I was anonymous. The only situation I dreaded was running into someone from Saint Paul. When I saw Colleen O'Brien talking to one of her friends at her locker, my heart sank. I thought about being without Thomas and wondered how she would treat me all by myself.

Colleen smiled brightly when she noticed me. "Hey, Gary."

I froze, a little shocked that she remembered my name. I walked over near her. "Hey, Colleen." As we talked, I realized it didn't matter that we hadn't been friends in eighth grade. There was an automatic bond because, among the hordes of high schoolers who came from all different schools, we had gone to the same grade school when we were kids. I thought about how she was always one of the prettiest girls in our class. Her blond hair was sprayed out a little fuller than it used to be, and she was wearing silver earrings that looked like spider webs. I thought about how cool her earrings were, but then instinctually stopped myself. I remembered how J.D. had laughed with Doreen about how 60s looking her hair was and how he told Mom that he loved how she did her eye makeup.

I smiled at Colleen. "I love your earrings. They're really cool."

She beamed. "Aren't they? Thanks!"

I leaned my head against the cool glass as the bus bumped along and the radio played. "When I'm feeling blue… all I have to do… is take a look at you… then I'm not so blue…"

When I got home, I dropped my book bag on the counter and opened the refrigerator. Mom walked in "Gar, guess where we're moving?" I paused. We'd only been in Marlboro a few months.

"Where?"

"We're moving to Florida. Isn't that exciting?"

Mom's Trip to the Bahamas

"The Beach Boys were around when I was a kid!" Mom proclaimed. As she turned up the radio – "Bermuda… Bahama… come on, pretty mama" – I remembered our kitchen in Marlboro. When the video with the curly, red-haired kid had come on, Mom had told me, "Rod Stewart has been around since I was your age, Gar." As I watched him snuggle with the annoying red-headed boy in the back of a pickup, I thought, this is the same guy that sang "Do Ya Think I'm Sexy?" He shouldn't be making new songs, and Mom had no idea what cool was.

Mom didn't care if the song was a number one hit or how many young people thought it was great. She smiled happily as she sang to Michelle. "Key Largo, Montego – Baby, why don't we go?"

Michelle giggled and began singing right along with Mom. Christina and Vincent enthusiastically joined in. Everyone's excitement about our new home, Florida and the song, which was actually really good, got to me. I started singing as well. Michael gave me a cocked eyebrow look, like the four of us had gone insane, but I just shrugged. Even though he did it in a goofy, exaggerated way, which I knew was making fun, Michael started singing, too.

As the song ended, we turned down the street where our new home was. I touched my forehead to the glass, warm from the bright sun.

Christina asked Dad why all the houses were so light. The yellow, peach, and tan houses looked pale compared to the hard brick homes in New Jersey. Instead of shutters and black metal porch lights, the homes in Cape Coral had screen doors and palm trees.

"I'm not sure. Maybe people like lighter colors so they feel like they're on vacation."

Michelle leaned up from the middle to look out the window. "Are we on vacation?"

Mom laughed. "It's like we're on vacation forever, Honey. We live here now."

As we turned into the driveway, the reality of our life settled back in. I thought how of course, for us, it would be like a vacation. We even brought a house full of people to party with.

When we were packing up the house in Marlboro, Michelle had asked, right in front of him, "Mom, why does Anthony have to move with us?"

Michael and I both looked at each other. Woah! We were surprised and eager for Anthony's reaction. He gave a nervous chuckle, then spoke in a soft tone. "What? You don't like me?" He stuck his bottom lip out to make himself look sad like he was dealing with a baby.

Even at six years old, Michelle was too smart for his juvenile manipulation. She looked right at him. "You need to find your own house and stop living with us, Anthony."

Michael and I held in our laughter as Mom gasped. "Michelle, that's not nice, Honey."

Besides Anthony, Uncle Dan was also moving to Florida with us. Of course, because she'd had a baby with him, so was Bernadette. She didn't seem to care how many times Uncle Dan called her a fat whale or even when he told her that he'd just used her for sex. She yelled back, "I may not have had bigger, but I've had better!" Uncle Jim laughed louder than anyone at Bernadette's crude comeback. It was slight, but one of the only ways to get back at Uncle Dan since he had beaten him up.

Mom had told everyone the best way to handle Uncle Jim when he began drinking was to ignore him. Uncle Dan didn't even try. Uncle Jim's drunken tear that began with the demolition of Aunt Peggy's modern glass table ended a few weeks before we left New Jersey. Uncle Jim began giving his usual drunken speech about how everyone was full of shit. Uncle Dan snarled at him. "You better watch yourself, Jim. I'm tellin' you."

The threat only made Uncle Jim bolder. "You think you're so tough, don't you Danny? You're a real tough guy."

Uncle Dan clenched his fists and teeth. "I'm warning you, Jim. I'm warning you."

Mom screamed, "Danny, no! He's an alcoholic," but it didn't matter.

When Uncle Jim taunted Uncle Dan with, "You gonna beat me up like one of your girlfriends?" Uncle Dan swung. After he hit him, Uncle Dan opened the front door and threw Uncle Jim out onto the lawn.

Uncle Jim, with blood running from a gashed eyebrow, got up and stumbled toward him. "Danny... you..." Uncle Dan threw one last punch that knocked Uncle Jim out cold. Uncle Dan walked inside and slammed the door.

The next day, Uncle Jim didn't say anything about his black eye. He even asked Uncle Dan about The Giants, like the fight had never happened. I realized that, just like the rest of us, Uncle Jim hated Uncle Dan but was afraid of him. When Bernadette made her joke and Uncle Jim cracked up, I wasn't surprised. I also knew, when Uncle Dan said he was going to Florida, Uncle Jim was going to stay in New Jersey.

The one couple I never expected to move with us was Sharon and Ted. Unlike Uncle Dan and Anthony, who only went to work when they felt like it, Ted was at our house every morning with red thermos and brown paper lunch bag. I was pretty sure it was because Sharon expected him to be a good husband, father, and provider. She had said many times that she liked Uncle Dan, but she'd never be with a man like him. Anthony, she called "pure trash." She mostly ignored him and told Mom that she didn't understand why she kept him around.

When Mom had told Sharon we were moving, she'd also told her about the office cleaning company she had been planning to start for years. Mom proudly opened the big leather binder to show Sharon the logo she'd had made. It was a leprechaun holding a broom. Mom, like a happy kid, stated, "Nick just had it incorporated, Sharon – Shamrock Sanitizing Service. You should come to Florida and help me start it."

As we turned into our new driveway, I asked, "Are you excited about starting your cleaning company, Mom?"

She nodded. "I am. Maybe you can work with me on the weekends, Gar."

The white, tiled foyer felt cool as we walked in from the humid air. I looked at the sunlit living room to the right. That's where Mom's plastic covered furniture would go. Christina's, Vincent's, and Michelle's footsteps echoed as they took off through the kitchen.

"Look!" Michelle squealed, as Vincent heaved to pull the glass door open. I knew Michael was as excited as I was, but he didn't run either. As we walked into the kitchen, we saw the step down to the huge family room, where there was a pool table. Through the glass doors was a screened in swimming pool, and our backyard ended at a canal as wide as a river.

Michael let out a "Wow" as he smiled at me.

Vincent laughed, but Christina was serious as the two of them flung balls around the pool table, trying to crack them into each other.

Vincent looked around. "I'm gonna get a stick." As he reached to pull a cue off the wall, Uncle Dan stepped into the room.

"Nuh-uh. Gimme that. You two aren't gonna destroy this table."

Anthony walked in. "Let's shoot a game, Dan." Christina placed the yellow ball down on the green cloth and stepped back. She knew to stop.

Vincent's lips tightened, and he crossed his arms.

"You better wipe that look off your face," Uncle Dan said, "unless you want me to bust your ass."

"But we were playing!" Vincent yelled.

Uncle Dan tilted his head down and motioned to Vincent. "Give me the ball." Vincent didn't look at him. Uncle Dan's voice deepened. "Give me the ball. I'm not gonna tell you again." Vincent tossed the ball where it knock knock knocked onto the table.

Uncle Dan lunged for him. Vincent ran, but Uncle Dan caught him before he got out of the room. He yanked Vincent's arm and whacked his butt. My heart dropped as I remembered being hit by Uncle Dan when I was his age. Unlike me, the look of shock on

Vincent's face quickly turned to anger. He screamed "I hate you!" then ran down the hall and slammed the door.

Mom hurried out of the kitchen. "What's going on?"

Uncle Dan pointed. "Your son. You better watch your son."

Anthony pulled out the rack, started dropping balls on the table and smirked. "He'll listen next time you tell him what to do." When he pulled the cue stick off the wall, it made me angry. If Uncle Dan and Anthony hadn't moved with us, Vincent would have been playing pool with Christina, not crying in the bedroom.

I walked down the hall and thought about how Vincent was able to push it further with Uncle Dan, but there was still a limit. I knocked lightly and opened the door. Vincent was sitting on the floor between two boxes playing with his Michelangelo Ninja Turtle. He didn't even look up. I knew exactly how he felt but didn't know what to say to him. I gave a slight smile as I crouched. "Hey, Vincent."

Michael walked in, shut the door behind him, and whispered, "Vincent, you can't talk back to him. He's crazy." I wouldn't have said that, but I knew it was the truth.

Vincent was still mad. "I don't care. We were playing."

As the sky turned from afternoon blue to orangey purple, Uncle Dan, Anthony, and Dad worked on the dock trying to figure out how to use the crab cage while the five of us sat in the grass watching. Mom hollered from the back door. "Nick, I don't want the kids on the dock."

I knew, as Dad continued to clip the chain, that he thought Mom was being overprotective.

Mom called out again. "Nick?"

"What?" he yelled back.

"I'm serious. I don't want the kids near the water."

Even when Dad was annoyed or angry, he wasn't scary. He was calm as he stood up and handed the chain to Ted, who had just walked out.

Ted said, "Ah, she's serious Nick. She wants the kids inside."

Dad answered, "Thanks Ted, I think Danny and Anthony almost have it figured out. I'm going to take the kids around front."

We stepped through the grass and followed Dad around to the front of the house. The mild, yellow, street lights humming felt like any neighborhood we'd ever lived in. It was the smell of salt water and the strange buzzing sounds that made it feel like Florida.

Michelle asked, "Dad, what's that noise? Is it a bug?"

Dad pulled a cigarette from the Pall Mall pack in his shirt pocket and listened. "I think it might be a frog," he said.

"Really?" asked Christina. She smiled and then began looking intently at the grass.

Vincent squatted and turned his ear. He gave a puzzled, doubtful look. "That's not a frog."

Dad grinned. "It's a frog. I'm telling you. Mike, Gar, you guys saw the frogs today, didn't you?"

Michael smirked at me, but then said, "It's frogs. We saw them."

Christina, who was examining the grass with Vincent, popped up. "Dad, you're teasing."

Michelle's confident voice boomed. "Nuh-uh! I found one!"

It didn't look like a frog that might buzz. It looked like the fat toads from New Jersey that Uncle Dan said would give you warts if they peed on you. It hopped. Michelle squealed, and Vincent and Christina darted over to catch it.

"Look at that!" Dad said. "You found one. Alright guys, we better get inside before your Mom starts looking for us."

The air inside was cold enough to make me shiver, but it felt good coming in from the warm, heavy air outside. Mom was in the kitchen talking with Sharon and Bernadette. The glass door opened. Uncle Dan and Anthony walked in, followed by Ted holding the crab cage. He placed the wire contraption on the counter. The crabs holding onto the sides fell backward, causing their legs to move like spiders, which creeped me out.

"We got ten crabs," Anthony said.

As Christina's eyes moved around the cage, I could tell she was mentally counting. "There's seven," she said as she stepped back for Mom to walk by.

"What do we do with them?" Mom asked.

Uncle Dan said, "We cook em'. They're blue crabs. They're good."

Sharon began reaching in and grabbing the dark crabs with the pale blue legs by the back of their bodies. She was intent as she dropped them one by one into a pot.

Michael asked, "Do you cook them alive?"

Sharon didn't look away from the pot as she answered, "Yep, that's the only way to cook them."

I was happy when Mom ordered pizza, too. As we ate our sausage and extra cheese slices, Uncle Dan sucked the legs of his crab. Sharon broke her crab apart over the sink and scooped a yellow mush out with her fingers.

"That looks gross," Michael said.

Sharon smiled then popped her fingers into her mouth. "It's delicious."

Vincent made a face. "Eww."

Mom held her hand up in front of her face as she looked away. "I don't want to see that."

Uncle Dan laughed. "Sharon, gimme one of those." Of course, he had to show everyone that nothing was too disgusting for him. He ripped his crab apart and sucked the inside right out of it.

Bernadette gave a sick look. "I don't know who you think you're impressing."

Uncle Dan wiped his chin and shot back, "Shut up and eat your pizza."

Mom and Dad explained that the new school was Christian, not Catholic. "Actually, it's Baptist," Dad said. I didn't care what kind of Catholic school it was. As long as it wasn't a public school full of vagrants and delinquents, I was happy.

When we pulled up to the tiny, gray building, Christina asked, "Is that the school?" followed by Vincent's, "Why's it so small?"

"It's a little, private school," Mom said. We slammed the doors and walked past three white vans parked in the dusty lot, up to the building. Dad opened the door. It was as quiet as a church and smelled like one, too.

The two ladies who greeted us both had curly, auburn hair and wore blue dresses that went to their ankles. The younger one, who looked like she was in her thirties, introduced herself. "I'm Mrs. Watts. My husband is the pastor."

Michelle asked, "Are you a nun?"

The older of the two women adjusted her glasses and leaned over toward us. "We are not nuns. We are normal ladies just like your mother."

Michael caught my eye as we both realized the school was going to be different.

The next morning, the white van pulled right into our driveway. I said, "Michelle, don't forget your lunch," as we scurried to the front door. The driver wore a white polo that stretched tight over his belly and arm fat. And his stringy brown hair, which was parted way on the side, looked wet. He smiled. "I'm Brother Bailey. Come on in. Take a seat." After we smushed ourselves in among the other kids, a little boy, probably Michelle's age, stood right in front of me. "Ah'm Georgie!"

"Hi, I'm Gary."

He held up his hand. "Ah'm this many. How old are you?"

I answered, "Fifteen," as the driver strained to turn around.

"Georgie!" Brother Bailey's face was red, and his kooky smile was gone. "Did I not tell you to sit your behind down!"

The little boy let out a big sigh and squeezed in next to Vincent. "Ah'm Georgie!" he said again, but Vincent didn't answer him. He was talking to a blond girl named Noel, who was explaining how everyone in her family was named after Christmas.

When we stepped out of the van, Michael whispered to me, "Is that boy retarded?" I quickly shushed him even though I was wondering the same thing.

When we got inside the school, Mrs. Watts took Michelle to a different room. The lady who was definitely not a nun handed me, Michael, Christina, and Vincent a book that felt like it was made of phonebook paper. "You study this section. You take the test, then you go to the table in the middle of the room and check your answers."

Michael, in disbelief, asked, "We check the answers ourselves?"

She answered, "Yes, Jesus watches everything you do. He knows you'll be honest."

After the lady walked each of us to a dark blue cubicle that had only two pencils and a tiny lamp, I opened my book. I thought about how easy it would be to cheat, then looked across the room at Christina. She was studying her book – no cheating for her. Vincent was gazing up at the wall, probably thinking about recess.

Michael was the one. After what couldn't be even ten minutes, he walked up to the table with a smirk on his face. He's *so* dumb, I thought. The lady's going to know he didn't have time to read anything yet. She wasn't paying attention, though. She was sitting at her desk staring intently at her Bible.

Mom beamed when she told everyone, "I got a contract for the Sanibel Sonesta!"

Sharon asked, "The whole hotel?"

Mom explained that it was just the clubhouse, to begin with, but if they did a good job, Manny (the person who supervised the cleaning companies) would give her more work. I thought the job was perfect for Mom. She, Sharon and Dad left right before midnight and came back early in the morning, right before the sun came up. It made sense for Mom to sleep all day.

When Mom said she'd pay me twenty dollars for working Friday and Saturday nights, of course, I was excited, but mostly I was curious to see what the hotel looked like. When Mom said we were cleaning the clubhouse, I expected a dull shack filled with dirty baseball uniforms, not a three-story, octagon-shaped building. The ornate trim and blue roof made it look like a Southern mansion. As we walked up the stairs, I heard the ocean, and even though the sky was black, I could still see the white foam as the waves rolled onto the beach. Mom pulled a small manila envelope out of her purse, took a key out, and unlocked the door. I knew she took the responsibility seriously as she placed the key back in the envelope and tucked the flap.

The door clicked, and I followed Sharon inside. Mom flipped the lights on. "Nick, Sharon and I are going to start in the kitchen. You work on the bathrooms upstairs."

"What do you want me to do, Mom?" I asked.

"You're gonna help us in the kitchen. Then I'm gonna have you vacuum out here."

Mom and Sharon scrubbed the counters and floors, and it took me half the night to spray and wipe all the stainless-steel refrigerators. I was exhausted by the time I began vacuuming, but at least I didn't have to crouch anymore. I only needed to pull chairs out to suck up the crumbs under the tables. When we were finished, we piled into the car and drove home. The sky was just starting to turn light when we pulled into the driveway. I flopped onto my bed and slept till late afternoon.

As we all got ready for school Monday morning, I couldn't stop yawning. After we packed into Brother Bailey's white van, I leaned my head against the door hoping to close my eyes and sleep – but knowing I wouldn't be able to. I listened as one of the girls explained to Michelle that the two white boxes she had were full of cupcakes that her Mom had made for her birthday. By the afternoon ride home, my tired had gone away. I had been half paying attention to the debate between Michelle and the cupcake girl. She had one box left to take home, and she told Michelle, "I can give whoever I want one. They're my cupcakes."

Michelle, intent on correcting the girl's bad behavior, commanded, "You need to share with everyone."

The girl yelled at her. "I do not!" She reached past Michelle to hand a cupcake to Vincent.

David, the only boy older than me, who smiled all the time, and who I was sure was gay, asked, "Can I have one?"

As I turned back toward the window, the girl with the cupcakes screamed. I looked back. She had a pink frosted cupcake smushed on her chest. I immediately recognized Michelle's serious, that's what you get, face. It was the same look she had when Billy got pushed down for not sharing. Before I could scold Michelle, the box was flying across the seat, and dark cake pieces were being thrown throughout the van. Christina loved it. She was all business as she ducked and threw a cupcake at every kid besides us. David screamed like a girl as Georgie began smearing cupcake frosting on the window.

I hollered. "Guys, guys, stop!"

Brother Bailey screamed, "What's going on? Georgie!" He screeched the van to a stop. Everyone froze but Georgie, who kept giggling hysterically as he threw cupcake pieces. Brother Bailey grunted, panted, and pulled himself around. He grabbed Georgie and yanked him to the front seat. He jerked Georgie's pants down, exposing his bare butt, and started whacking, "I... told... you...!"

The next day at school when Mrs. Watts whispered, "Gary, I need to speak with you," I held my breath. I was sure we were being expelled. My mind raced as I followed her. Should I blame the girl with the cupcakes? No, we were the new kids. She'd never believe us. Should I beg for forgiveness? Tell her I'd make sure we all said Hail Marys' every night before bed? I let out my breath. I just knew we were going to end up in a public school.

Mrs. Watts looked sternly at me. "You and your brothers and sisters will be taking a different van to school – just the five of you."

As I flung the rod, I wondered why neither the pastor nor Mrs. Watts called Mom about the cupcake fight. The reel buzzed before the lure plopped into the water. As hard as I flung, I couldn't make it more than halfway across the canal. I was still happy I could cast farther than Anthony, though. I cranked the reel, anticipating a hard tug.

The first time I had caught one, Dad had said, "That's a Jack."

Ted looked through the fishing book and announced, "It's a Crevalle Jack."

"It's small," said Anthony.

Uncle Dan chimed in, "Nice job, Champ. That's a good fighting fish."

As the yellow, plastic fish with hooks for fins appeared in the dark water, I heard Uncle Dan. He sounded serious, but I couldn't tell what he was saying. I placed the pole on the dock and listened to make out what he was talking about. Was it about Bernadette?

I walked up toward the house. Uncle Dan was telling Mom, "We have to get her out. The car has Jersey plates."

Get her out? Was Bernadette in jail? I slid the door shut behind me. Sharon was sitting on the couch with Elizabeth Grace's face pressed to her boob. Yuck, I thought. How old was she? Two and a half? Three? I remembered when Mom had whispered to Bernadette, "When Jack is old enough to tell you he wants your boob, it's time to stop breastfeeding."

Mom was standing in the doorway. "Do we even know why they stopped her?"

Uncle Dan answered, "She's an idiot. She said it was because a tail light was out."

"A tail light?" Mom questioned, "they don't arrest you for a tail light."

Two days later the phone rang. Mom picked it up. "Hello?"

"Oh, Hi Manny."

"Ok… is everything alright?"

"Ok, I'll see you soon. Bye, Manny."

Mom looked worried as she hung up the receiver. Dad asked, "What does he want, Kath?"

Mom pressed her fingers to her lips and stared at the counter.

Dad asked again. "Kath?"

Mom blinked a few times before she responded. "I don't know, Nick. He sounded serious."

Even though my stomach had an empty feeling, I smiled at her. "It'll be fine, Mom. He probably wants to give you more rooms in the hotel."

Mom gave me a sad smile, then pulled the envelope with the key to the Sonesta out of her purse and stared at it for a couple of seconds. "I guess we should go, Nick."

When they walked in the front door an hour later, seeing the black mascara smudges around Mom's eyes made my heart sink. I asked her what happened.

She sat down, leaned her head into her hand, and choked to keep from crying. "I'm… sorry, Gar… I shouldn't be crying."

Dad told Uncle Dan, "We lost the contract. He wouldn't even tell her why."

As Mom turned her head away, I remembered her pulling out the refrigerators to be sure the floor was clean under them, how she checked the bathrooms two and sometimes three times. She even gave the door handle a final polish after she'd locked it before we headed home in the early morning. The pit in my stomach consumed my chest until the sadness turned to anger. I hugged her tight as she sobbed. "I'm sorry Mom. I'm sorry."

A few days later at school, I found a mistake in the religion section of our workbook. I raised my hand, and the older lady came over.

I whispered, "This says you only pray to God and Jesus. What about Mary?" The lady gave me a look like I'd just smashed a rosary with a hammer.

She answered in a calm, but very serious tone. "Mary is just a woman."

I held myself from smiling and spoke like I was talking to a child. "But she gave birth to Jesus."

The lady motioned with her hand. "Come with me."

After she shut the door to the office, she sat down and pointed for me to sit. She explained how Mary and Peter and all the apostles were just people. I gave a puzzled look and said, "They're saints." She proceeded to lecture me until I finally just agreed, "Yes. They're all just people. There's nothing special about any of them." I tried my best not to sound sarcastic.

As we got into our van, Michael asked, "Gar, why were you in the office?" I wasn't about to get into the debate all over again with Brother Bailey.

"It was nothing." I scooted into my seat. I smiled as I thought about telling Mom. She'd say, "Mary wasn't a saint? Is she nuts?" We'd both laugh about how loony the woman was.

When we walked in the house, Sharon was waiting for us in the front hallway. She smiled. "Kids, guess what? Your mom and dad won a free trip to the Bahamas!" Michael looked at me like he didn't quite believe it. Sharon kept the forced smile as she said, "Go, go, put your book bags in your rooms."

As the others ran to the bedrooms laughing, Sharon pulled me into the living room. She sat down on Mom's plastic covered white couch. "Gary, your Mom and Dad were arrested today."

Normal Someday

The night of the arrest, Sharon scrambled eggs for dinner. She made a happy face as she handed Elizabeth Grace her plate. "There you go!"

As she set down plates for the rest of us, Michael asked, "Sharon, when are Mom and Dad gonna be home?"

Sharon answered in an annoyed tone. "I already told you. I don't know." She took a breath, smiled, and tried to sound sweet. "I'm not sure when they'll be home."

When Sharon walked back to the kitchen, Michael gave me a look like, is she crazy? I never really liked Sharon, but I knew she had to be stressed. She had come to Florida to start a new life, complete with jobs and a place to live for her, Ted, and Elizabeth Grace – all provided by Mom and Dad. I was sure their being arrested had her in shock. I gave Michael a shrug and a halfhearted look to at least acknowledge what he'd said, then took a bite of my eggs.

As we finished dinner, Michelle asked, "Sharon, can we watch TV?" Sharon dropped the pan in the sink and turned on the faucet.

"Yes, for an hour. Then everyone needs to get ready for bed."

Michelle ran to the family room. "I get to choose!" She changed the channel and plopped on the couch. Vincent followed after her, stood in front of the TV and clicked the channel.

Michelle hollered, "Vincent!"

Sharon shouted from the kitchen. "No arguing or you're going to bed now."

Vincent crossed his arms and flopped on the couch. "I hate Full House."

Sharon stepped into the room as she dried her fingers with a dish towel. "You're watching Full House. And one more thing – I don't want any one of you wetting the bed tonight."

Michael, Christina, and Vincent had each sporadically wet the bed their entire lives. I assumed it was a nervous condition due to moving so much, changing schools, or having people live with us. We all just accepted and dealt with it. I had a rule that I'd never sleep with Michael or Vincent, which was easy to follow with three boys. We usually had at least two beds. Michelle, when she did have to share a bed with Christina, would sleep at the far edge so the wet spot wouldn't touch her legs.

Mom had told us that she had wet the bed until she was a teenager. She also told us a horrible story how Grandma, one time when she was drunk, told Uncle Jim and Jack's friends that "Kathleen still pees the bed."

Mom had never said anything embarrassing about Michael, Vincent, or Christina wetting the bed, and she never tried to make them feel bad about it. The only person I ever heard her discuss it with was Dad. I knew she'd be furious when I told her what Sharon had said.

As soon as the organ theme music started for the *Father Dowling Mysteries*, Sharon said, "Alright, it's time for bed."

Michael got right up. I was sure, after what Sharon had said, he couldn't wait to get out of the room. Christina and Michelle followed, but Vincent stayed where he was. He didn't care who knew he peed the bed.

Sharon gave Vincent a stern look. "Vincent, bedtime."

He let out a sigh and whined. "I don't want to go to bed. It's only nine o'clock." The bed wetting comment and her increasingly annoyed tone made me feel there was something dangerous about making Sharon angry. I stepped toward him.

"Vincent, come on. I'm going to bed, too." I smiled. "Goodnight, Sharon." Then I said in a sweet baby voice, "Goodnight, Elizabeth Grace."

How stupid, I thought, as I listened through the wall. Only Sharon would believe Tom Bosley could be a priest solving mysteries. The bedroom door quietly clicked open, and Christina and Michelle snuck into the dark.

Christina asked, "Gar, why would Mom and Dad leave without saying goodbye?"

I spoke softly. "It was a fast trip. They had to leave right away. They might even be home tomorrow."

Michelle questioned further. "Did Uncle Dan go with them?"

Before I could answer, Vincent piped up. "I hope they're home tomorrow. I hate Sharon."

I wanted to whisper, "We all hate Sharon," and tell them it was wrong for her to say something about wetting the bed, but I didn't want to rile them up about it until Mom was home. I ignored Vincent's outburst and answered Michelle's question. "Uncle Dan went back to New Jersey." No one would have been surprised to hear he'd been arrested, but it would have seemed suspicious that it happened the same day Mom and Dad won their trip to the Bahamas. I didn't feel bad lying about Uncle Dan. I just wanted to be sure everyone behaved for Sharon until Mom, and hopefully, Dad, came home. I whispered, "They could be home tomorrow, or it might be a few days. I'm not sure, but we need to listen to Sharon. Vincent, do you understand that?"

The front door opened, and I heard Anthony and Ted talking.

I whispered, "Christina, Michelle, go back to your room." They crept over to the door, slid into the hall, and clicked the door shut.

I heard Anthony through the wall. "I need to take a piss. Are the kids already in bed?"

I lay in bed and thought about how crazy it was that the five of us were in the house alone with Anthony, Sharon, and Ted. I remembered the panic on Sharon's face when she'd told me, "Gary, I have no idea why they would arrest your mom and dad." I had wondered if she might just pack up her car and leave us with Anthony. I didn't think Sharon knew about Dad being in jail in Iowa, and I wasn't sure if she knew that Nick Mele wasn't even his real name. She was probably just as shocked by his arrest as Mom's.

Mom's arrest was the only one I couldn't make sense of. I thought maybe they had arrested her to get information on Dad or Uncle Dan. Or maybe they arrested her as a scare for associating with criminals. Mom had been a housewife her whole life before she started her cleaning company. I couldn't imagine anything illegal she might have done at the Sonesta. Everything was locked shut – even the refrigerators. Plus, Mom had so much pride about the job. I knew she wouldn't have done anything to jeopardize it. I was sure they would let her out.

The next morning, I woke when Sharon opened the bedroom door.

"Come on. Get up. If you don't get up, you're not getting breakfast." She stood with her fists on her hips in the center of the room. "Come on, pull the blankets down. Did you wet the bed?"

As I sat up, blinking, I tried to comprehend that she was actually telling Michael and Vincent to show her their beds. They both looked at me, horrified, but I didn't know what to say. Sharon commanded, "Come on. Let me see."

409

Michael lifted his blanket and scooted so Sharon could see the middle of his bed. Vincent just sat up.

Sharon snipped, "You're not gonna show me?" She pulled back Vincent's blanket as he gripped to hold on. I jumped up, but she had already seen.

Sharon barked, "Take your sheets off and put them in the washer. Where's Christina?" As I pulled the light blue, fitted sheet with the dark spot from Vincent's bed, Christina walked into the room.

Sharon said, "Good job not wetting the bed last night. If any of you wet the bed tonight, you're taking your mattress to the backyard to dry out."

After a breakfast of scrambled eggs (again) Sharon said, "Michael, take Christina, Vincent, and Michelle, and go play in the room." I knew from his curious look, Michael thought it was weird that Sharon was sending him to the room with the kids. I gave him a pleading look without saying a word.

Michael turned to Vincent, Christina, and Michelle. "Come on, guys."

Once they closed the door, Sharon took out The Yellow Pages and opened it on the table. She picked up the phone and began dialing.

"Hi. I'm trying to get information about a person who was arrested yesterday…"

"Ok…"

"Kathleen Mele."

"Nick Mele and Daniel Canaley were arrested, too."

The bedroom door clicked. Michelle stuck her head out and called, "Sharon, I need to go to the bathroom." Sharon shot me a look that meant – get her!

I jogged down the hall. "Michelle, it'll be just a few minutes. Please wait in here."

Christina asked, "Gar, what's going on?"

I smiled. "Everything's fine. Sharon just needs to make a private phone call."

Sharon walked up behind me. "If you need to use the bathroom, use it now." Michelle bolted. Sharon clenched her jaw into a phony grin while she waited. After the toilet flushed, and the water ran, Michelle opened the door. Sharon asked, "Are we good now?" then turned. "Anyone else?" Christina shook her head. Sharon shut the door, walked back to the kitchen, and began dialing again.

I watched and waited for a smile of relief or some indication that Mom was getting out, but Sharon kept her serious stare and answered, "Ok," "I understand," and "No, I'm not." When she hung up the phone, she gave me a cold look. "They're not giving me any information." She dialed someone she knew in New Jersey. I listened as she told them, "The police surrounded the house. When Kathy answered the door, they pulled her out to the front porch and put her in handcuffs. Her brother Danny was hiding in a closet. He got arrested, too." Sharon walked to the far end of the kitchen and whispered, "She owes me almost two weeks' pay. I don't think she's getting out. I think they're taking her back to New Jersey."

I stepped back as her words repeated in my mind. I pictured two policemen, just like the ones who had arrested Uncle Dan in New Jersey, holding Mom's hands behind her back as they locked handcuffs on her. I imagined her crying and pleading, "But I haven't done anything wrong," and my throat closed. Suddenly it was all real. *Could it be true that she wasn't getting out?* My heart started beating fast as I reached for a kitchen chair to steady myself and sit.

Sharon finished her conversation and came back to the kitchen. "Ok, I will," she said then touched the button with her thumb to hang up the call. She looked down as she dialed. I remembered how Mom had said Tampa was just under three hours away.

"Sharon, do you think we should call my Aunt Peggy?"

She ignored me and put the phone to her ear. "Hello?"

I quietly stood, pushed in the chair and walked out to the backyard.

I sat on the dock and stared at the sunlit shimmering water as a white yacht cruised by. An old man wearing a captain's hat waved, while his wife, wearing big sunglasses, sunned herself behind him. I looked up, smiled, and moved my hand back and forth. Waving my hand didn't feel real. The water, the boats, and the bright green palms moving with the breeze didn't seem real either. I stared at the water as the light wake splashed against the sea wall. None of it felt beautiful or tropical or like a vacation anymore. It all felt empty.

Sharon called from the house. "Gary, come inside." I walked up through the grass and pulled the glass door closed behind me. I heard the bedroom door open.

Michael asked, "Sharon, can we come out now?"

Sharon's footsteps echoed as she stomped to the edge of the hall. "Michael, I told you I'd let you know when you can come out."

I saw the receiver on the counter as I stepped up into the kitchen.

Sharon walked back and said, "Your Aunt Peggy is on the phone. She wants to speak to you."

I picked up. "Hello?"

"Hey Gar, how're you doing?"

I smiled. "Good, Aunt Peggy."

"I've been trying to call for hours, but it's been busy."

I could see, off to the side, Sharon watching me. I answered, "I don't know why."

413

Aunt Peggy asked, "How's Sharon treating you guys? She said your mom never paid her."

I felt my voice get slightly higher. "Good. Good. Everything's good."

"I'm going to come down tomorrow and give her some money for you guys."

After the calls were done, Sharon opened the door to the bedroom. "You can come out now."

Michelle ran for the family room and leaped onto the couch. Michael and Vincent giggled about something as they walked to the kitchen.

Christina asked, "Do you want to play pool, Gar?"

"Sure," I answered, then turned toward Sharon. "Do you mind if we play pool, Sharon?"

Sharon kept her eyes focused on the open cabinets. "You can play until dinner's ready."

Michael made a goofy look and commented, "Dinner? It's still light outside." Vincent laughed.

Sharon gave a curt answer. "Well, normal people eat at five o'clock."

Christina stared intently as she cracked and sank ball after ball. She beat me two times. We were just about to start our third game when Sharon announced, "Dinner's gonna be ready in a few minutes. Come and sit down." Michelle popped down from the couch and ran for the kitchen. Christina and I followed.

Even though I wasn't hungry, I was happy to see the Kraft Macaroni and Cheese boxes after having eggs for dinner and then breakfast.

Sharon turned on the sink and began filling a measuring cup. I asked, "What's that for, Sharon?"

"I need to save the milk for Elizabeth Grace." She dumped the water into the macaroni.

As she clinked the fork around the pot to mix in the cheesy powder, Michael whispered, "Doesn't Elizabeth Grace get enough milk from Sharon's boob?"

Vincent chuckled. I quickly stood, shot them both a stern look then turned toward her. "Sharon, do you need help with anything?" I watched her face, as she scooped out the macaroni, to be sure she hadn't heard them.

The next morning, the phone began ringing early. Sharon motioned for me to gather the kids into the bedrooms, which I did. I knew they would begin questioning what was really happening as I told them, "Guys, just wait in here. It'll only be a few minutes."

Vincent grumbled. "That's what Sharon told us yesterday. We were in here all day." I got annoyed at him for exaggerating, then reminded myself that it had to be scary for all of them. I was sure they knew we were hiding something.

I tried to speak calmly. "It was only a couple of hours, Vincent. Please, just don't make Sharon upset." I closed the door, shut my eyes for a couple of seconds, then turned down the hall.

Sharon was speaking on the phone when I walked back into the kitchen. "That would be great. Yeah, he's right here. Hold on." She put her hand over the mouthpiece. "It's your Aunt Lorraine. She wants you to go live with her."

I answered. "Hello?"

"Gar, this is so crazy. How is everyone?"

"We're good, Aunt Lorraine. It is crazy."

"Listen, I was talking to your Uncle Mike. You can come stay with us if you want, Gar."

I answered before I even processed what she said.

"Oh, ok. That would be great. Thanks, Aunt Lorraine."

She told me to think about it and said she loved me. I told her I loved her, too, before we said goodbye. As I hung up the phone, I thought about all the times I had wished and prayed that I could live with her. I remembered us laughing about Uncle Dan stealing quarters from her change jar as we drove to Bradley Beach with the top down in her convertible. The idea of living with Aunt Lorraine usually made me

416

smile, but this time, I thought about Christina, Michelle, Vincent, and Michael. Imagining leaving them put an empty, sick feeling in my gut.

Sharon seemed excited. "Are you going to go live with her? Are you?"

I forced a smile and tried to put a thought together. "I don't know. What if Mom gets out? And what about the other kids?"

Sharon turned deadly serious. "She's not getting out. And no one's going to take all five of you – you know that, right? Besides, they'd split you up if you went to a foster home, anyway." The bedroom door closed.

My mind raced as I walked down the hall. They'd been listening. *What had they heard?* From outside the door I heard a soft noise that sounded like whimpering. I took a deep breath and walked into the room. Christina had her hand on her mouth, trying to muffle her crying. I ran over. "Christina, what's the matter?"

She wiped the tears with her wrist. "I… don't… want… to go to a foster home."

I grabbed her and squeezed tight. "You're not going to a foster home, Christina."

As I tried to figure out exactly what they had overheard, Michelle started crying. I reached out and pulled her close to me. "Shh… shh…" I whispered, "It's ok, guys. It's ok."

Vincent's mouth was tight. I could tell from his heaving chest that he was about to cry, too. I stretched my hand out for him, but he pulled away.

Michael stepped protectively toward Vincent and directed his words to me. "I heard Sharon tell you we're going to a foster home, and Aunt Lorraine wants only you. Where are Mom and Dad?"

The feeling in my chest went hollow again. I wasn't sure if it was true, but I still said, "No, I'm not going with Aunt Lorraine, Michael. We're all staying together."

Sharon walked into the bedroom. "This is why you shouldn't be listening at the door. Your mom and dad were taken to jail. That's why your Aunt Peggy is coming this afternoon."

Michelle sobbed. "Are we going to live with her?"

"I don't know. We're trying to figure everything out."

I felt relief that everyone knew the truth, but I also felt intense hate – stronger than I'd ever felt – toward Sharon. I knew she was angry at Mom and probably despised her, but Christina was ten, Vincent was seven, and Michelle was only six years old. I thought about Elizabeth Grace. As much as I loathed Sharon, Elizabeth Grace was a baby – innocent. What kind of evil person would I be if I took my feelings for Sharon out on her? I wanted to kill Sharon, but I forced the anger from my mind and focused my thoughts on Aunt Peggy's coming to visit us.

The five of us sat around the family room as Sharon walked back and forth through the kitchen with Elizabeth Grace on her hip.

Michael asked, "Where's Anthony?"

"He's out with Ted somewhere," I answered.

Michelle said, "I hate Anthony," as Sharon walked into the room.

Sharon reached for a red shirt that was draped over the back of the couch. "Why do you hate Anthony, Michelle?"

"I just do."

We had another lunch of scrambled eggs before filing back onto the couch to watch the sun, which was bright and still high in the sky. When Aunt Peggy's car pulled into the driveway, Sharon said, "Wait here," as she slipped on her flip flops. Once she was outside, the five of us ran to the window to watch. Aunt Peggy closed the door to her shiny, red Mustang that we hadn't seen since she'd left New Jersey.

As Sharon walked up to the car, a man got out of the passenger side. He was tan, with dirty blond hair and a mustache. He was also just a little shorter than Aunt Peggy.

Sharon gave a phony, "Hi," as Aunt Peggy walked around. "Hi, Sharon. Thank you for everything you've been doing."

As Aunt Peggy talked to Sharon, she took the sunglasses from the top of her head and casually ran her hand through her long black hair to be sure it looked tousled and carefree, I assumed to remind Sharon, that even though Aunt Peggy's teenage modeling days were behind her, she still knew how beautiful she was. The man walked proudly to Aunt Peggy's side as she finished her chit chat. "I want to see the kids, Sharon," Aunt Peggy said. "Let's go inside."

When Aunt Peggy walked in the door, I realized, even though her face and physique were slimmer, how much she looked like Mom. I hugged her and breathed in the scent of her neck. Her perfume was different, but her skin still smelled similar to Mom's which put a slight lump in my throat.

After Aunt Peggy hugged each of us, she turned toward the man. "This is my boyfriend, Terry."

Terry grinned, obviously proud that she'd just named him her boyfriend.

As Aunt Peggy introduced us, she added things like, "Michael always helps around the house," "The nuns in Catholic school loved Vincent," and "Christina is great at sports. She can beat all the boys in kickball." I watched his eager smile and realized Terry wanted us to like him as much as Aunt Peggy wanted him to like us.

I asked Terry, "What do you do for work?" He told me that he manages the grounds at Innisbrook Resort and Country Club.

I had no idea what that meant, but I still acted impressed. "Wow, the whole resort?"

Terry gave a humble smile then explained a little more about the job. After I told him that Christina and Vincent sometimes played golf with a plastic cup in the backyard, he chuckled and said, "Maybe I can teach you both to play for real someday."

Aunt Peggy's eyes moved from Terry to Christina and Vincent and then back to me. I knew she was proud that I'd engaged Terry and got him talking. She gave me a slight, acknowledging grin and put her arm around my back. "Gary is my godson, Terry." I smiled.

After a couple of hours of talking and laughing, Aunt Peggy said, "We have to get going, guys."

Michelle begged, "No, please, don't go."

Aunt Peggy bent down and hugged her. "I'll come back, Michelle. I promise." She stood and said to me, "We're gonna get your Mom out, Gar. You guys just need to stay strong."

I appreciated her trying to make me feel better, but I knew it wasn't true. If Mom were really getting out, Sharon wouldn't be working to ship us off to different relatives. Aunt Peggy hugged each of us one more time, then handed Sharon some folded money and thanked her again.

Ted and Anthony came home about a half hour after Aunt Peggy had left. After Sharon questioned Ted about his and Anthony's efforts to find quick work, she gave Ted two of the twenties that Aunt Peggy had handed her and sent him to the store for groceries.

Ted picked up his keys. "Ant, come take a ride." Anthony jogged toward the front door. Even before her lips tightened, I knew Anthony's going was not part of Sharon's plan. Still, she didn't say a word. She only stared out the window with Elizabeth Grace on her hip as they drove away.

Over two hours later, we all sat quietly in the family room as the sun set. No one got up to turn any lights on as shadows stretched through the room, and it got cool and dark outside. Sharon nursed Elizabeth Grace as she sat motionless, staring toward the front door.

Elizabeth Grace turned her head to take a breath, leaving Sharon's long, pink nipple exposed. Sharon broke from her trance, pulled her shirt over her boob and turned toward us. "Alright, it's bedtime." Everyone looked puzzled.

"Sharon," I said, "we didn't even eat dinner."

She stood up. "They're not back from the store yet. We don't have any food."

I calmly stated, "We have bread. Can we at least have toast?"

Sharon popped eight pieces of toast and cut three in half. We ate our piece and a half of dry toast before going to our rooms.

As we lay down, Michael whispered, "Sharon's nipple looks like E. T's finger."

Vincent laughed as I snapped, "Michael!"

Michael turned toward the wall. "It does. No wonder Ted didn't come home. He probably hates being married to her."

I sighed. "Yes, I'm sure he does, but he had the money Aunt Peggy left for food." I pulled my pillow under my head, closed my eyes and remembered the smell of Aunt Peggy's skin. I imagined Mom walking through the door.

The muffled screaming startled me awake. I could make out Sharon's hysterical voice. "Fucking nice, Theodore! You went to a bar – with him?!"

I propped myself up on my elbows and blinked, as shadows appeared in the dark.

Vincent whispered, "Gar?"

"Yeah, Vincent?"

"Why are Sharon and Ted fighting?"

"I'm not sure. Just stay in bed and stay quiet, ok?"

After the arguing stopped, Michael asked, "Gar, do you think we're gonna live with Aunt Peggy?"

I didn't know what would happen, but I knew I needed to sound confident. "Yeah, I'm pretty sure. If Mom and Dad don't get out, I'm sure we will."

The door flung open, and I blinked to adjust to the morning brightness. Sharon stomped into the bedroom, flipped back Michael's blanket and then Vincent's. "You both wet the bed. Take off your sheets and grab your mattresses."

Michael and Vincent both bolted up and out of bed. Sharon commanded, "Out to the backyard. Then get clean clothes and get in the shower."

I helped Vincent turn his mattress on its side to push out of the room, then noticed Christina struggling with her mattress in the hallway. I gave Michael a look. He offered to help Vincent. I took a side of Christina's mattress. We slid it through the house, out to the backyard, while happy birds chirped. As Michael and Vincent pushed and pulled through the open glass door, I couldn't help but smirk. Michael grinned, and then Vincent and Christina started laughing. I began cracking up as I asked myself, how much more absurd could our lives get?

That afternoon, Sharon called me from the family room. "Gary, I need to speak to you alone." She raised her eyebrows and pointed toward the living room. I followed her to Mom's plastic covered white sofa. She sat down, looked to be sure no one was near, and asked in a hushed voice, "How long has Anthony lived with your family?"

Why did she want to know about Anthony? I wanted to say, "Too long," but I knew she wouldn't appreciate my being funny, and I didn't want to joke with her, anyway. I knew she hated Anthony. So did I. But I hated her just as much

I answered. "He would spend the night once in a while. This is the first time he's actually lived with us. Why?"

"No reason."

A few days after Sharon asked me about Anthony, he left and didn't come back. It was almost two weeks after he was gone when the man from the Florida Department of Health and Rehabilitative Services came. Even before Sharon told me, I knew it was the man's job to find out if we had been neglected or abused.

I told Michael, "Don't tell him about all the people that have lived with us and how much we've moved. He's going to try to keep us from going back to Mom and Dad."

Michael nodded with nervous energy and explained it to Vincent while I explained it to Christina and Michelle.

The social worker sat in Mom's spot at the kitchen table, which made me remember Mom laughing about Sharon eating crab guts while the rest of us ate greasy, sausage pizza. The man gave a phony smile and wrote my name in black ink on his clipboard as I pulled out a chair. He began the conversation with questions about things I knew he didn't care about, such as my favorite television show and my favorite subject in school.

Then he said, "Tell me about your life."

I smiled at him. "I have a great life. My parents are very supportive. They want me to make good grades and do my chores before I go out with my friends. I hope they come home soon."

The man wrote much more than what I had told him. His next question was, "Has your mother or father ever hit you?"

Even though they really hadn't, I still gasped to emphasize how shocked I was. "Never!"

When I was done, I knew I had answered every question perfectly. My only concern was how the other kids would do. Michael was great. Christina and Vincent were both good. Michelle's answers were the only ones I thought he could probably see through.

"My Mom and Dad are the best parents ever," Michelle proclaimed.

The man shuffled his papers neat and placed them in his tattered, brown briefcase. He turned toward Sharon. "That's everything I need. We'll be in touch with their aunt."

It was a week after that when Sharon called, "Gary, it's your Aunt Peggy on the phone."

I hustled to the kitchen. "Hello?"

"Hey, Gar. How are you guys?"

"We're ok, Aunt Peggy. How are you?"

"Good. Listen, Terry wants to take everyone in. He's being interviewed by H.R.S. tomorrow."

"All of us? And you? In his house?"

"Yup! Keep your fingers crossed. I love you, Honey. I'll call you in a few days."

"I love you, too, Aunt Peggy."

As I hung up the phone, relief welled up in my chest. I wasn't sure if I wanted to laugh or cry. I let out a deep breath and gave Sharon a hug. She smiled. I ran to the bedroom. "Guys, we might all be going to live with Aunt Peggy!" Seeing Michael, Christina, Vincent, and Michelle smile and laugh with giddy excitement made me the happiest I'd ever been in my whole life.

Dysfunctional Normality

I got irritated as I counted the bags at the front door. There were already six, including a Hefty trash bag. Aunt Peggy had told us that Terry's house was nice, but it wasn't that big. She said we should only bring what we could fit in one bag. I was sure the extra bags were Michael's. I pulled one of the black garbage bags open. Inside was his Nintendo and his two boxes of Garbage Pail Kid cards.

"Michael!"

He huffed, "What?" as he walked out with a stack of VCR tapes. I knew they were the movies he'd recorded from HBO. I reached for one, but he pulled away and yelled. "Stop! Aunt Peggy!"

I marched down the hall to Christina and Michelle's room where Aunt Peggy was helping them pack their clothes.

I stopped in the doorway. "Aunt Peggy, Michael already has three bags."

Michael came up behind me as Aunt Peggy held up Michelle's black and neon yellow bathing suit. "Oh my God, this is so cute." Then she told me, in a sweet voice, "Gar, I told him he could bring the Nintendo."

"He's bringing all his videos, too."

I grabbed one of the video cassettes and read the white label where Michael had neatly written the titles. "Lethal Weapon, Robocop,

Good Morning, Vietnam. He's never even seen Good Morning, Vietnam."

Michael snatched it back. "I'm gonna watch it."

Aunt Peggy said, "Michael, why don't you just pick your favorite two or three videos? You can always record more. Terry has a VCR."

After Aunt Peggy told Michael that he could only bring three of his videos, I got a slight guilty knot in my stomach. Even though she assured us that Terry was having everything put in storage, I suspected we'd never see anything we left behind again. I questioned whether I should have said anything about Michael's bags but then reminded myself how crazy it seemed that Terry had agreed to take in five kids that he didn't know. I thought about his forced grin when he told us that he was so happy we were all going to live with him. I felt bad about Michael's movies but knew it was more important not to push the rules with a strange man whose house we were going to be living in.

I walked into my bedroom to grab my bag and take one last look. I remembered when Mom had whispered, "Uncle Danny wanted my stereo, but I told him I already promised it to you." She winked and gave me a sweet smile to let me know it was mine. I stared at the dual tape deck and thought about the Madonna mixtapes I'd made. I felt cool, like a D.J., when I'd recorded "Material Girl," "Papa, Don't Preach," and "Causing a Commotion" on the same cassette. Thinking about leaving the stereo in our deserted house, along with our furniture,

TV, and all of Mom's and Dad's clothes, made me sad. I picked up my stack of Madonna cassettes and placed them next to my neatly folded Madonna concert shirt. I zippered up my bag and walked out to the kitchen.

After we'd loaded the back of the van that Aunt Peggy had rented with our backpacks, duffle bags, and Michael's garbage bags, Aunt Peggy said, "Alright guys, let's get in." I followed her back to the house as the kids piled into the van. I stopped in the kitchen as Aunt Peggy walked to Mom and Dad's room. I'd already spent so much time sitting on their bed wishing they would come home. I didn't need to see it one last time. I opened the refrigerator. It was bare except for the remains of our last stick of butter, a half-empty ketchup bottle, and Mom's bottle of Diet Coke.

Aunt Peggy came back into the kitchen. "Gar, do you know what happened to your mom's fur coat and her necklaces?" I knew from the suspicious look that she thought Sharon had taken them. I hadn't seen Sharon take anything from Mom's room, but I wouldn't be surprised if she had. She told every person she spoke to that Mom owed her two weeks' pay.

I shrugged. "I don't know, Aunt Peggy. I know Sharon was upset that Mom owed her money."

Aunt Peggy looked off as she thought for a moment. "Ok, let's go."

As we passed through the living room, I thought about how Mom's white furniture had never actually been sat on. I touched the thick, clear plastic and wondered what she was saving it for. I started to get a lump in my throat. I took a deep breath. I was tired of feeling like everything was terrible. I reminded myself that the five of us were together and about to start a new life with Aunt Peggy. I pulled the front door closed behind me and walked out to the van.

As we drove north on Highway 75, I thought about nine people squeezing into Terry's three-bedroom house. Besides the five of us, Aunt Peggy and Billy had just moved into Terry's house. Aunt Peggy told me Terry also had a son who was Billy and Michelle's age, but he was only there on the weekends. I wondered what he would think of having six more kids living at his dad's house. I couldn't imagine where we were all going to sleep. I snickered as I thought how Mom could have told Terry how to make it work.

I looked out the window at the marshy fields that stretched for miles with no houses at all. There were tall, bushy trees that looked like something from a swamp and a lot of pine trees.

"I didn't realize pine trees grow in Florida."

Aunt Peggy looked out her window. "Oh yeah, I didn't realize either."

Vincent asked if it snowed in Florida. "No," Aunt Peggy answered, "it's beautiful all year long."

When we got off the highway, Aunt Peggy told us, "This is Dale Mabry highway. It's the main road through Tampa."

Vincent asked, "Dale what?"

Aunt Peggy gave a silly look but tried to answer seriously. "Mabry, like maybe or baby – or babery." She cracked up.

I smiled, and Michael said, "Whatever it is, it's a weird name."

As we turned into Terry's neighborhood, I rolled my window down. The air smelled like fresh cut grass and two boys about Michael's age watched us as they walked their Huffy bikes along the sidewalk. The stucco walls of Terry's white house were bright and clean, and the rose bushes in his yard looked like they'd been trimmed the day before.

Terry unlocked the front door and led us into his home. The kitchen was small, seemingly designed for a single person, and it was separated from the living room by a tiny, two-seat breakfast bar. Through a glass door, was a pristine, aqua pool that I was sure smelled like chlorine. Terry smiled and motioned for us to follow. He showed us a sparsely decorated room with a neatly made bed, clearly the spare bedroom.

Terry spoke in a baby tone. "Christina, Michelle, this will be your room."

Michael cocked his eyebrow as if to ask me if Terry was really speaking to Christina and Michelle like they were toddlers. I quickly shook my head to make him stop and turned away. Next, Terry walked us into what was obviously a little boy's room. He cooed, "This is my son T.J.'s room. He's here on the weekends." He grabbed the railings of the two sets of red bunk beds. "Michael, Vincent – you two are in this bunk. T.J and Billy are in this one."

Finally, Terry pulled open double doors in the living room to reveal a small room with a couch and a TV. He looked at me. "This is the den. It's going to be your room, Gary."

I examined the dark paneled walls and touched the tan, woven fabric of the couch and smiled. "Thank you, Terry."

Terry gave a quick, forced smile then walked to the kitchen. Aunt Peggy popped her head in. "Isn't this nice, Gar? You've got your own room!" I imagined how proud she was for negotiating the deal with Terry, unaware that he'd give her anything she wanted.

I smiled, gave her a hug, and said, "Thank you, Aunt Peggy."

Aunt Peggy followed Terry to the refrigerator, where he clicked the top of a Coors Light can. "Terry, I think we should get Pizza Hut for dinner."

As I sat on the couch, which was going to be my new bed, Michael said, "At least you get your own room, Gar. We have to share a room with Billy and Terry's son."

Vincent asked, "Why does Terry talk like we're babies?"

434

Michael whispered, "You're lucky he didn't ask to change your diaper."

Even I wanted to tell Terry that we'd experienced alcoholism, abuse, neglect, and our parents being arrested. None of us needed to be spoken to like two-year-old's. Even though I agreed with Michael and Vincent, I knew if I let them know, it would just encourage Michael's jokes and Vincent's laughter.

Instead, I explained, "Some normal people speak to children, regardless of how old they are, like babies."

When the pizza was delivered, Aunt Peggy sniffed the boxes. "Mmmmm… we got an extra cheese and a super supreme." She placed the brown boxes on the dining room table and then went to the kitchen to begin popping cans of Caffeine Free Pepsi. She poured each of us a glass as we all filed around and took our seats. Terry clicked the top of another Coors and took a huge gulp. He sat and smiled.

As everyone reached and grabbed for their slice of pan pizza, nudging and pushing each other's arms out of the way, Terry stiffened, and his grin became tense. His eyes scanned every kid at the table before he settled on Michelle. "Let me get that for you, Baby."

Terry then focused on Billy. "Are you going to eat all three of those slices?" Aunt Peggy ignored Terry's apparent frustration and laughed as Billy pulled at his cheese with only his teeth.

It had been years since we were able to wear whatever clothes we wanted to school. Christina quickly picked out a tee-shirt to go with her jeans and white Nike sneakers. Michelle was as excited as Aunt Peggy as they dug through her clothes for the cutest outfit they could find. Aunt Peggy told her, "We're going to T.J. Maxx this weekend. It's right near my salon. They have the cutest girls' tops. Christina, you're going to come, too."

I knew the last thing Christina wanted to do was go girly clothes shopping with Michelle and Aunt Peggy, but she agreed. "Ok."

As I fingered through my clothes, I debated which shirts would call the least amount of attention. I pulled my Madonna shirt out of its fold and held it in front of me. Even though Mom wouldn't let me go to her concert, the "Who's That Girl World Tour" black tee-shirt was my favorite. I knew there was a chance some of the teenage boys might think I was gay if I wore it. Even though we had been wearing uniforms to school for years, I still knew boys weren't wearing Madonna shirts. They thought of her as a singer that only girls liked. I examined the white image of Madonna, the leather jacket falling off her shoulders and only a bra on underneath. She didn't care what anyone thought of her. I took a breath and pulled the shirt on. When I walked out of my den, Aunt Peggy exclaimed, "Gar, I love Madonna!"

I walked to my economics class and thought about the three schools I'd attended since I started ninth grade. The Catholic school in New Jersey was full of snooty rich kids, but at least there were a few people I knew, like Colleen O'Brien. The Baptist school in Cape Coral was weird but fun, with the five of us experiencing the craziness together. Ben Hill was considered junior high, but it went up to ninth grade. It had been so long since I'd been in a school where I didn't know even one person.

It was late in the afternoon when I walked by a group of teenage boys who were also wearing black concert tee-shirts – but theirs were Metallica and Van Halen. One kid hunched against the wall, in the middle of the group, stared as I walked by. I kept my eyes forward as if I didn't know they were there, but I still heard him. "Is that kid really wearing a Madonna shirt?" His friends snickered.

I wanted to turn and confront the ugly kid with the black curly hair. I imagined telling him, "Yeah, I'm wearing a Madonna shirt. Why don't you go sneak another cigarette in the bathroom?" but I just kept walking. On the bus ride home, I held my bag so nobody else would see Madonna. I stared out the window and wondered if I'd ever stop being afraid.

As the weeks rolled by, Terry got comfortable creating and enforcing rules. He walked into the dining room, where we were all already sitting, holding a platter and a bowl. He smiled. "We're having pork chops and applesauce for dinner." He set down the plate of meat, dunked a spoon in the applesauce and walked back to the kitchen.

Michael leaned back to be sure Terry couldn't hear and then imitated Peter Brady's "pawk chopsh and apple shaush." Everyone snickered, including Aunt Peggy.

When Terry came back in, he placed glasses of water in the center of the table. Michael and I looked at each other. We quickly figured it meant no drink with our meal. Christina, Vincent, and Michelle followed our example and pretended the water wasn't even on the table. Billy either didn't get it or didn't care. He reached for the water, which made Terry snap, "Billy!" Terry calmed his voice. "You may drink your water when you've finished your dinner."

Aunt Peggy took several bites of her pork chop. "Oh," she said, in a raspy voice, "This is delicious – dry, but delicious." Christina and Vincent both let out a chuckle. Then it was completely quiet.

After about thirty seconds, Terry slammed his first, which made the silverware on the table pop. He got up and dropped his dish in the sink and walked back in with a beer.

Aunt Peggy yelled, "Have another beer, Terry. Why don'tcha?" and stormed off to the bedroom.

Terry pointed at Vincent, then Billy. "You finish your dinner before you take a drink." He followed Aunt Peggy to the room and slammed the door.

The next afternoon, Terry called all of us into the living room. "Family meeting," he said, as he clapped twice. Aunt Peggy stood next to the breakfast bar brushing clear polish onto her nails. As Michael walked into the room, I knew that he was thinking the same thing I was. Does Terry really think we're *The Brady Bunch*? Everyone took seats on the couch, but Vincent and Billy scuffled over who would get the rocking recliner. Vincent shoved Billy away, but Billy pushed him right back and squeezed in.

Vincent yelled, "Billy, get off!"

I clenched my mouth and commanded, "Both of you, stop," but they ignored me.

Terry said, "It's ok." He forced a smile. "You can both sit there."

Once everyone was settled, Terry started. "Your Aunt Peggy –" He turned to Billy, "– or your mom – and I should not be arguing in front of you guys. We're a family now, and we have to have rules." He scanned everyone for an objection before going on. "Everyone will make their beds right after they get up."

I quickly glanced at the sheet and pillow on the couch in the den, open for everyone in the house to see.

He continued. "Christina, you and Michelle will clear the plates and load the dishwasher. Vincent, you and Billy will take out the trash and skim the pool every day. Michael, you will mow the lawn on the weekend."

Michael blurted, "What about Gary?" I wanted to yell back, "Gary watches you guys. Don't worry about Gary!" but Aunt Peggy interjected, "I got Gary a job. He's going to clean my salon on Sundays."

Aunt Peggy and I met Sal, the salon manager, around eight o'clock in the morning. As he unlocked the door to Executive Quarters, I remembered Mom letting us into the Sonesta. Unlike the resort on the beach, the salon had long fluorescent bulbs that flickered on, and it stank like hair chemicals.

Sal led us through the salon, as he explained, "You need to sweep under the salon chairs to get all the hair out onto the floor. Then you vacuum, then you mop. It's going to take you about four hours. There's a check for twenty dollars on the reception desk when you're done." After he showed me the cleaning supply closet, he asked, "Do you have any questions?"

I asked, "Are you going to meet me up here to let me in and out?"

Sal smiled and held up the same key he had let us in with. "This is yours. Be sure you lock both doors and turn out the lights when you're done."

I realized that even if you sweep the same spot five times, you'll never get all the tiny hairs, and the vacuum seemed to blow more around than it picked up. Frustrated, I finally decided I'd gotten as many off the tile as I could. I filled the yellow, rolling bucket and bobbed the dirty gray mop up and down. I slopped the mop on the floor and began pulling back and forth when I realized the water had sloshed out patches of hairs that were stuck in crevices and under counters. I wanted to scream. Instead, I let out a long, aggravated breath, then kneeled to wipe up the hairs with paper towels. By the time I was finished, it was two thirty in the afternoon. I thought, four hours, yeah right! I took my envelope, locked the doors and headed home, exhausted.

As I walked through the shopping center parking lot, I thought about Aunt Peggy always having a job and making enough money to take care of herself. She paid for her own apartment and didn't let anyone who was an alcoholic or a criminal live with her. I wondered why it was so easy for her but so difficult for Mom.

I turned down the street to our neighborhood and wondered if Mom would get a job when she got out of prison. Aunt Peggy said the reason Mom was arrested and taken back to New Jersey was because of things Dad had done. She'd explained that the police didn't believe Mom was innocent, so they had to look for something to charge her with and lying on a credit card application was the only thing they could come up with.

Why would the police want to arrest a mother with five children for lying on a credit card application? I was sure if Mom had had her own career, instead of a cleaning company that she'd just started, they would have believed she was innocent.

441

As I walked along the sidewalk of our street, Terry's house came into view. He was clipping bushes on the side of the garage, and Michael was pushing the lawn mower, sweating. When I neared the driveway, the lawn mower sputtered down. Michael wiped his face with his forearm.

Terry marched around to the front of the yard. "What are you doing? You're not done."

Michael panted. "I am. It's finished."

Terry gave his phony smile. "I want you to go over it again, the opposite direction. Here, I'll show you." Terry set his Coors Light down on the driveway, yanked the cord, and began pushing up and down the yard, the same direction as the driveway. He hollered over the motor. "It's easier because the grass is already cut." I felt bad that Michael had to mow the lawn twice, but I was too tired to get involved. I walked in and plopped down on the couch.

When Michael was finally finished, he came in and dropped into the recliner. We were both too exhausted to argue about what to watch, so MTV went on. As the music started, I livened up and started rocking to probably the best dance song I'd ever heard in my entire life. Michael groaned. "I hate Milli Vanilli," then imitated their crazy shoulder moves.

I didn't care. I perked up and sang along. "Girl… you… know… it's… true…"

Terry walked in from the garage. His usual phony smile had melted into a dumb, drunk grin. He walked by us. "Those boys can really sing." He grabbed another beer from the refrigerator and headed to his bedroom. A few minutes later, he stumbled out to turn the air down. I wasn't sure if he was too drunk to realize or too drunk to care that Michael and I were still in the living room. He was wearing only tight, white underwear that he'd obviously gotten for Christmas. There were red and green Ho Ho Hos printed on them.

After Terry went back in his room, Michael leaned toward me and said, "His underwear's laughing because there's nothing in them." We both cracked up.

When our first report cards came, Michael's grades were as bad as they always were. Vincent and my grades were ok. Michelle's were good – but everyone's grades were good in the first grade.

It was when Aunt Peggy pulled out Christina's report card that she practically shouted. "Christina! You made the honor roll!"

Christina smiled, humble but proud of herself. Aunt Peggy squeezed her. "Oh my God! We have to celebrate. We're getting Pizza Hut."

Michael whispered. "We get Pizza Hut every Friday."

I snapped, "Shut up. You're just jealous no one's celebrating your D's and F's." I smiled and hugged Christina, too.

It was the first week of summer. Terry was in the pool throwing T.J., Billy, and Vincent toward the deep end as they screamed. Michelle paddled around with her orange floaties, spitting water, and Christina was serious as she held her nose and cannonballed off the diving board. I sat in the lawn chair next to Aunt Peggy as she dried in the sun.

"Aunt Peggy, what made you want to be normal?"

"Well," she answered, "I started going to Al-anon after Bruce and I broke up."

"What's Al-anon?"

"It's a twelve-step program for when you're in a dysfunctional relationship with an alcoholic." After she explained what dysfunctional meant and that the alcoholic didn't have to be a husband or wife, she told me she was going to ask her friend, Mary Ann, about meetings in North Tampa.

There weren't any Al-Anon groups in the area, but Aunt Peggy found an ACOA meeting.

I asked, "What's ACOA?"

"Adult children of alcoholics."

"But Mom's not an alcoholic, Aunt Peggy."

She whispered to me. "She doesn't have to be. Terry is an alcoholic."

We both laughed. She wrote the address for me on the back of an envelope. "It's just up the street, Gar. You should think about going."

My heart pounded in my chest as I walked up Northdale Ave. to the business park. I walked into the courtyard and around the four-sided clock. The three clocks that were working all had different times, and the one that was probably the closest to the actual time made me a half-hour early. All the offices were dark except one. It was bright, like a doctor's office waiting room, and I could see people inside.

Fear spread through my arms and legs as I thought about approaching the door. What was I doing? This was crazy, I told myself. I didn't even think that Mom was an alcoholic. I was just about to turn and walk home when a strength pulled at my chest. I didn't want to be dysfunctional. I didn't want to be afraid. I took a deep breath and let it out – two times. I walked over and pulled the handle of the door.

As I stepped inside, three of the four ladies smiled. They looked like normal people. I stuttered. "I… I'm… Is this the ACOA meeting?"

The shorter of the three ladies walked over. "Yes, it is. Is this your first time?"

It was dark by the time I walked home. I replayed the meeting in my mind. The person who started the meeting explained that nothing that was said would ever be repeated outside of that room. Every person took a turn to talk. They spoke about whatever they wanted, and no one interrupted them. I told them about Mom and Dad going to jail, Uncle Jim being an alcoholic, Uncle Dan being a criminal, and the many people who lived with us. When I couldn't think of anything else to say, I let out a breath and just felt good. I had never told any stranger, let alone a group of them, about my life. Everyone smiled at me, and most of the people hugged me before I left.

It was a restless weekday afternoon. Terry was working. Aunt Peggy had taken Christina, Michelle, and Billy shopping. It was supposed to just be girls, but Billy whined, "I wanna go."

I was glad he didn't stay home with us. Michael and I were watching TV when Vincent came out of the bedroom in his swim trunks. "Guys, do you want to go swimming?"

I shook my head. "Terry doesn't want us swimming when he's not home."

Michael had a different response. "We'll go swimming... if you put on Michelle's bathing suit."

Vincent furrowed his eyebrows in a serious, there's no way he'd do that, type of look, but his slight smile made Michael's eyes light up. "Really. Just go try it on. I promise if you do, we'll go swimming. Right, Gar?"

I mentally debated for a quick second, then decided I was going to enjoy being an evil older brother. "Yeah, Vincent. Just try it on. No one will see but us." He walked to the girls' room and closed the door.

When the door clicked open, Vincent peeked his face out.

Michael asked, "Do you have it on?"

Vincent nodded, and we bolted toward him. He slammed the door, but I grabbed the handle before he could lock it, and we pushed our way inside.

"Grab his legs!" I said as I took Vincent's hands. We picked him up and struggled to maneuver him to the back door.

Vincent screamed, "Not outside! Not outside!" laughing the whole time.

Michael reached behind him and managed to pull the door open. "On the count of three. One... Two... Three!" We heaved Vincent, in his yellow and black one piece, through the air, as his arms and legs flailed.

SPLOOSH!!

Vincent flipped his head out of the water. He tried not to smile as he yelled, "That wasn't funny!"

I laughed as Michael cracked up. Vincent paddled over to the side and started pulling himself out.

Michael got serious. "The neighbors are gonna see you."

Vincent plunked back down, so the water was at his chest. "Stop! Get me a towel." When we got bored of the teasing, Michael got him one of Terry's blue striped beach towels from inside.

Aunt Peggy, the girls, and Billy came home while the three of us were smushed into the couch, watching *Adventures in Babysitting*.

Aunt Peggy placed her keys on the counter. "What did you guys do today?"

I answered, "Nothing."

Michael and Vincent both shook their heads. "Yeah, nothing."

Michelle called from the bathroom. "Why is my bathing suit wet?" She walked out holding it.

Vincent immediately answered, "I don't know."

Michael shrugged, and I said, "Maybe you left it in there from the weekend."

Michelle put her hand on her hip, "It was dry, and I folded it. It was in my room."

I stood and changed the subject. "Aunt Peggy, what're we having for dinner?"

Her eyes moved from Michelle to Michael and Vincent, and, finally, to me. "I have to work, Gar. Terry will be home in a little while. He'll make dinner."

Aunt Peggy reached for Michelle's wet suit. "Michelle, give that to me, Honey. I'll put it in my bathroom."

The level of tension around Terry amplified when Aunt Peggy wasn't home. When the front door opened, I felt a slight stiffening in my shoulders. I nervously rocked in the recliner as I waited to examine his scowl to determine which mood he was in: angry and quiet, angry and phony happy, or angry and ready to yell. He walked around the corner, took a Coors Light from the refrigerator, and glared intently into the living room. He pulled out a pan and opened the refrigerator again as Billy called from the bedroom, "Why is there a wet towel behind the door?"

Terry's face turned disgusted. "What?!" He dropped the package of cubed steak and marched to the boys' room.

I wanted to slam Billy for being stupid, as he denied, "It wasn't me. It wasn't me."

Terry stomped out clenching the damp towel. He growled. "Who left a wet towel on the carpet?" Everyone was quiet. "Who?" he yelled and started toward Vincent. I popped up in front of him. "Terry it wasn't–"

As I rolled backward out of the tipped recliner, I tried to make sense of what just happened. Had Terry pushed me? Hard enough to knock the recliner backward? I pulled myself up from my hands and knees. Michael, Michelle, and Vincent's eyes were wide and their mouths open. Terry's rage melted into a phony smile. "Oh, I didn't mean to push you. You're alright."

My heart pounded. I grabbed my sneakers and headed for the front door. Terry pleaded. "You're alright. It was an accident."

I focused on tying my laces as my hands shook. I stood up and opened the front door. Terry walked up behind me. "It was an accident," he said again.

As I walked down the path, Terry's voice turned angry. "Jeez! I told you it was an accident!" He slammed the door, which made me jolt. I walked down the street steady as I breathed. I kept repeating in my mind that I had to get to Executive Quarters and tell Aunt Peggy.

It was dark by the time Aunt Peggy and I pulled into the driveway. My heart sank as I imagined Terry's face screaming violently. I got out of the car and followed Aunt Peggy to the front door. As she walked in my mind raced with thoughts, such as Terry telling me he wants me out of his house. Aunt Peggy slammed the door behind me and called, "Terry!"

She turned to me. "Gar, go in your room, and shut the door." As I pulled the double doors to the den closed, I could hear them screaming from their bedroom.

Aunt Peggy hollered, "You're an alcoholic, Terry. Admit it!"

He yelled back. "I said I'm sorry." It made me shiver as I listened.

The next morning, after Terry left for work, Aunt Peggy knocked on my door. "Gar, he was wrong, and he feels terrible. He's been under a lot of pressure at work."

I looked in her eyes, which were hopeful and optimistic, just like her slight smile, and realized she wanted, no, she *needed* me to be ok with it. I thought about everything she'd done for us, including giving up her freedom to become Terry's girlfriend so that she could keep all five of us together.

I smiled as reassuringly as I could. "Aunt Peggy, I'm sorry. It really wasn't that big of a deal. I probably overreacted."

She hugged me "I love you, Gar."

"I love you, too, Aunt Peggy."

For my sixteenth birthday, Aunt Peggy brought me home a vanilla ice cream cake with chocolate crunchies.

Terry exclaimed, "Hey! Sixteen – you're practically a man."

I thought about the anger, the push, the argument – and then Aunt Peggy. I smiled sincerely. "Thank you, Terry!"

An Angel without Wings

I missed Mom's humor. I chuckled as I remembered her teasing Dad while at the same time putting on a show for everyone in the kitchen. "Avoid the Noid? Avoid Nick!" she had quipped, then asked, "How do you manage to get the cheese stuck to the top of every pizza box?" Everyone cracked up. Even Dad smiled, as he scraped at the glop of cheese with a fork.

As I lay on the couch in my bedroom den, I thought about how loudly Mom would laugh when she thought something was really funny and it made me smile. I knew she'd be happier than she'd ever been to be out of prison. I imagined her in the car ride from the airport, putting on her mascara, rolling on her lipstick, and turning her head from side to side to be sure her big, curly black wig was perfect for when she saw us. The excited feeling, knowing I was going to see her the next day, kept me awake like it was Christmas.

When Aunt Peggy turned into the driveway, we all bolted to get outside. I counted. Had it really only been eight months since we had last seen Mom? It felt like years. As Mom got out of the passenger side wearing a simple cream blouse and white slacks, I was surprised to see she wasn't wearing her wig. Her thin hair was pulled into a short ponytail near the top of her head. I noticed, and wondered, how long the hair at her temples had been white. How long had it been since I'd seen her without her wig? Was it months? Years? She wore it constantly, like a proud crown, and she was confident that most people believe the thick black curls were her real hair. Her lips were plain – barely a shade pinker than her skin, and she only had on a light coat of mascara which, I imagined, was only applied because Aunt Peggy must have said, "Kath, you have to put a little makeup on."

"Mom, what happened to your hair?" asked Michelle.

Mom turned her head, so we could completely see her new hairstyle. She explained in a soft, gentle tone, "It's my natural hair. Don't you like it?"

Michelle scrunched her eyebrows and gave a puzzled look at the absurdity of the question – Mom was meant to have giant curly hair that matched her personality. But it didn't matter what Mom looked like. Michelle broke into a huge smile, ran over and squeezed Mom's waist.

Michael's face was relaxed – no humor, no jokes. He simply smiled, and said, "Hi, Mom," as she reached for him. Vincent beamed and practically bounced like he'd just found his long lost best friend. He jumped toward Mom. She caught him and laughed.

Christina acted shy. I thought back to what it used to be like. Mom was always quicker to get angry at Christina than any of us. Living at Terry's was probably easy for Christina. Terry had never directed his anger toward the girls, and Aunt Peggy made a special point of praising how well Christina did in school and how good she was at kickball. I realized that Christina's life now was probably the most comfortable it had ever been.

454

"Christina," Mom said, "give me a hug, Honey." Christina's face melted with hope that it would be different. She stepped forward. Mom grabbed Christina, pulled her to her chest, and rested her cheek on the back of Christina's light brown ponytail.

I looked at Mom and knew the connection we'd shared my whole life was still there. She gave me the same sad smile that she'd given me so many times before. This time it felt real. I looked in her eyes and saw a deep hurt – hurt from her having been away from us for so long. It was one of many moments that I realized how strongly I loved her. I gave her a happy smile back to let her know it was all ok. Even though I wanted to feel like a little kid, safe with his mother, she was the one who rested her head on *my* shoulder. I closed my eyes and hugged her tight.

As we walked into Terry's house, everyone chattered over each other. Vincent asked, "Mom, do you wanna see my room?" at the same time as Christina's, "Mom, you can sleep in our bed if you want."

Michael said, "Mom, I have a bunch of movies recorded. Do you want to watch one?"

Aunt Peggy knew everyone was excited, but she tried to calm it down for Mom. She raised her voice. "Guys, why don't you give your mom a few minutes to relax? She just got here. She's not going anywhere."

That night, because T.J. wasn't there, Mom was going to sleep on the bottom bunk of his and Billy's bunk bed. I lay awake in my bed, listening to the adults.

I heard Terry. "Make yourself at home, Kathy." He walked down the hall to his room.

Aunt Peggy and Mom talked and chuckled quietly for a few minutes before Aunt Peggy said, "I love you, Kath." She left and walked down the hall, too.

After the house had been quiet for several minutes, I turned the handle, and the door creaked open. The muffled sound of Johnny Carson came from Aunt Peggy and Terry's bedroom, but the rest of the house was dark and quiet. I tiptoed toward the boy's room where a soft, orange light warmed the hallway.

I stepped in and whispered, "Hey, Mom."

A quick scan of their open mouths and heavy breathing assured that Michael, Vincent, and Billy were all asleep.

Mom set the yellow pad she had been holding down on her chest. She smiled and whispered back, "Hey, Gar. Come on in."

I walked gently over and sat with my back against the wall between the bunk beds. "What are you doing?"

"I'm writing a book."

"Really? About what?"

456

"About my life. I started when I was in jail."

"That's neat. Do you have a lot done?"

"I'm about halfway through."

"What are you gonna call it?"

"An angel without wings."

I wanted to tell her that people might think the title was a little self-centered, but I remembered how defeated she had looked when she got out of the car that afternoon. Regardless of the mistakes she'd made with Uncle Dan, Uncle Jim, and the many people who lived in our houses, I knew it was never her intention to hurt us. I was sure, whatever Dad had done illegally, that Mom wasn't a part of it. I didn't think the whole world would see it, but to me, Michael, Vincent, Michelle, and even Christina, Mom really was an angel. I smiled and asked, "Does it begin when you're a child?"

A couple of weeks later, Aunt Peggy came home from work, put her keys and bags on the counter and said to Mom, "Kath, one of my clients is an Area Manager for Barnett Bank. He manages the Visa MasterCard division. The office is in the same shopping center as my salon."

Mom had explained that her probation officer expected her to find employment quickly. She'd applied for office manager and receptionist positions but hadn't heard anything back. She'd shared her fear with Aunt Peggy: "Oh God, Peg, am I going to have to bag groceries at the store?" Aunt Peggy gave Mom the same determined look she had given us when she said, "They're not splitting the five of you up."

Mom asked, "Really, Peg?"

"Yeah, he has an open job. We've got to go to T.J. Maxx tomorrow and buy you a suit."

When Mom and Aunt Peggy came home from shopping, there was a familiar looking round box. Mom stepped out of the bathroom in a sleek navy suit and curly, black wig.

"How do I look?"

Michelle exclaimed, "You look beautiful, Mom!"

I added, "You really do, Mom. You really do."

Mom came home from work, took off her heels, and leaned back on the couch. She lifted her pantyhose covered legs and said, "Mike, I'll give you five dollars if you rub my feet."

Michael answered, "Sure!" and crouched down to begin the foot massage. Squeezing Mom's ankles and toes, in the air conditioning, to earn some money was an easy decision. Michael had to do a week's worth of chores, including the double lawn mow, before Aunt Peggy could hand him money without getting a dirty look from

Terry. Mom laid her head back and closed her eyes as Michael massaged.

I asked, "How do you like your job, Mom?" She opened her eyes and smiled. "Good. My boss already wants to make me a supervisor."

I was kind of excited to be out of the junior high, where I finished my last few months of ninth grade, and to be going to an actual high school again. Plus, Gaither High was within walking distance, across the street from the shopping plaza where Executive Quarters and Mom's office were. As I scanned the course schedule of electives, I contemplated classes that I'd heard students talk about. Speech seemed like it would be boring, and I had no idea why anyone would take marketing. I thought, I could learn to sing in chorus, and with drama, the idea of getting to pretend I was someone else seemed like a dream come true. Plus, I'd been acting my whole life. I was pretty good at playing a kid whose family wasn't crazy.

I hesitated and wondered if I should just pick classes that no one would question. As I stared at the sheet, I thought about the woman at ACOA who had said, "The definition of courage is being afraid but doing it anyway." She also explained how she'd always been terrified to tell her boss that she couldn't take extra shifts because of things her mother had told her when she was growing up.

I asked myself why I was afraid then thought about Uncle Dan. I imagined the nasty look he'd give and knew he'd say, "Chorus is for pussies," or "Drama's for fags." He had gotten out of prison, too. I reminded myself that he was far away, and hopefully, I'd never have to see him again. I took a breath and wrote the course code for intro to drama.

Drama ended up being first-period. When I walked into the room, I realized it wasn't the type of class where you listened to a boring teacher and wrote a lot of notes. The teacher's desk was all the way on the far side, and the students' desks were on one half of the room, facing the empty opposite half. As I walked across the blue, matted carpet, I looked at the bare walls. I knew the area was clear so that when a student stood up to act, there would be nothing to distract everyone's attention. *What had I gotten myself into?*

When I got home from school, I closed and locked the bathroom door. I opened my mouth and examined my teeth in the mirror.

I heard a knock – and then Michael's voice. "Gar, I need to use the bathroom."

I turned my head as I stared at the spaces between my front teeth. Mom had a job. I was sure she could afford to get me braces. Michael pounded again. "Just a minute!" I shouted, then deliberately waited about thirty seconds before opening the door to go find Mom.

Mom was standing at the breakfast bar talking with Aunt Peggy. I cut in with, "Mom, do you think I can get braces?" before I realized they were having a serious discussion.

Aunt Peggy was trying to sound convincing. "I'm done with Tampa, Kath. Terry wants to look for a job on the East coast, anyway."

Mom sounded like her old self – smart and protective. She spoke softly. "Do you really want to marry him, Peg?"

Aunt Peggy opened the refrigerator, grabbed a Caffeine Free Pepsi and gave a look as unconvincing as her voice. "Terry has been good to me. He's been good to all of us. He even said you guys can stay here until Nick gets out."

I asked. "Aunt Peggy, when are you getting married?"

She forced a smile. "In October."

"And you and Terry are moving? What about your job?"

"There are a lot of nice salons in Jupiter, Florida."

Of course, she had to clarify Florida. Wanting to marry Terry was enough to make all of us think her mind was on another planet.

Mom stood. "Peg, you can still move. You don't have to marry him."

Aunt Peggy smiled again, sweetly, aware that Mom was trying to protect her. "Kath, it's already set. I'm even flying Danny and Jimmy down for the wedding."

I lay back in the orthodontist's chair and thought about Uncle Dan and Uncle Jim coming. Mom had said Uncle Jim had stopped drinking and was part of a union, but I didn't trust it. The pattern seemed like every time everyone believed he'd stay sober; he'd show up sloppy drunk, ready to argue with someone and shatter a glass table. My times at the meetings made me realize Uncle Dan was just pathetic. He hit his nephews, beat up his girlfriends, and took pride in making everyone afraid of him. I decided I'd be polite, speak as little as possible, and avoid both of them until they were gone.

The orthodontist walked in. "How are we doing?"

I imagined how ridiculous I must have looked with the clear retractors holding my jaw and lips open. I started to speak, "Gud," then just smiled with my eyes and nodded my head.

I didn't care when he had jammed the tiny, red rubber bands between my back teeth the week before. When he said, "These might cause a little discomfort," I had no idea it was going to feel like I had huge hunks of steak between all my molars. Still, every time I was tempted to grab a tweezer and yank them out, I made myself imagine having a perfect smile. Even sitting there with my mouth flared open like a suckerfish, I was happy. I relaxed as he began gluing brackets to my teeth.

When I came home with a sore mouth full of braces, the kids were fascinated.

Christina asked, "Can I see?" I smiled wide, proud of the metal wires and brackets.

Vincent flinched a painful grin. "Does it hurt?"

Even with the two Tylenol I'd taken; my gums were still throbbing. I said, "Not that much."

"How do they stay on?" Michelle asked.

"Cement," I said, and added, "Guys, I'm going to lie down for a little while." I shut the doors to the den and propped my head on the arm of the couch. I ran my tongue over the tight gear and remembered the acidic taste of cement before I shut my eyes to nap.

My first tightening was a couple of days before Aunt Peggy's wedding. When we opened the front door, I smelled pizza and recognized the familiar bluster of Uncle Dan's voice. "Ter, you could do a lot with this house to increase the value before you sell it."

As we walked around the corner, Terry, I'm sure ignorant to the type of schemers Aunt Peggy's brothers were, gave an engaging answer. "I was going to paint it. I was also thinking about taking down the dark wood paneling in the dining room. Your sister thinks it's outdated."

Aunt Peggy added, "I never liked it. It's so seventies."

Uncle Jim offered, "I can paint it for you. I'm part of the painters' union in Jersey."

I smiled without opening my mouth. "Hi, Uncle Dan. Hi, Uncle Jim."

Uncle Dan smirked. "Hey, let me see your teeth." I took a short breath to keep from rolling my eyes and opened my mouth. Uncle Dan said, "You know if you kiss a girl who also has braces, you're gonna get locked," then laughed like a fool and nudged Terry. "Am I right Ter?" Terry smiled big and took a bite of his pizza.

As Aunt Peggy walked back and forth through the house, I thought about how grateful I was, how grateful we all were, that she had taken us in. I remembered how pretty she had looked in her white, lace wedding dress with her black hair pulled up. After the ceremony Mom sniffled and wiped tears with her fingers, telling her, "Peg, you are beautiful." I knew she wasn't referring to Aunt Peggy looking prettier than Scarlett O'Hara in a wedding gown. She was talking about her strength, courage, and determination.

I asked, "Are you excited about moving to the other coast, Aunt Peggy?"

She looked frantic as her eyes darted around the room. "I'll be excited if I find my Ray Bans with the gold frame. Have you seen them, Gar?"

I looked at her hair, flared out by mirrored lenses on the top of her head and questioned, "Do they look like the ones on your head?"

She reached up, pulled the glasses off, and started laughing so hard she almost lost her breath. I smiled as she answered. "Yeah, I'm excited. I just need to keep Gestapo from having a stroke about money."

Once the car was packed, Aunt Peggy clicked on Billy's seat belt for him. She took a deep breath and looked up and down our street.

I asked, "Do you think there will be more palm trees in Jupiter?"

Aunt Peggy smiled. "I hope so. This is nice, but it doesn't feel like Florida."

I agreed with her. There wasn't anything about Terry's neighborhood that felt like a vacation. The adults worked, the kids went to school, and everyone pulled weeds and hedged their lawns on the weekends.

Aunt Peggy gave me a hug. "Gar, my godson, you're so tall and handsome. Keep going to the meetings." Then she whispered, "Especially with Uncle Danny and Uncle Jimmy here." We both chuckled.

After Aunt Peggy gave Michael and Vincent hugs, she told Christina, "Keep doing great in school!" She turned to Michelle, "Make sure Mommy does your hair before your school picture." She said to Mom, "I want a five by seven of each of their school pictures. No – make it eight by ten."

Mom laughed. "Sure, Peg. Why don't I just send them all to you? Is it ok if I keep a wallet size for myself?"

Aunt Peggy began laughing, too, until they both started crying.

"Peg, thank you," Mom said. "I love you so much."

Aunt Peggy shrugged like she'd done nothing anyone else wouldn't have done. "I love you, too, Kath."

She got in the car with Terry, waved and screamed a happy "Bye!" as they drove up the street.

I hadn't actually seen it happen, but I wasn't surprised. The drinking and late-night parties had begun within a couple days of Aunt Peggy's leaving. Before Mom left for New Jersey, she told Uncle Dan, "Danny, I don't want the kids in the pool. Jimmy broke a glass bowl out there."

"Don't worry about it, Kath. Just go take care of business with the parole officer. I've got this."

The very next morning, Uncle Dan asked Michelle, "Hey, Squatbox, you wanna go swimming?"

Michelle squealed as she ran to put her bathing suit on.

It aggravated me how irresponsible he was. I asked, "Uncle Dan, didn't Mom say there's glass in the pool?"

"Don't worry about it. I'm watching the kids." Christina and Vincent raced past me and jumped into the water.

It was cool but sunny. I decided I'd go swimming, too, but I wouldn't touch my feet to the bottom of the pool. The water only took a few minutes to get used to. After an hour of laughing and splashing, Christina screamed, "Ow!" She began paddling across the pool with her foot behind her. I pulled myself out of the deep end as Uncle Dan lifted Christina.

"Let me see your foot," Uncle Dan said, as he examined the gash.

I ran over to help. "In my health class, they said if you're bleeding, you should elevate it."

Uncle Dan ignored me and pressed the padding of Christina's foot.

Christina winced and whispered, "Ow," as blood ran along the creases in the bottom of her foot.

I stepped forward to help her. "You have to lift her leg, so the cut is above her heart."

Uncle Dan growled. "Leave it! If I have to tell you again!"

I didn't say anything to him after that, but I smiled at Christina and mouthed the words, "It'll be ok."

Uncle Dan placed her in the car and said, "I'm taking her to the emergency room, Jim, to see if she needs stitches." Christina gave me a sad smile as they drove away.

The class gasped when the teacher said, "We're going to make lip sync music videos and have them recorded in two weeks." Wow! This teacher really did take drama seriously. She had asked me, and only one other student, to record the monologues we had done a few weeks before. When I had finished, she exclaimed, "Oh my God, that was amazing." She even clapped. I didn't think there was anything difficult about pretending to be an eighteen-year-old Vietnam soldier hallucinating and dying. There was a comfortable ease to becoming a young man, who had probably had a great life before being shot in the stomach.

The students quickly began teaming up into threes and fours. I turned and looked at the kids around me. There were the two boys, in heavy metal tee-shirts, who only showed up three or four days a week. They were obviously only taking drama to get an easy, passing grade. I knew none of the serious drama students would want to be paired with them, and I didn't want to end up without a team, so I asked if they wanted to group up. One said, "Sure," and the other one, "Ok."

And the blond foreign exchange girl behind one of the boys darted her eyes around the room in an anxious manner. She didn't have a group yet. I asked her, "Do you want to be in a group with us?"

She looked slightly relieved. "Yeah, but I don't sing." I realized she probably had no idea what she'd signed up for when she chose drama, and it probably wouldn't do any good to explain that we weren't really singing.

I said, "I'll be the lead singer. I've been in the video room before anyway."

She smiled. "Thanks, I'm Helena."

The moment I opened the front door, the smell of hours old fried eggs closed my nose. I held my breath as I walked around the corner to the kitchen where a greasy frying pan was balancing on a stack of dishes in the sink. Uncle Jim was lying on the sofa, reading *Raise the Titanic*, for probably the fourth time, and Uncle Dan was covered by a sheet, snoring on the couch in my room. A knot tightened in my stomach as I realized that a month had passed since Aunt Peggy had moved, and they still hadn't left. I pulled the glass door open, let out my breath and sat on the lawn chair by the pool – which was now green and full of black leaves.

When I heard Mom pull into the driveway, I walked to the front of the house. As she grabbed her jacket from the back seat, I asked, "Mom, why haven't Uncle Dan and Uncle Jim left?"

"Gar, it's not my house. Terry said they can stay here."

I sighed. "Can they at least get a job, Mom, and clean up after themselves?"

"Gary, I can't deal with this right now. I'm leaving tomorrow to see my probation officer."

"Again? Already?"

The morning after Mom left I woke to a CRACK. I blinked and tried to process what I'd heard as it cracked again then again. I opened the double doors and realized the splintering sound was coming from the dining room. Michael, Vincent, and Christina were ripping the dark wood paneling off the walls, as Uncle Jim directed. I could tell from his slow blinking that he was drunk. He probably had never even gone to bed.

Vincent giggled as he yanked the planks backward.

Christina whined. "Michael, let me use the hammer."

He ignored her, jammed it under to lift and crack another piece of the paneling. Uncle Jim sat at the dining room table, grinning like a drunken fool. "Make sure you put all the pieces in a pile in the middle of the carpet."

I thought about how insane it was but couldn't help from smirking. Mom's words, "Terry said they can stay," repeated over and over in my mind as I watched Uncle Jim orchestrate the destruction of Terry's dining room.

Within days, Uncle Jim also had the inside of the garage spray painted a shiny black, and the humor I found in the situation was replaced by concern. I huffed as I walked to the kitchen. Uncle Dan was buried in the sofa with his dirty socks on the coffee table. He ordered, "Don't start with the attitude."

I took a deep breath. I couldn't imagine hating any person more than him. I calmly spoke, "He's destroying Terry's house. The garage looks crazy. There are frogs in the pool."

Uncle Dan stood and pointed at me. "If you think you're a man, you better be ready to step up."

I knew Uncle Dan didn't respect Terry – probably because Terry had a job, a house, and wasn't a criminal. And even though Mom said it was Terry's decision, I knew Terry was holding her responsible for Uncle Jim, Uncle Dan, and his house. He'd been calling and leaving messages for Mom every few days. Uncle Dan would say, "The Midget called for you again. I deleted it."

I looked at Uncle Dan, frustrated that he didn't get that it wasn't about respecting Terry. It was about protecting Aunt Peggy. Was Uncle Dan really that stupid, or was he just oblivious because Terry didn't scare *him*? Was it possible he didn't realize Terry could be dangerous to Aunt Peggy? I didn't respond to what he said. I looked at the clock. "I need to get ready for my meeting."

I sat on the couch with Michael and Vincent, switching the TV back and forth between MTV and VH1 before settling on "Oh... think twice... it's just another day for you and me in paradise..."

As I told them, "We're recording a music video tomorrow," Uncle Dan said, "Jim, the Celtics game is about to start. Put it on."

Uncle Jim answered, "Dan, they're watching TV."

I interjected, "I like this video."

Uncle Dan marched over, took the remote from Uncle Jim, changed the channel, and walked back to the kitchen. "We're watching the game."

My heart started racing. I thought about the lady at the meeting who explained that abusive parents who don't respect their children are what causes low self-esteem. I inhaled a deep breath and told myself over and over: *courage is, courage is.*

Almost as if watching myself from outside my body, I stood, grabbed the remote from the coffee table, and typed in the number for VH1. My heart pounding in my chest kept me acutely aware that I was still there – and I had just done the unthinkable. Michael and Vincent both looked at me, shocked.

The moment Phil Collins flicked back on the TV screen, Uncle Dan slammed the cabinet. He was standing in front of me in the time it took for me to draw one more breath. As his angry, contorted face came right up to mine, I fell backward onto the couch. When I stood up, he pushed me down and snarled. "Sit there!"

Michael jumped up. Vincent started crying. I stood again.

Uncle Dan's voice became even deeper. "Sit there!"

Uncle Jim cut in. "Danny! Danny! What're you doing?"

Christina and Michelle came running out of the bedroom. I stood again, and the front door slammed. What? Who? I realized Uncle Jim was gone right before Uncle Dan pushed me down again. He leaned in. "Don't... get up... again!"

I turned my face away as my imagination played out the scene of me standing – one last time – and Uncle Dan grabbing my shirt and throwing me, before beating me bloody. I made the decision. It was better to be a humiliated coward, so I stayed seated and thought about Michael, Vincent, Christina, and Michelle – all looking at me. I wanted to die.

When I heard Mom's car, I ran outside from my room. She was getting out, and Uncle Jim was with her. Mom said, "Gary, please just go to your room. I'll handle it."

The argument with Uncle Dan lasted for hours. He told Mom, "It's those meetings. They're fucking up his head."

Mom pleaded. "Danny, please! Why do you have to do this?"

Uncle Dan screamed. "Just you wait! You'll see! He doesn't respect anybody – including you!"

I lay in bed wondering why Mom was pleading with him. I couldn't understand why she didn't just tell him to get out.

I jolted awake. As I realized I had forgotten to set my alarm, my heart sank. I thought about how first-period was just ending. I was sure the heavy metal boys, if they showed up at all, had made Helena be the lead singer.

The next day in drama, the teacher proclaimed, "Every single one of you who participated yesterday, which was almost the entire class, did a wonderful job." She looked at me. "Gary, I'm sure you regret not making it. Why don't you perform your lip synch for the class?"

I slowly got up from my desk as she clicked the tape deck on the boom box. I waited. The beat started. I began moving my feet and snapping, sure that I looked like a complete idiot. I lip synced, "I wanna know… what you're thinking… there are some things you can't hide." Helena turned her head and wouldn't look at me. I wasn't sure if it was mercy or hate.

When Uncle Dan went back to New Jersey, Mom said it was to see his parole officer. I was just glad he was gone. I knew Mom was frustrated about Uncle Jim drinking when I told her about the wheelbarrow incident. Uncle Jim had loaded all of Terry's power tools, including his drill and saw, and had sent Michael and Vincent around to ask the neighbors to buy them. I told her, "Mom, you're the one that said they could stay."

She snapped, "Gary, I don't need this shit."

I was mad as we sat down for dinner. Mom had a job and a chance to make our life right, but she was ruining it by allowing Uncle Dan and Uncle Jim to stay with us. Christina and Michael bickered and pushed each other with their elbows.

Mom growled, "Christina."

Uncle Jim stood and grabbed the empty scalloped potato bowl and two plates. Of course, I thought, he's sober and helpful a day after making our family look ridiculous to the people on our street. He asked, "Kath, do you want me to load the dishwasher?"

Mom sighed. "It's ok, Jim."

Christina pushed her plate toward Michelle. "Give this to Uncle Jim."

Michelle pushed it back. "You give it to him."

Mom stood. "Christina, I'm gonna beat your ass if you keep it up!" Christina crossed her arms and kicked her feet under the table.

Mom growled "God damn it!" as she reached toward Christina. Christina ran from the table to the corner of the dining room. Mom darted toward her. I exploded.

Images of Mom's snarly face as she hit Christina's bare legs – at five years old, seven years old, ten years old – ripped through my mind. Her clenched grip on Christina's hair and the petrified look on Christina's face caused the rage. Uncle Dan, Uncle Jim – Mom never saying anything to them when they were wrong, never getting angry with them – but Christina, *always* Christina.

My chair flew back as I stood. In a moment I was in front of Christina, who was cowering on the floor. My voice, guttural, deep, like a monster: "GET AWAY FROM MY SISTER!" I stared at Mom's face as my chest heaved. The fear, yeah, finally the fear was in her face.

Uncle Jim panicked. "What the hell is going on?" I gave him a glance and knew he wouldn't dare approach me. I looked back at Mom with her mouth open, in shock. She knew, if she ever touched Christina again, I would kill her.

Mele?

I sat in my room and thought about how I'd never screamed at Mom before. I replayed the full force confrontation until I couldn't get the stunned look of her face out of my mind. A lonely emptiness filled my gut as I wondered if I had destroyed the bond we had always shared. Maybe I shouldn't have jumped up. I imagined sitting quietly as Mom hurled toward Christina, who was desperately crawling backwards to the corner. The image of Mom's clenched teeth and Christina's terrified face brought the rage again. It was small, in my stomach, but still strong enough to clear my mind. I had to make a decision, and I had chosen right. I wasn't sorry I'd done it, even if it meant my connection with Mom was gone.

I was sure Uncle Jim was going to tell Uncle Dan when he got back. And Uncle Dan would probably wait until Mom was at work to confront me. He'd push his chest into me, hoping I'd push back or swing at him so he could throw a punch. Even if I didn't, he'd still hit me. Changing a channel was one thing. Standing up to, screaming at and confronting, Mom was something else. Anxiety consumed my chest as I imagined myself down on the carpet – bruised, bleeding and humiliated – and Uncle Dan above me, snarling, "You're not so tough now, are you?"

I leaned back and wondered why we could never live normal. The desperate feelings swirled through my mind until my stomach felt nauseous. I remembered what I'd heard at ACOA: "It's ok to cry. It's not healthy to hold it in." I told myself it was fine, breathed deeply, and waited for my eyes to water. I choked up slightly, but the emotion froze in my throat, which made me angry. I imagined screaming into the dingy couch pillow, but that felt ridiculous. I couldn't cry. I wouldn't yell.

As the hopeless feeling crushed into my chest, I pictured myself sneaking out really late into the cool night. The idea of tiptoeing through the wet grass until I stepped onto the sidewalk excited me. I imagined running under the buzzing, white street lights – away from Mom, Uncle Dan, Uncle Jim, and the insanity of our home. The fantasy relaxed me. I closed my eyes and let my thoughts float. I just wanted to sleep.

I was the first one home from school. I heard Uncle Dan's booming voice as I gently pushed open the front door. I took a deep breath, as my book bag slid off my shoulder. I mentally guessed how many hours he'd been home alone with Uncle Jim. My chest tightened as I realized Uncle Jim had to have told him. I told myself to just get it over with. I inhaled deep, stepped in, and walked around the corner to the living room where Uncle Dan and Uncle Jim were talking.

Uncle Jim made genuine eye contact, in a way that he never did, as if to communicate with me that everything was ok. "Hey, Gar."

I quickly answered. "Hi, Uncle Jim." My heart bounced in my chest.

Uncle Dan said, "Hey."

Relief flooded me as I processed that the tone of his voice was normal. I paused. "Uh, hi Uncle Dan." I walked into my room and dropped my bagful of textbooks on the couch.

Maybe Uncle Jim hadn't said anything? I could feel my heart rate slowing. But then I began hearing their conversation.

Uncle Dan was serious. "Jim, you don't understand. For her to be hooking up with this guy? Is she fucking crazy?"

"Jacky thinks she's had a nervous breakdown."

Uncle Dan scoffed. "Jacky?" His voice tensed. "He's the one that introduced her to him. Nervous breakdown? She's fucking lost her marbles. I'm telling you, this guy is an asshole. He's a nasty fuck."

Who was Uncle Dan talking about? Was Mom really cheating on Dad? I listened intently as I slowly unzipped my backpack and removed my science book.

Uncle Dan was suddenly in my room. "Listen, don't you repeat this to your brothers and sisters. I don't know what your mother is thinking."

I stammered, "No, no, I won't."

Uncle Dan gave me the most concerned look I'd ever seen. "Your dad is a good guy. He's doing time for her. Your mom's head is just fucked up from going to jail." I nodded, then eased down to the couch.

Could it really be true? My heart sank as I thought about Mom not being with Dad. I got a choked up – but not able to cry – feeling again. Was our life before they went to prison completely gone?

When Mom got home from work, I gave a half smile. "Hi, Mom." My chest was tight with anticipation of her ignoring me like Uncle Dan would have.

Instead, Mom smiled sweetly. "Hi, Gar." She put her keys and purse on the counter and walked to the dining room. I followed. She sat sideways on a dining room chair and stared blankly out into the empty backyard.

The coldness I was prepared to give her back melted. I just felt sad for her. "Mom, are you looking forward to Dad getting out?" I could tell by the steady breath she took that she was about to lie.

"Yeah, Gar, why?"

"Is it Dad's fault you went to prison, Mom?"

Mom seemed to soften. "It's not just that, Gar." She whispered, "Nick cheated on me when we were first together – a few times."

I remembered their arguments. I knew he had cheated, even before I completely understood what cheated meant. But it was so long ago when they were first together. Ten years later they were a happy, married couple. Mom would tease Dad and make him laugh. He always listened to her and told everyone, "Kathy's the boss." She had even told me how relieved she was when the officers handcuffed the two of them next to each other for the van ride back to New Jersey. I thought about Uncle Dan saying Mom was messed up from going to jail.

"Mom, you guys are really good together. Dad loves you. You know that, right?"

She forced a smile. "I know, Gar."

When the overly taped up boxes arrived, we knew Uncle Tub was coming to visit. It had been years since we'd seen him.

Vincent asked, "How old is Uncle Tub? He looks like he's ninety."

Michael whispered, "I think he's closer to a hundred."

"Guys, stop," I said. "Mom wants us to be respectful."

Michael answered, "Mom's in New Jersey again."

I snapped at him. "She's there for her parole officer. She'll be home on Monday. Don't make Uncle Tub mad."

In the few days that Uncle Tub had been there, Vincent, and especially Michael, entertained themselves by asking him the same dumb questions over and over. They'd snicker when he answered, unaware that they'd just had the same conversation a moment earlier. When he realized they were making fun, he'd start grumbling. "God damn, mother fucking brats. They need to have their asses beat."

481

Michael and Vincent would laugh under their breath as they ran to the bedroom.

I was lying down reading about Madonna's new movie, *Dick Tracy,* and how she wanted to be a serious actress. Uncle Dan was in the kitchen seasoning cubed steak. Michael was in the dining room talking to Uncle Tub.

I sat up as I heard Michael, sounding puzzled, call my name. "Gary?"

I stood and walked out to the living room. I heard "My father, Gary? Don't you mean my brother?" Michael walked in from the dining room with a confused look on his face. When he saw me, he motioned with his finger to make a cuckoo sign. "Uncle Tub is going crazy. He said my father's name is Gary."

Bam! Uncle Dan slammed the frying pan on the counter. "Go in the room, now!" He mumbled under his breath, "Mother fucker," and then yelled, "Your mother doesn't need this shit!" Michael looked justifiably shocked. He knew he hadn't done anything wrong, but he still ran for the bedroom.

I tried to figure out when I had stopped caring about the other kids knowing the truth. Was it the summer we were supposed to see Gary? When Mom said he couldn't meet us, I suspected she might be lying. Still, why didn't he contact me on his own? I had stopped caring about ever seeing him after that, but I had still thought the other kids should know the truth.

482

I realized the change happened when Mom and Dad got arrested, and we were left with Sharon. Dad had been there for all of us our whole lives, and then he was gone. Some man, the man who was actually my, Michael, and Christina's biological father, was suddenly insignificant. I realized he had never mattered to any of us.

I thought about the shock the other kids would be in. Michelle was only seven, and Vincent was nine. Would they even understand? Would it make them feel less connected to me, Michael, and Christina, their older siblings? I remembered how angry I would get when people would subtly treat them better because Dad was really their father. Now, none of us had a father.

The five of us watched TV to pass the time. It had been several hours since Uncle Dan left to pick Mom up from the airport. When we heard the muffled slams of the car doors, everyone got up. Uncle Dan walked in, followed by Mom. Even before I saw the smudged mascara, I knew she would have been crying. Finally, after years of being angry with her, I understood her reasoning. She had created a lie and made everyone go along with it to protect us. She wanted to be sure there would never be a question that there was a difference between the five of us. She stumbled into the dining room, sobbing. "Come on, guys."

Mom sat next to the pile of cracked and broken wood paneling. She stared away as the five of us gathered around her. As the tears streamed down her cheeks, I noticed she seemed different, slower, like

Uncle Jim when he had been drinking. She took a deep breath, sighed, and began to speak. "I was going to tell you guys."

Was she slurring her words from crying? Or was she drinking? I examined her face as she sat motionless. She was drunk. I looked at Michael. He knew. Christina and Vincent saw it.

Michelle looked at me and then at Mom, puzzled. "Were you drinking, Mom?"

I'd seen Mom drink one or two wine coolers before when it was hot in the summer. She'd usually leave them unfinished, with an inch of pink juice and white foam at the bottom of the bottle. It wasn't like Uncle Jim's hidden beer and vodka bottles that were always as dry as dust. I'd never seen Mom drunk. None of us had.

Mom stared until I said something. "Mom?"

She kept crying. "I was going to tell you guys." She sniffled. "When you were older... I'm sorry... I'm sorry."

I stood to hug her. As I pulled her toward me, the hot, boozy fumes caught my breath. I said, "It's ok, Mom." My stomach flip-flopped with the same feeling I had when I smelled Uncle Jim drunk.

When Uncle Dan announced, "Bern's coming to visit," I thought, yeah right. She's coming to sleep on the floor in the living room.

Vincent asked, "I thought Uncle Dan didn't like Bernadette."

I shushed then answered, "They have a baby together. He probably just wants to see Jack."

I remembered back in New Jersey how Uncle Dan had lectured me and Michael about scrubbing blackheads out of our faces.

Michael had asked, "What's a blackhead?"

Uncle Dan leaned in close to us and pressed his nose to the side. "You see those?" We both nodded quickly as he continued. "You see Bern's face? She's got beautiful skin. She scrubs every day with soap and water."

When Uncle Dan finished lecturing us, Michael leaned toward me. "We don't have blackheads. Uncle Dan does. Why doesn't he scrub his face?"

I mumbled, "You're right," as I processed what I'd just realized. Deep down, in some tiny way, Uncle Dan cared for Bernadette, too.

When Bernadette arrived, she gave Uncle Dan a quick glance, like he was the last person in the world she wanted to see.

Uncle Dan smirked at her. "What? You've got an attitude now?"

Bernadette looked at me and winked. I smiled, not because of her game with Uncle Dan, but because she reminded me of Cape Coral and the happiness of Florida. Then I thought about how Mom had told Aunt Peggy, "Bernadette sung like a canary. She ratted out the whole house."

I wondered if Mom would be cold to Bernadette as Bernadette reached out to hug her. "Hey, Kath."

Mom smiled warmly. "Hey, Bern," and hugged her back.

Of course, they're not here, I thought. Bernadette was at work, but Uncle Dan and Uncle Jim were both just gone – who knows where? – when Terry pulled into the driveway. Mom yanked Uncle Dan's sheet from the coach and handed Vincent the pillows from the floor.

"Vincent, put these in your bedroom – quickly." Vincent ran, as I scooped up glasses with brown stains at the bottom from the coffee table. The front door opened.

Mom gave me a panicked look before turning toward the front hallway with a shaky, "Hello?"

The master bedroom was immediately to the right when you entered the house. I knew, when he didn't answer back, Terry was in there probably looking through Mom's makeup bags and perfume bottles in the bathroom he used to share with Aunt Peggy.

Terry walked out of the bedroom and headed toward the dining room. His lips tightened as he grabbed a piece of dark paneling. "What have you done to my house?"

Mom started, "Terry, Jimmy said you wanted him to paint–"

"This isn't painted," Terry interrupted. He walked into the kitchen next. He picked up the handle of a pan that had been in the sink for several days. "This is filthy. Look at these counters. Don't you people clean?"

Mom followed him as he walked through the house. "Terry, I'm sorry. I've been working. I've been busy-"

Terry snapped at her. "What about your brothers?" He looked at me. "Or your kids?"

Mom begged, "Terry, please. We'll clean. I promise."

Terry cursed under his breath as he walked through each bedroom, pulling dressers away from walls and lifting mattresses to see what was under the beds. When he slammed the last door, he walked back to the living room.

"I need you out of my house."

Mom stuttered, "I… I… Terry… please!"

Terry ignored her as he walked to the garage. He whined, "Jesus Christ – *black?*" He yanked the lawn mower from behind the wheelbarrow that was full of power tools.

487

As Terry plowed through the overgrown lawn, Mom started frantically scrubbing Uncle Dan's and Uncle Jim's food-crusted plates. I grabbed a rag from the sink and began digging at the dried on coffee rings on the counter. Christina and Michelle ran to the bathroom.

Michelle yelled, "Christina, I want to wipe the mirror!"

Christina said, "Start cleaning the toilet, Michelle."

Michael made the beds, which included tucking tee-shirts and loose socks under pillows. Vincent bolted to the backyard, grabbed the skimmer, and began dredging sludge out of the pool.

The next day, Mom spoke to Aunt Peggy on the phone.

"Peg, are you sure?"

"But he said he wants us out."

"Oh, I could tell he was mad."

"Ok, I'm really sorry Peg."

"I'll make sure Jimmy starts painting."

"Alright. I love you, too."

I asked, "Does Terry want us out, Mom?"

"No, Aunt Peggy calmed him down. But we're moving, anyway. Uncle Danny and Uncle Jimmy are going to stay and finish everything."

"Where are we going?"

"My friend Bobby from New Jersey is coming down. He's going to help us get a place."

Michael whispered, "How tall do you think he is?"

It was a couple of weeks before my seventeenth birthday. I knew I was full grown at five feet eleven inches. I figured Bobby had to be a foot taller than me.

"I don't know. Seven feet, maybe."

Bobby wasn't just tall. He was scary. His forehead sloped like a Neanderthal, and his bristly blond goatee was only a shade darker than the thinning hair that went down to his shoulders.

When Vincent asked, "How many tattoos do you have?" Mom interjected, "Vincent, that's not polite."

Not polite? I thought. How would a nine-year-old know it was rude to ask a man with tattoos that covered his arms, neck and fingers how many he had?

The craziest part was when Mom introduced us. She had smiled. "Guys, this is my friend, Bobby."

Michelle gasped, and Christina squeezed her arm to quiet her. I smiled and nudged Michael. We all grinned and pretended Mom hadn't just introduced us to the most terrifying man we'd ever seen.

I understood exactly what Uncle Dan was thinking when he had said, "I don't want to be around that fucker," before leaving with Bernadette.

After Vincent's tattoo question, Bobby smiled awkwardly at us.

Vincent asked another question. "Do you know our Dad?"

My breath stopped as I scanned Bobby's face. He inhaled deeply through his nostrils before answering.

"No, I don't know your Dad." Suddenly, the pretend niceness stopped. "Let's get moving," he said.

The kids ran to their rooms. I hurried into the den and began untacking the Madonna posters and magazine covers I had on the walls. Bobby took long strides as he walked through Terry's house.

He told Mom, "I want to get out of this faggot's house tonight."

Mom winced. "Bobby, the kids."

Bobby looked at Christina. "Oh, sorry."

He continued with Mom, "He'll be lucky if I don't burn this fucker to the ground after you're out."

Once we were completely packed, Bobby looked at me. "Get the kids in the car and help me grab this shit."

After loading the car, I walked back inside where Bobby was unhooking the cable from the TV. "Bobby," I said, "that TV is Terry's. He left it for us to use."

Bobby didn't even look up. He answered in a gruff voice, "We're still using it."

As we drove to the new house, Michael said, "I guess Uncle Dan's not watching any more Celtic games. Now he has to talk to Bernadette."

Vincent giggled. I held my finger up and shushed them. "I don't think they're staying there much longer, anyway."

Michael whispered, "I heard Bobby tell Mom we were all looking at him like a freak."

I answered, under my breath, "We need to just act normal with him."

We usually got pizza or McDonald's cheeseburgers to celebrate our move to a new home, but not that night. Bobby dumped out a paper bag full of Lay's chips, pretzels, and packs of spicy, red peanuts that he'd gotten at the liquor store.

After we'd all grabbed our dinner and began eating, Michelle held out her tongue and made a face, "These are hot."

I popped open a bag of chips. "Here, eat these. I'll get you some water."

As the faucet plock, plocked to get the air out of the pipes, I glanced over at the bottles of whiskey and vodka on the counter.

The next morning, the sun shone in through dingy windows. I looked through the dust and grime covered glass out at our new neighborhood. The houses were smaller than the ones in Terry's neighborhood. The lawns were overgrown with dandelions and jagged weeds, and the front porches were littered with rusty, folding chairs, broken toys, and garbage.

Christina asked, "What are we gonna have for breakfast?"

Michael was trying to get the TV working as he maneuvered the antennas around to get one of the staticky channels to come in.

Vincent gave a puzzled look, "Is Bobby sleeping in Mom's room?"

I answered, "I'm sure he's sleeping on the floor," but I knew from the suspicious look on Vincent's face that he didn't believe me.

As the morning rolled past noon, everyone began getting restless and hungrier. Michelle marched over to Mom's door and began knocking. "Mom, we haven't eaten breakfast."

I could hear Mom's slurred voice through the door. "Just a minute."

An uneasy feeling knotted in my stomach, and I decided, even as late as it was, waking Mom was a bad idea. I said in a low tone, "Guys, just leave Mom alone."

Christina asked, "Why is Bobby in Mom's room?"

My heart sank as I put together an answer. "It was late. I'm sure they were talking and fell asleep. Just stay away from her door, guys."

I walked toward the kitchen, and called out to the kids, "I'm gonna look through the boxes to see if we have any cereal," already knowing we didn't but hoping they would follow me.

I grabbed a loosely packed box from the floor and set it next to the empty whiskey bottle and half-empty vodka bottle on the counter. I noticed the brands weren't any that I'd ever heard of. Did they make generic alcohol, like canned corn, I wondered? I lifted the wet, clear plastic bag, with red letters spelled "ice," out of the sink. As I squeezed the water out to throw it away, I heard Mom's bedroom door open.

Of course, I'd heard Michelle cry when she was a baby. When she was old enough to start running, she'd fall and scrape her hands and knees like every kid. She would cry, but it was almost as if she did it because she knew she was supposed to. If you asked, "Do you want some soda?" with a bright smile, she'd stop in an instant.

This time was different. Michelle was the one I heard first. Her moan was deep and emotional like someone had died. I had never heard it before. My chest tightened, and my mouth dropped open as I ran toward her.

The moment I saw Michelle's face, already crumpled into a hard cry, I heard Christina's whimpering sobs. I pulled Michelle close and reached for Christina.

"What happened? What happened?" I asked.

Vincent screamed, "I hate her!" and ran to an empty bedroom and slammed the door.

Michael had a stunned look on his face.

Bobby yelled, "Fucking kids that's what they get!" He slammed Mom's door hard enough to shake the whole house.

I asked again quietly, and desperate, "Michael, what happened? Did you go in the room?"

He looked at me and answered without any emotion. "Mom and Bobby were in the bed naked."

The 21 Brutal Moves that led to my Sanity

Bobby's voice was deep and aggressive. "If you don't, I will. I know people in there. He'll get the message."

Mom pleaded, "Bobby, please. He's in prison."

Bobby pointed at her and snarled. "You better fuckin' tell him, or I'm outta here."

The five of us were sitting in the living room watching each other but still listening to the argument. I knew from the desperate, but hopeful, looks on both Christina's and Michelle's faces that they were thinking the same thing we all were: let him go.

Mom sighed. "Alright, alright. The next time he calls, I'll tell him."

The phone rang. Mom answered, "Yes, operator, I'll accept the charges." Mom told Dad that she was going to let him talk to the kids first. She called out, "Mike."

Michael spoke quietly and finished quickly. "Bye. Ok. Love you, too, Dad." He handed off the phone.

Vincent – defiant to Bobby's presence – asked, "When are you coming home, Dad? We all miss you."

My eyes darted to Bobby's face. His upper lip curled under before he huffed at Mom. "Hurry them up. I want him off the phone." Mom gave a nervous smile and motioned for Vincent to hand Christina the phone.

Dad must have started asking what was wrong because Christina said, "Everything's ok, Dad."

Michelle told Dad, "I'm fine. We're all fine."

After Michelle finished, I took the phone. "Hi, Dad."

I recognized the familiar, complete trust in his voice the moment he asked me, "Gar, what's going on with your mom? I know something's wrong." My chest tightened as Bobby watched me.

I took a breath and forced a normal voice. "There's nothing wrong, Dad." I changed the subject by telling him it was too bad he'd never seen Terry's house, then, as Bobby stared (I lied) I told him the new house was even better. I tried to wrap the conversation up. "I should probably get going, Dad. I'll give the phone to Mom."

"Gar," Dad said, "remember, you're the man of the house. You have to take care of everyone… I love you."

My throat hardened with a deep hurt that I knew was going to break my measured voice. I closed my lips, inhaled through my nose and told myself that I couldn't get upset. I couldn't cry. My eyes moved to a matted, gray stain on the carpet. My thoughts contemplated what kind of filth it could be – throw up? Garbage juice seeped from a torn

Hefty bag? I decided it had probably been there for years, the remnant of another dysfunctional family, just like us, who had existed in this house. I blinked the gaze away, let out my breath, and willed myself to speak. "I love you, too, Dad." I handed Mom the phone.

Mom cupped her hand over the mouthpiece and whispered, "Gar, make the kids go in the room."

Vincent whined, "I don't wanna go in the room." His desperate attempt to stop the moment, along with Michelle's anxious eyes and the alarmed look on Christina's face, told me that they all realized Mom was about to tell Dad.

I whispered, "Guys, its ok. *Please*, just until Mom finishes talking to Dad."

Michael put his hand on Vincent's back, "Come on, Vince."

I clicked the bedroom door behind me, took a deep breath, and walked back toward Mom and Bobby. At the edge of the hall, I heard Mom. "But Nick, I don't love you anymore. I can't stay with you."

The nervous feeling in my gut turned hollow and empty, like everything below my rib cage had disappeared. *Did she really just tell Dad?* I stepped back into the living room where I could see her. She was sitting, hunched on a kitchen chair, staring out the window with tears streaming down her face. She was completely quiet. What was Dad saying to her? Was he begging? Crying? I realized the empty feeling was shock. It was really over. Our life was gone. As the shock settled, I began to feel anger or hate or some other intense feeling that made my fists tight and my jaw clench. I breathed heavily – in and out, in and out. *What had she done? To Dad? To all of us?*

After a few days, the reality of our new surreal life began to hold. We expected Bobby to finish a bottle of vodka or whiskey every night. Sometimes Mom would drink with him. Other times, she'd plead with him, "Bobby, my job. I *have* to work."

After the second glass of booze, the hatred would cement a deep scowl on Bobby's face. He'd growl at Michael or Vincent. "Go to your fuckin' room."

I'd hurry everyone into one of the bedrooms and direct in a soft voice, "Just go, and be quiet."

Mom and Bobby would then either lock themselves in the bedroom or scream at each other in the living room. Most of the arguments were about Mom's boss.

Bobby threatened, "I'll snap his fuckin' neck if he says you look nice again." Mom went to work late, tired, and in clothes that she hadn't had pressed at the cleaners, or at least ironed at home, several days in a row. Then she just stopped going.

Michael opened the refrigerator, "Mom, there's nothing to eat."

Mom answered, "Bobby's bringing home dinner, Mike."

Michelle whined, "I don't want hot dogs again." Bobby had brought home a pack of generic hot dogs and buns for dinner the last two days.

The second night, Vincent had said, "There's not even any ketchup or mustard."

Michael whispered, "No amount of mustard is going to make this taste like a hot dog."

Everyone snickered except Michelle, who didn't find joking about an incomplete dinner even one bit funny. She dropped out of her chair and marched over to Bobby. "Bobby, we can't eat hot dogs without ketchup or mustard."

When Bobby came home with hot dogs (again), he stretched tall to dig into his tight jean pockets. He pulled out two big handfuls of mustard and mayonnaise packets and dropped them on the table. "I got these from the gas station. Are you happy now?"

None of us were happy but wouldn't dare say it, not even Michelle. I bit open a mustard packet and squeezed and pressed until every last bit was on the dog. Mom joked under her breath. "If I eat one more hot dog, I'm gonna turn into a hot dog." Everyone laughed.

It was nice to see a glimpse of Mom's former self, but it disappeared the moment Bobby snapped, "What do you want me to do? The checks haven't come yet." He slammed his dish into the sink and walked to the bedroom. Mom got up and ran after him.

Christina asked, "Can't he just use money?"

Vincent responded, "How would he have money? He doesn't have a job!"

I smirked at the irony of Vincent's accurate remark. He didn't even realize how right he was. But then the reality of how dangerous Bobby could be returned. I clenched my teeth and scolded under my breath, "Vincent!"

He pushed his plate away and folded his arms. "Well, he doesn't."

I knew when the rectangle shaped box with the bank logo came that Bobby's mood would improve. He strutted around smiling. "I'm going shopping tonight."

Mom asked, "Bobby, why don't you take Gary to the store with you?" which reminded me of when she had first met Dad. She did all sorts of things to get us to like each other. With Dad, though, none of it was necessary. I did like him, and he liked me.

I wanted to beg, "Mom, please, stop with the games. Bobby hates us, and we hate him. Nothing you do will change it." Instead, I silently sighed and waited for his response.

Bobby answered, "If you want to go, come on."

I pulled myself up from the musty, medicine smelling couch. No matter how many minutes Mom had sprayed, and no matter how soaked the fabric got, Lysol could not completely mask the mildew scent. When Bobby had brought the sofa home, Christina sincerely asked where he got it. His abrupt answer was meant to stop the questions. "The store." I knew he'd probably pulled it from a pile of broken furniture – that was meant to be trash – out of a neighbor's yard. I reached for my sneakers. "Ok, if you're sure you don't mind."

My heart thumped in my chest as we drove. I tried to think of something to say but had no idea what might make Bobby warm up. All I could think of was, "How do you like Florida, Bobby?"

Bobby kept his eyes forward as he turned into the grocery store parking lot. "I don't put up with kids sitting home all day. Didn't you just turn seventeen? How old is your brother Mike?"

"Yeah, I'm seventeen, and Michael's fourteen."

"You should be out doin' shit, fuckin' girls, hanging out with guys. When I was your age, you'd never catch me at home."

He pulled in near the edge of the parking lot as the Kash n' Karry sign flickered on. He turned to me before we got out of the car. "Don't call me Bobby in there. Just keep your mouth closed and follow my lead."

"Ok, uh, ok."

We walked in past ladies tugging to free shopping carts. As the baskets clanged behind us, Bobby walked up to the service desk and smiled. "Hey, is Phil the evening manager here? He helped me sign up for a check cashing card. Tell him it's Ryan."

A pudgy, young man with neat, black hair walked up from the back. He stuck his pen behind his ear when he saw Bobby. "Ryan, hey, you should be all set. Give me a sec." The guy walked behind the counter and began looking through papers.

As he flipped through, Bobby asked him, "So, how's Mary? It's Mary, right?" I watched the guy smile and wondered how old he could be – twenty-one? Twenty-two? Did he really believe the scary man that towered over him – "Ryan" – cared about Mary?

When the guy handed Bobby a card, Bobby took his hand, shook it, and gave a wide, phony smile. "You're the man, Phil." He pointed. "I'm gonna talk to Kathleen about having you and Mary over." Phil laughed.

As we walked up and down the aisles, Bobby grabbed boxes of spaghetti, cans of tomato sauce, loaves of bread, and pancake mix. He pushed the cart up to the fluorescent-lit back of the store where there were all sorts of red meats wrapped onto Styrofoam trays. He began loading packages into the cart.

"Go grab another cart," Bobby ordered.

As I started to leave to go get one, he added, "Get some cereal... and shit for the kids."

I jogged to the front of the store. Phil made eye contact and smiled. I gave a slight grin back and wondered if he would get fired when Bobby's check bounced.

I pushed a cart with a squeaky wheel into the cereal aisle. I grabbed Count Chocula, Honey Nut Cheerios, and Alpha Bits before heading to the dairy section to get three gallons of milk. When I brought the cart back to Bobby, he said, "Good," then switched carts with me and finished piling the second one up before heading toward the register.

Bobby leaned towards the checker, read the girl's name tag, and commented, "My daughter's name is Amber."

The girl flashed a quick, disinterested smile as she began sliding food over the scanner. When she finished, she said, "I need to get approval for this, Mister…?"

Bobby smiled, "Call me Ryan. Phil knows me."

Phil walked over and took the check. He bit his bottom lip as he stared, "It's just the amount, Ryan – almost five hundred dollars. My limit is a hundred."

Bobby chuckled. "Phil, you know it's good. I was approved." He pointed at the check. "You've got my address right there on the check. Where am I gonna go?"

I leaned in and saw that the check had Terry's house address. Phil began nodding his head, clearly trying to convince himself. "Yeah, it's good. It's good." He wrote his initials at the top, gave a proud smile and handed the check back to the cashier.

August felt hotter in our new neighborhood. Instead of making the house brisk and cold, the air conditioner blew air only slightly cooler than the room. Even though it was stuffy and warm in the house, Michelle still wanted to stay home with Mom. I was pretty sure she expected Mom to wake up permanently from the bad mother she had become.

Mom would laugh and say, "Hey, Michelle!" like the mother she was before she went to prison.

Michelle would smile brightly, but then get serious. "Mom, we need to clean the kitchen, then go to T.J. Maxx. I need to buy new clothes for school."

Vincent and Christina just wanted to be with me and Michael. We walked along the long main road that bordered woods overgrown with tall tan grass. Christina reached for a stick and began swinging at swarms of tiny gnats.

Vincent asked, "Is that water?"

I looked into the grassy filled ditch. "Yeah, it looks like water. I bet there are even tadpoles in there."

"Really?" Vincent smiled.

Christina said, "We should get a jar and bring some home."

Michael was quick to respond. "Why? So Bobby can flush them down the toilet?" then added, "He'd probably make Mom do it."

I sighed as the reality of our life came back to me.

Christina asked, "Is everything ok, Gar?"

"Everything's fine. We just need to stay out of Bobby's way."

Christina and Michelle yawned and pulled themselves out of bed. I opened Michael and Vincent's door. "Guys, it's time to get up."

Vincent lifted his head, "It's still dark out."

Michelle asked, "Should we wake Mom up?"

I whispered, "No, let her and Bobby sleep, Michelle. You can get yourself ready for school."

Michael sighed, "I don't want to go back to school."

"Nobody does," I said, "but we still have to."

I closed the bathroom door to think. Actually, I didn't mind going back to school and getting away from Bobby. I just wondered if any of the students in my eleventh-grade class would notice I was wearing the same tee-shirt and jeans from the year before. I looked in the mirror and opened my mouth to examine my braces. Even though they hadn't been tightened in the three months since Bobby came, at least the tiny gaps were closed.

I grabbed my bag. "Michael, make sure you guys are outside fifteen minutes before."

When I got home from school, Mom was talking to Bobby about Uncle Dan. She said, "He got a trailer in a park off of 41. He told me they have a three bedroom."

Would Bobby want to live near Uncle Dan? Even though they were always friendly to each other's face, Bobby despised Uncle Dan as much as Uncle Dan hated him. The discussion twisted Bobby's lips into an angry snarl, but Mom still insisted – in a sweet, pleading tone. "Bobby, we have to be out of here. And we can move right in."

Bobby stated flatly, "Ok, but we're only staying until I figure something else out."

As we drove along Route 41, tall, dark pines were only broken with a random rusted gas station sign. When I realized a railroad track, deep in brown grass, ran parallel to the road, it didn't cheer me – even slightly. I leaned my forehead on the glass and remembered the times Dad had stopped and waited so I could see a train. My heart had raced when the bells started, and the gates came down. I also thought about Gary showing me how to click the tracks together, so my tiny silver and red engine would hum along smoothly without popping off the tracks.

As I wondered whether I even cared about trains anymore, Michelle asked, "We're not living in Tampa? Are we going to a different school?"

Mom answered, "It's in Lutz. It's north of Tampa, Honey. Yeah, you're gonna go to a new school."

We slowed as the sign came into view: Pine Tree Village Mobile Home Park. We turned onto the white stone littered road that led into the park. I imagined that the rocks had been dumped from bags, at some point in the past, to add a level of class to the dirt road leading into Pine Tree Village. As we drove down the path, there were less and less welcoming white rocks until the drive was just tire-tracked dirt. Our trailer was at the end of the drive, at the far back of the park. There were papers, plastic cups, and sun-bleached, crushed beer cans mixed in with tall grass along the twisted, rusted fence that surrounded the "village." I got out, waited for Michelle to hop down, and then slammed the door. I waved away the hot, dry dust as I looked at our metal box-shaped home.

Christina said, "There's dents in the walls," as Vincent crouched down to examine the space between the trailer and the ground. "What's underneath?" he asked. We followed Bobby and Mom inside.

Once we were in, Vincent said, "It feels like a spaceship."

Michael muttered, "That's because the walls are aluminum."

507

Michelle scrunched up her nose, "What's that smell?"

I questioned, "Is it mold?" I knew from science class that breathing in mold was bad for your lungs. I was also pretty sure that Bobby, who had dropped out in the fifth grade to begin his life of crime, would have no idea the filthy rug in our new home could cause us to get sick.

After Bobby walked down the skinny hall to the back bedroom, I said, "Mom, if that smell is mold, we shouldn't be breathing it."

Mom took a deep, annoyed breath, as if I'd just asked for a ride on The Great Space Coaster, and pleaded, "Gary please, we're only gonna be here a few months until we find another place."

CLUNG CLUNG CLUNG

Mom opened the door to Uncle Dan. He stepped up and walked in. "Hey, Murph." He hugged Mom and then smiled at us. "Hey, guys!"

Christina ran up and threw her arms around him as he asked Michelle. "Whatcha doin' there, Squatbox?"

I watched how genuinely happy Uncle Dan seemed to be to see us, and my thoughts drifted to his life as a young teenager – both parents dead, his older siblings either drunk, married, or running away to Florida. He had learned to survive on the streets. I never thought about his young life before then, but he had probably been beaten up, mugged, and who knows what else, before fighting back to survive. He wasn't like Bobby, who I knew despised us. Uncle Dan didn't think his crazy ways were mean or abusive. He thought he was teaching us to survive the vicious, terrible world that had devoured his childhood.

Bobby walked out of the bedroom with the same phony smile that he had given Phil. "Hey Dan, you were right. This place isn't bad." Then he whispered, "So, what's going on with this guy across the way? Is that a bar? Anything else goin' on there?"

Uncle Dan laughed, just as phony. "That's Don. Yeah, he's got some kind of set up for these fools in the park. You should try to get in on that action."

The next day, when Bobby told Mom, "You need to get these kids back in school," I knew it wasn't because he cared about our education. He wanted all of us gone.

After Mom finished registering the other kids for school, I asked, "Mom, is there any way you can drive me to Gaither? I can't start another new school in eleventh grade."

Mom looked at me with hopeless eyes. "Gar, we're so far away."

I pleaded, "Mom, please."

As we drove down Highway 41, I mentally calculated which period classes would be in at that hour. The first time I had to wake Mom at 6 a.m., she got right up. I knew she had probably been up until 4 o'clock by the number of times she yawned as we drove through the dark morning. Still, when we pulled into the school drive, she smiled brightly and proud. "Have a good day, Gar. I love you."

I smiled back, as I got out of the car. "I love you, too. Thanks, Mom."

By the fourth morning, I had to knock three times over an hour. I heard Bobby grumble. "Can't he take the fuckin' bus?"

Mom came out of the room and closed the door behind her. I held my frustration as I whispered, "Mom, it'll be third-period by the time I get to school."

She yawned. "I'm sorry Gar. You've got to make sure I'm up."

As I walked up the sidewalk to the entrance to the school, I put my hands in my pockets and tilted my head down. I knew, through the two stories of sun-shiny, blue tinted windows, the students in the classrooms could see me. I imagined Helena, the foreign exchange student who hated me, sitting in her third-period class – probably social studies or psychology – glaring with a tight-lipped smirk, to keep herself from snickering.

I took a breath as I pulled the door open. I wasn't going to sign myself in again. I headed up the stairs to the bathroom on the second floor. I closed the stall door to hide and wait for the bell. I thought about my third-period teacher. The first time I had walked in late, when I apologized, she smiled and said, "Please, take your seat." The second time her tone was curt. "Thank you for joining us, Mr. Mele. Now please take your seat." The third time, she kept her chalk on the board and continued her lecture about molecular structure, as if there was no interruption. I knew I'd never step into her class late again. The bell rang. I walked to my next class wondering if I could still pass high school if I failed my first three periods.

Bobby's criminal activities put a knot in my stomach until I realized they made him much less angry – almost happy, even. I pretended not to notice when he took a thick stack of twenties from his jean pocket and showed Mom. When he came home with a box of Reebok sneakers and said, "Pick your size. The thirteens are mine," I gave a phony, happy chuckle like I was thrilled to be getting a pair of hot sneakers.

"I'm only a ten and a half, Bobby," I said then added, "Oooooo, these are awesome." I lifted a pair of brand new stolen Reeboks that I knew I would only wear in the trailer when he was home.

Sometimes Bobby would leave for several hours during the day. Other times it was at night. He even began going places with Uncle Dan, which I thought meant they were getting along. I was surprised when I walked in from outside to Bobby shouting at Mom. "I don't give a fuck that he's your brother. He's a scumbag piece of shit."

Mom pleaded, "Bobby, just talk to him. I know you two can work it out."

Bobby growled, "You think I wanna talk to him? I'll talk to him when he gets on his knees and sucks my cock."

Bobby getting along with Uncle Dan made it much less dangerous for all of us. My thoughts raced with how I could help? What could I say? I did my best to be polite, respectful and soft-spoken when I butted in: "Bobby, Uncle Dan can be difficult, but he doesn't mean it."

Bobby turned and bent toward me, so his face was mere inches from mine. He snarled, "Oh yeah? You know what your Uncle Dan thinks about you?"

I froze. Silent. Bobby squinted, as he looked right into my eyes. "You're a fag."

Mom yelled, "Bobby!"

He ignored her, stood straight up, and continued, "That's right – a fag. He said you're a stone-cold fag."

I stuttered. "I'm… uh… I'm not–" My thoughts raced – laugh! Laugh like it's too crazy to be true. I chuckled. "Uncle Dan…"

Mom screamed at Bobby as I began walking backward toward my room.

Christina asked, "Gar, are you ok?"

I chuckled again and nodded. "I'm fine, Christina. I'm fine."

As I sat on my bed, Michelle popped her head in. "Gar, do you want anything?"

I forced a smile. "No, thanks. I'm ok, Michelle."

As I lay in bed, Mom and Bobby continued to yell. I stared at the ceiling and imagined what I could have said back. Uncle Dan's a criminal? Uncle Dan beats his girlfriends? Bobby would have probably said, "So what? At least he's not a fag." I turned toward the wall, closed my eyes, and wished I were dead.

When I woke in the morning, I turned over and stared up at the warped, white ceiling panels that were discolored from water stains. Thinking about knocking on Mom's door for a ride to school twisted my stomach into knots. I kept replaying Bobby yelling, "That's right – a fag. He said you're a stone-cold fag."

Plus, the idea of listening to teachers blather on about how exciting living in a dorm was going to be felt ridiculous. I knew I was never going to live on a college campus and bring my laundry home on the weekends for Mom to wash and fold.

I pulled myself up and looked through the dingy, scratched up window at Don's bar. It was actually just a blue cooler on the side of his trailer. *Had I ever seen him with a shirt on or without a cigarette dangling from his sun cracked face?* He took pride in his illegal bar, but Bobby had huffed and told Mom, "He's small time."

Well, he probably is compared to Bobby, but why would Bobby care? Was it because the criminal activity was right across the dirt drive, and it wasn't his? Why did *I* care enough to even think about it? I sat up, thinking. I have to get away from these crazy, dysfunctional people.

I looked up Adult Children of Alcoholics in the phone book. When I told the lady that I was in Lutz, she said, "I'm sorry, dear. The closest meeting is in Tampa. It shouldn't be a far drive." After I explained that I was seventeen and didn't have a chance to buy a car yet, she practically cried. "Oh, my sweet dear, let me see if I can get you a ride."

I quickly cut in. "No, no, it's ok. You know, I think I will be able to get a ride. Thank you so much." I hung up. I sighed, closed the phone book and rested my weight on the flimsy card table that Bobby had surely pulled from someone's garbage. As I breathed in the musty, flat air, I wondered if my life could possibly get any more hopeless.

After a few minutes, the heavy despair caused a tiny angry knot to start pressing at my gut. As the feeling spread to my chest, my thoughts pulled into focus. I tightened my lips, inhaled a deep breath and demanded of myself that I stop feeling defeated. My brain raced with ideas. What else? There has to be another way. Mom? No. Aunt Peggy? Yes, Aunt Peggy. I tried to remember when Aunt Peggy had first told me about meetings. It wasn't ACOA. What was it? What was it? I knew it was affiliated with A.A. I opened the phone book again, scanned for the number and dialed.

"Thank you for calling A.A."

"Hi, uh, I'm looking for a meeting. I'm not an alcoholic, but I heard there's something."

The woman on the phone said, "We have an Al-Anon meeting right off of 41 in Lutz."

The lady had explained that the meeting was north after the railroad tracks crossed 41. I walked out to the street and looked down the highway. It was probably over a mile away, I figured. There wasn't a sidewalk on either side of the road. I took a breath, crossed the highway, and walked over to the railroad tracks. The smell reminded me of flattened quarters, deafening bells, and Dad. I began walking, one step at a time, forward on the dark wood planks.

The room in the building off to the side of the white Baptist church had about twice as many people as the ACOA meeting. The person who began was older, about fifty, with a gray braided ponytail. She had big eyes that looked even bigger behind her glasses. As she read information that seemed like it was read before every meeting, I realized Al-Anon was more structured than ACOA. She explained the importance of anonymity and made eye contact with me and two other people. I assumed they were new, too. I thought how, if I ever wrote a book, she would probably want me to change her name.

Valda didn't just have an interesting name. She was a bit quirky and by far the smartest person in the room. She responded to things people said by telling her own stories in a subtle way that they could relate to. I watched over several weeks as people who came in with desperate looks left with hopeful, bright smiles. Unlike the people at ACOA, and many of the people at Al-Anon, who gushed about how wonderful I was to be looking for help at such a young age, Valda asked, "What's your part in it? What are you doing to make your life better?" I asked myself those questions every night as I walked home along the railroad tracks.

When Bobby said, "I got us a place up in Land O' Lakes," Michelle asked Mom, "Is that where they make the butter?"

Mom chuckled and told her, "Maybe. I don't know for sure."

Michael whispered to me, "Do you think we're moving because of Don's bar?"

A week before, two police cars had driven all the way to the end of the dirt road between Don's and our trailers. After they left, Don started yelling, "You fucking nark! Bobby, I know it was you."

Bobby slammed the door open, walked right up to Don, and growled. "I'll kill you where you stand, little man!"

I said to Michael. "Maybe. I don't know for sure."

As we drove north on 41, we crossed the railroad tracks and then passed the Baptist church where the Al-Anon meeting was.

I asked Mom, "You said it's off of 41, right?"

"Yeah Gar, but it's in Land O' Lakes."

I watched as we drove by a Winn Dixie grocery store. I wondered how many bad checks Bobby had written there. After the grocery store, we passed a Burger King, a bank, and then drove for a long time with nothing but marshy fields passing by.

The homes in our new neighborhood reminded me of the first grimy house Bobby had moved us to. Some had old rusted cars parked on their front lawns, and others had torn screens.

As we pulled into the driveway of our latest new home, I noticed the blue paint was chipped and peeling, exposing gray boards underneath.

When we walked inside, Mom smiled at me. "Gar, this can be your bedroom."

I looked through the open doorway to the den, connected to the living room. "But Mom, the laundry room is in here, too."

She pointed to the upper part of the doorway. "We'll put a curtain here for you. Everyone will have to ask before going in to use the washer and dryer."

I looked at Michael to be sure he'd heard her. "Ok, thanks, Mom."

I stacked my Madonna tapes next to my Panasonic boom box. When Aunt Peggy had given it to me, she said she wasn't using it anymore, but I knew it was because she felt bad that I hadn't brought my stereo when we left Cape Coral. As I stuffed my tee-shirts into the dresser, I heard happy screams and giggles outside. I peered through the window. Christina, Vincent, and Michelle were running across the front lawn with some neighbor kids, including two girls, Michelle's age, with exactly the same Dorothy Hamill bowl haircut. I wondered if they were twins. They had to be sisters, at least.

Bobby left for the store as Mom and I unpacked. Once I was finished in my room, I walked out to the living room. "Mom, do you need help with anything?"

"No, I'm ok, Gar." I walked to the bathroom and flipped on the light. I looked at myself and thought about school.

The thought of walking into any one of my classes after being away for more than a month twisted my stomach tight. Weeks before I knew we would be moving from the trailer, I had stopped knocking on Mom's bedroom door to go to school. After a couple of days, she had asked, "Gar, don't you want to go back to school?"

I told her, "I don't feel like it, Mom."

She said, "Ok, Honey. Let me know when you do. I promise I'll get up early to drive you." I knew she meant it and she probably would for at least a few days, but I didn't care about school anymore.

518

After a few weeks, the anxiety about getting dirty looks from teachers and scoffs and snickers from a room full of juniors got replaced with a panicked realization – I couldn't drop out. This is crazy, I had thought to myself. It was then that Bobby began talking about moving. I decided that once we were moved and settled, I'd go back.

I examined my braces in the mirror. It had been over six months since I'd had them tightened. I tugged at the wire and remembered the orthodontist saying the cement scrapes off easily. I then ran my fingers through my thick brown hair. I needed a haircut. I walked to the kitchen and dug through the box of tools until I spotted the red rubber handle of the pliers.

"Mom do you still have the clippers Aunt Peggy gave you?"

She looked around. "I think they're in that box over there, Gar." I grabbed them, walked back into the bathroom, and locked the door.

I breathed in and out and told myself; you can do this. I knew I was never going back to the orthodontist again anyway. I clasped the thin, metal wire with the dirty needle nose pliers and tugged. I felt pressure, but it didn't hurt. I clenched my jaw and pulled steady and slow. The wire clicked out of one back brace and was sticking out of my mouth like I'd been munching on a hanger. I grinned big and examined the brackets with no more wire. I gripped and yanked the wire out of the other side, did my bottom jaw, then clenched the bracket on my front tooth with the pliers. It popped right off. After an hour of popping and scraping, I ran my tongue over my smooth teeth, smiled at myself and thought, wow, I really am handsome. Now for the haircut.

I opened the black plastic case, took out the clippers, and examined the fittings. 1/2 inch, 1/4 inch. I decided I was tired of thick, wavy hair and clicked the clipper on without any fitting. It hummed as I placed it up to my ear. I pushed back then chuckled at the bare skin that extended back from my temple. I did both sides of my head and then the back, before deciding that going completely bald would look crazy. I remembered Aunt Peggy cutting hair. I followed what she did: 1/4 inch, 1/2 inch as I graduated up. I finished the top off with 1 inch. I examined myself in the mirror. I looked like a military guy, and my head felt cold.

When I came out of the bathroom, Christina's eyes lit up. "Wow, Gar, you cut your own hair?"

"Yup."

Michael asked, "Did you take off your braces?"

I smiled. "I did. What do you think?"

Michelle reached up. "Can I feel your head?" I bent down as she placed her warm hand on my scalp.

Vincent exclaimed, "I want a haircut! Will you cut my hair?"

I laughed. "I don't think Mom will let me, Vincent."

By the time Bobby got home, the excitement had died down about my removed braces and crew cut. I knew he wouldn't care or notice anyway. He came in with a brown paper sack and slammed a bag of ice into the sink.

The five of us sat motionless, staring at the TV, in the living room. As Doogie Howser put on his stethoscope, Vincent questioned, "How can a kid be a doctor?"

Michelle said, "Change it. This is stupid."

"The only other show is Jake and the Fatman," Michael said.

Bobby walked out of the kitchen with a soda glass full of whiskey and ice. "Give me the remote. You kids need to go in your rooms."

I shot Mom a look, expecting her to jump up and tell Bobby that we were watching TV, but she only stared blankly from the kitchen table where she'd been sitting for hours. Bobby barked again. "Go to your rooms!" After everyone pulled themselves up, he fell into an arrogant sit, with his arms on the back of the couch and his legs wide open. He snatched the remote and started changing the channel.

Vincent murmured, "He acts like he's the king, and Mom doesn't even care."

I was so tired of shushing Vincent for things he said that were true. I told him, "Come on. I'll go in your room with you and Michael."

I knew Mom was drinking, too, when the yelling started. Through the wall, I heard her slurred words. "You're a fucking bastard, Bobby. You're rotten!"

Bobby screamed back. "You don't think I'm a bastard when I feed you and your fuckin' kids." He continued, "And Danny–"

"Oh, stop it, Bobby." Mom interrupted, "You think you're so tough. You're not impressing anyone."

Bobby's voice got deep. "I'll fucking kill that brother of yours. Then you'll think I'm a real bastard!"

Mom yelled, "Yeah, try it, and you better sleep with one eye open." She muttered something else and then screamed.

The familiar, violent sound, like boxes toppling against the wall, put a panicked look on Michael's face. He stood. I jumped between him and the bedroom door. "Michael, no. They're both drunk. Stay in here!" I closed my eyes for a moment and begged God to please not let Christina or Michelle open their door. I breathed in and out steadily, waiting for the next sound.

Mom screamed again. "Bobby no! My wig!" His footsteps were fast and boomed down the hallway. Their bedroom door slammed.

Mom begged at the door. "Bobby, please… please let me in." Her begging turned to cries, then sobs. "Bobby please, please!"

Hours later, after the house had gotten quiet and Michael and Vincent had both fallen asleep, I closed my eyes.

I shuddered awake when the door clicked. I blinked as light came in from the hall. It was Mom. She had her wig back. She guided Christina and Michelle into the bedroom. Christina rubbed her eyes and asked, "What time is it, Mom?"

Mom put her clumsy finger to her gaping lips, blinked slow, and shushed her. I sat up, alert. Mom whispered to me, "Gar, I'm gonna start the car. I want you to sneak the kids out to the car, through the window."

I started, "But Mom–" She closed the door.

Christina asked, "What's going on?"

My mind was racing, and my heart pounded. "Nothing, guys. Just be quiet." I turned and gripped the bottom of the window, terrified that Bobby would hear. I pulled up. When it creaked, I stopped. I saw Mom running from the front door to the car. I took another breath, closed my eyes and lifted again. As the window slid up, without a sound, the brisk night air, chilled my chest.

My heart beat hard as I whispered, "Michael, go outside first, and help me get the other kids out." Michael put a leg out and ducked through. As I put my hands under Michelle's arms, I noticed

Christina's face. She was about to cry. I gently lifted Michelle and tensed my jaw to hide the fear in my voice. I told Christina, in a forced, soothing voice, "It'll be fine. I promise." Once Michelle was outside, I helped Christina and then Vincent. We hurried quickly to the car.

Mom was sitting in the driver's seat. I ran around the front of the vehicle, sat in the front passenger seat and pulled Michelle to my lap. Michael, Vincent, and Christina carefully and quietly piled into the back. "Are you going to start the car, Mom?" I asked.

She stared forward for a few seconds, trancelike, then said, "Keep everybody in the car. I'll be right back." She got out of the car, and Michelle began crying.

I put my hand on the back of Michelle's head and rocked her. "It's ok, Michelle. It's ok." Christina started crying in the back seat, too. I could see Michael reach for her in the rearview mirror.

"Aaaarrrh!"

It was Bobby! *What had Mom done!?!* Vincent started crying. The front door flung open. Mom ran across the lawn, got in, and started the car. Seconds felt like hours. I was sure that Bobby was going to storm out – bloody, furious, and ready to kill each one of us. Mom backed out and skidded to a stop, jerked at the clutch, and shot us forward.

I hollered, "Mom, turn your lights on!" I turned to the back. "Michael, make sure you each have your seat belts on." I clicked the seat belt over me and Michelle as Mom veered out of our neighborhood onto the dark, 41, two-lane highway.

The car started swerving. Even though I'd never driven, I knew to hold the wheel steady. I reached and straightened the car. Mom barked, "Gary, I've got it!"

I pleaded, "Mom, slow down, please." We barreled up to the back of an old Volkswagen.

Mom smashed the horn and yelled, "Get out of the way," before pulling into the opposite lane and speeding up.

The headlights were too close. I knew we'd never make it. I screamed, "Mom, no!" as she clenched her teeth and dug her foot into the gas pedal. I grabbed Michelle's head and closed my eyes as everyone screamed. The car jerked back to the right as the oncoming car passed us with a loud horn.

When we turned onto the stony dirt road of Pine Tree Village, I thought I'd never be so happy to see Uncle Dan.

CLUNG CLUNG CLUNG

After a minute, he opened the door in his robe, blinking. "What the hell happened?"

Uncle Dan's trailer was close to the front of the park. From his kitchen area, you could see across the way where the washing machines and the pay phone were. It was late in the afternoon the next day when Mom walked back from talking to Bobby.

When she opened the door, Uncle Dan asked, "When are we getting your shit outta there?"

Mom sighed, "Danny, everything's fine. It was a fight."

Uncle Dan got flustered. "Fine? Kath, he hit you, and you busted a beer bottle over his head and drove here drunk. Are you crazy?"

I had never agreed with Uncle Dan absolutely about anything in my life. I blurted out, "Mom, Uncle Dan's right. We can't go back."

She ignored me and called out, "Michael, Christina, Vincent, Michelle – come on."

I turned to Uncle Dan. "I don't know what to do."

He looked at me, "Just keep your brothers and sisters out of that asshole's way."

I nodded, "I know."

He gave me an approving grin. "I like the haircut, Champ. That's a high and tight." I smiled back, then walked out to the car.

The first day back, Bobby gave a lot of phony smiles. The second day, he mostly just ignored us. The third day, the kids had to go to school. Michelle played out front with the bowl haircut girls as they waited for their bus. I thought about what Michael had said to me: "Their father lets them watch porn."

I had asked, "Really? They're like eight – Michelle's age. Michelle shouldn't be playing with them."

Just then, the front door opened and broke me from the thought. It was Michelle. She told the girls, "You two go in my backyard. I'll be right back."

As Michelle ran to her room, I told her, "Michelle, you guys shouldn't be in the backyard. You might miss your bus."

She hollered back. "No, we won't," as she dug through her room for something. I sat on the couch and clicked on the TV. A minute later I heard the squeal of the school bus.

"Michelle, your bus is here."

Michelle zoomed out, straight to the front door. As soon as the door slammed behind her, I realized that the weird, bowl cut girls had their hands up to their faces trying to look in through the back glass door. I shot up and over to them. That was all we needed, their porn-loving father blaming Michelle for them missing the bus.

I yanked the door open. "Your bus is here!" They started to run around the side of the house. I hollered, "You can cut through!" and ran over to open the front door for them. They zigzagged through the house and chased the bus down the street until the tail lights came on.

I couldn't help but chuckle to myself, throughout the morning, as I pictured the two girls' noses pressed up against the glass with dumbfounded looks on their faces. Goodness! It had been so long since anything had made me crack up. I *knew* Mom would laugh, too, when I told her. I could hardly wait for her to get up.

It was early afternoon before Mom came out of the bedroom, rubbing the tired from her eyes. She walked into the kitchen and turned on the coffee pot.

I started, "The funniest thing happened this morning, Mom. I couldn't wait to tell you."

"What?"

I continued, "You know those two weird girls that Michelle plays with–"

BAM!

After Bobby slammed the hall closet door, he walked toward the den. He flung the curtain open and started banging around in the laundry room.

Mom sighed, "Bobby, what is it?"

He stepped out of the den. "It's my fuckin' sneakers. I can't find them. Did Vincent move them?" Mom just looked away.

I glared at her as I thought about Vincent. Bobby hated him because Vincent dared to, in his mind, disrespect him by telling Dad he missed him. Mom stared blankly as she poured her coffee, and I realized she didn't care about protecting us from Bobby. She brought us back. She wouldn't even *try* to defend Vincent from Bobby's ridiculous accusations. The anger tightened my shoulders, but I forced it to release. Exasperated, I closed my eyes for half a second, inhaled a deep breath and, in the most respectful tone I could muster, asked, "Bobby, why would Vincent touch your sneakers?"

He took an aggressive stomp toward me. He squinted his eyes and his lips contorted with rage. "You need to understand something. I *killed* a man and got away with it." My chest froze.

I answered, "Uh, ok. I was just saying."

Mom yawned, stirred her coffee and addressed Bobby – not like he had just threatened my life – like he had just told me I couldn't go out and play. "Bobby, please."

That evening I sat in my room and replayed the horrible things Bobby had done to each of us. I was absolutely terrified of him, but the memories would flare into anger. I told myself that I couldn't mouth off to him, no matter what he did and no matter what Mom didn't do.

From the living room, Michael asked, as politely as he possibly could, "Bobby, there's a show I want to record at nine. Is that ok?"

Bobby scoffed at him. "I'm watching TV."

Michael pleaded, "If you're done?" but Bobby ignored him.

The interaction stayed in my mind the whole time leading up to nine o'clock. Was Bobby going to let Michael record his show? I felt perspiration in my palms and wished that Michael wouldn't ask as the minutes ticked closer. Would Mom finally, without being drunk, yell, "Bobby, why can't he record?" My heart started racing as Bobby got up to turn the TV off – a minute after nine.

Michael darted over to the TV, smiled, and asked, "Bobby, is it ok if I record now?"

Bobby barked, "No! I said no!" The enthusiasm melted into disappointment on Michael's face. Mom stood quiet.

"It's ok, Michael. You can record it next time." The sarcastic words came out before I even realized how angry I was.

Within a moment, Bobby's face was above me, staring down and screaming, "I will break your fuckin' legs as you stand there." I turned my face to the side, away from him. I didn't step back. I didn't move. He continued, "Do you understand me? Your fuckin' legs!"

As Bobby's hot breath and spit battered the side of my face, I knew he had his hand above me, pointing down. I breathed in and out, waiting for Mom to say something, for him to hit me – I wasn't sure what.

When Bobby stopped screaming and stepped back from me, I looked for Mom. She was in the kitchen – desperate, pathetic and terrible – just standing there. I grabbed my sneakers and ran for the back door as she yelled, "Gar!"

I walked around the front of the house to the sidewalk and started walking up the street. I couldn't go back. I wouldn't. Ever. I folded my arms as the cold air chilled me. Why had I left without grabbing a sweatshirt? I walked along the sidewalk, where the streetlights created bluish, white half circles. I came to 41 and wondered how late it was. Maybe ten o'clock? I looked south to Lutz. The street was dark and quiet. I crossed over, walked through the grass, and onto the railroad tracks. How far away was Uncle Dan? I wondered. Six miles? Seven? I began walking at a fast pace, so I wouldn't shiver so much.

It had to be at least two hours before I made it to Pine Tree Village. I knocked softly on Uncle Dan's door. When he opened it, he didn't even ask what had happened. He just shook his head. "You must be freezing." He handed me his Giants jacket. "Here. Put this on 'til you warm up. I'm gonna make you some coffee."

I thought about what Valda had asked me, "What are you doing to make your life better?"

A few days after I got to Uncle Dan's, I walked up to Burger King, applied, and got a job as a cashier. I was proud the first time I put on the burgundy, polyester shirt and blue cap. Every time I asked, "How may I help you?" and searched for which colored button to press, I knew I was earning my paycheck. After a month, I'd saved enough to rent my own trailer. It was near the laundry and pay phone, far away from the place we had all lived with Bobby.

A few weeks after I'd gotten my own place, Uncle Dan knocked on my door. "Your Mom's moving back to New Jersey. She wants to come by and say goodbye before they leave."

"Ok, thanks."

When I saw Mom's face – her sad, blue eyes and childlike, innocent smile – a deep hurt clenched at my throat, and I wanted to cry. Her eyes started to water, and she asked, "What's the matter, Gar?"

I said, "Oh, nothing." We both cracked up as tears started streaming down our cheeks.

Mom looked at me. "Gar, I'm so sorry. I love you so much, and I'm so proud of you."

I took a breath, "I know, Mom. I love you, too."

Mom smiled. "You're still my biggest and best." As she squeezed me, I looked past her at Michael, Christina, Vincent, and Michelle.

I hugged Michael and told him, "You know you're the real man of the house now, right?"

He laughed and then looked down. He put his fingers on the bridge of his nose to keep from crying. I hugged him tight. "I love you, Mike."

He looked up with red eyes, chuckled, and grinned. "I love you, too."

I grabbed Christina. "You know you are so pretty and smart. Don't forget it. I love you, Chris." She squeezed me tight. I added, "So much."

Christina mumbled through her sobs. "I brought your Madonna tapes, Gar." I just kept holding her as tight as I could.

I took a deep breath, wiped my cheeks with the back of my hand and tried to cheer up. "You gonna give me a hug, Vince?" He smiled and stepped toward me. I bent down a little. "Listen, you're really smart with what you know. Just be careful who you tell."

He laughed as he started crying, "Like Bobby?"

I smiled as the tears started welling up again. "Yeah, like Bobby. I love you, Vince."

"I love you, too, Gar."

Michelle ran over and jumped toward me. I lifted her as I laughed. "You are so strong, Michelle and funny and smart and pretty and–" I gave her a big kiss on the cheek and squeezed her close as she began to cry. I whispered, "Don't cry, Michelle. I love you so much. Everything's gonna be fine. I promise."

I waved as the car drove over the crackling white rocks. As they turned onto 41 and disappeared, I realized I had a headache from crying. I pulled my door closed as I thought about Michael, Christina, Vincent, and Michelle – still a part of all the craziness. My throat started to tighten again, but I stopped it. I looked around my trailer living room, kitchen and down the skinny hall to my bedroom. I sat down on my couch and thought, this is mine. I work and pay for it. It'll be as clean as I want, and I'll have as much food as I want. I'm in control of my own life. I felt free and full of hope for the future. I knew, if I made it out, I would figure out a way to get them out too.

The Inexplicable Survival of a Happily Fallible Child

Michael, Christina, Vincent and Michelle, I could not have survived and become the person I am without each one of you. Your fortitudes, positive outlooks and incomparable senses of humor make me proud to be your older brother. You know I could not have written this book without your input and support. From the group text 'title debate' to the individual conversations and laughter over the absurdity of some of these stories, this is as much your story as it is mine. This memoir is dedicated to you. You know how much I love you.

To my mother, Kathleen Sarah Canaley: Despite the cruel and terrible things you endured as a child, you always wanted better for your children. You encouraged us to break free from the shackles of the destructive life that you tried so desperately to escape from. You wanted us to be the best that we could possibly be, which was evident by the endless pride you exhibited for our successes. Your strength, humor and limitless compassion live on within each one of us.

We love you forever, Mom.

To my husband, Anthony: Your support and encouragement as I wrote this story (and made you read chapter after chapter) made me realize how forever grateful you are to have me. I'm grateful to have you, too ;-)

Love you, Dink.

This memoir depicts the events of my childhood as honestly as possible from my perspective. All persons within are actual individuals. Some of the names of friends (and one school) have been changed to protect privacy. To anyone referenced in this book who feels they are portrayed in an unflattering light, they are welcome to write their own story.

Made in the USA
Middletown, DE
10 September 2018